Oswald Spengler and the Politics of Decline

# Oswald Spengler and the Politics of Decline

Ben Lewis

berghahn
NEW YORK · OXFORD
www.berghahnbooks.com

First published in 2022 by
Berghahn Books
www.berghahnbooks.com

© 2022, 2024 Ben Lewis
First paperback edition published in 2024

All rights reserved. Except for the quotation of short passages
for the purposes of criticism and review, no part of this book
may be reproduced in any form or by any means, electronic or
mechanical, including photocopying, recording, or any information
storage and retrieval system now known or to be invented,
without written permission of the publisher.

Library of Congress Cataloging-in-Publication Data

Names: Lewis, Ben (Benjamin Joseph), author.
Title: Oswald Spengler and the politics of decline / Ben Lewis.
Description: New York : Berghahn Books, 2022. | Includes bibliographical
  references and index.
Identifiers: LCCN 2022016082 (print) | LCCN 2022016083 (ebook) |
  ISBN 9781800735743 (hardback) | ISBN 9781800735750 (ebook)
Subjects: LCSH: Spengler, Oswald, 1880-1936.
Classification: LCC B3332.S44 L49 2022  (print) | LCC B3332.S44
  (ebook)
DDC 901--dc23/eng/20220605
LC record available at https://lccn.loc.gov/2022016082
LC ebook record available at https://lccn.loc.gov/2022016083

British Library Cataloguing in Publication Data
A catalogue record for this book is available from the British Library

ISBN 978-1-80073-574-3 hardback
ISBN 978-1-80539-707-6 paperback
ISBN 978-1-80073-575-0 web pdf
ISBN 978-1-80539-901-8 epub

https://doi.org/10.3167/9781800735743

# Contents

| | |
|---|---|
| *Acknowledgements* | vi |
| *Preface* | viii |
| Introduction | 1 |
| 1. Oswald Spengler's Life and Work: A Chronological Overview | 6 |
| 2. Spengler Reception and Research | 29 |
| 3. Decline, Determinism and Development | 42 |
| 4. Faustian *Zivilisation*: Prognosis and Perspectives | 67 |
| 5. Spengler's Prussian Socialism | 86 |
| 6. Rebuilding the German Reich: Illusion and Failure | 113 |
| 7. Decisive Years: Spengler and National Socialism | 144 |
| Conclusion | 173 |
| *Bibliography* | 177 |
| *Index* | 185 |

# Acknowledgements

This publication would not have been possible without the generous support of the Wolfson Foundation, which funded my PhD dissertation 'Oswald Spengler beyond the Decline of the West' at the University of Sheffield between 2015 and 2018.

At Sheffield, I benefited from optimal research conditions, friendly colleagues in the German Department and beyond, as well as several cohorts of engaged undergraduate students, with whom I discussed everything from the decline of the West to the decline of the German genitive case (and much more in between).

This book, and the efforts that went into it, will always be bound up with the city of Sheffield and my colleagues and friends there. There are far too many names to mention here, but it would be remiss of me not to acknowledge the support and friendship of colleagues such as Mike Braddick, Maxime Goergen, Dina Gusejnova, Giles Harrington, Nick Hodgin, Kristine Horner, James Lewis, David McCallam, Michael Perraudin, Sarah Pogoda and Bob Stern, as well as the warmth of my friends Carey Davies, Louise Dyason, Alex Evans, Reimund Kümpel, Chris Maccormac, Lawrence Parker, Alex Plant, Rebecca Roberts, David Sabbagh, Jamie Tedford, Ben Watkins and Tina Werkmann. I am most fortunate to have a family – spread across the world from Abergavenny to Istanbul, from California to Karaj – that has always been there for me throughout the entire process of working on this book.

I am particularly indebted to my main supervisor, Henk de Berg. Not only did he help conceive of this research project in the first place, but he also devoted hundreds of hours of his time to reading and discussing *The Decline of the West* with me, spending a few hundred pounds of his money on coffees at Jessop West Café in the process. His supervision was meticulous, his guidance always insightful and his faith in me as a scholar unwavering: I am truly grateful for all that he has done to help me in my academic career in general and this study in particular.

My co-supervisor Caroline Bland has also been a source of reassurance and inspiration ever since I first came to Sheffield as an eighteen-year-old undergraduate in 2003. She embodies everything that made studying German at Sheffield such a rewarding experience.

I must also thank my examiners Paul Bishop (Glasgow) and Craig Brandist (Sheffield) for an incredibly rewarding discussion of my thesis and for impressing on me the need for this study to be published as soon as possible. Here I must thank Sulaiman Ahmad, Marion Berghahn and Keara Hagerty at Berghahn Books for arranging for this book to be produced, and to Caroline Kuhtz for her thorough copyediting of the manuscript. Any outstanding errors or gremlins in the text are my own responsibility.

Since completing this project almost three years ago, my path has not always been a smooth one, as I have had to navigate the precarity of being an early-career academic with a young family during a global pandemic. In this regard, I must thank Angelika Ebbinghaus, Marcel van der Linden and Karl Heinz Roth at the *Stiftung Sozialgeschichte des 20. Jahrhunderts* for always returning to me as a translator, and Sebastian Budgen at *Historical Materialism*. Special mention must also go to the many supporters across the world who back my Patreon project *Marxism Translated*, as well as to the Leverhulme Foundation, which is currently funding my postdoctoral project on the social-democratic women's publication *Die Gleichheit* (*Equality*).

I would like to dedicate this book to my wife, Anahita Hosseini-Lewis, without whose encouragement I would have never embarked on this journey and without whose love and support I would have never finished this book. At a time when the decline of the West and, indeed, the capitalist mode of production makes itself felt in an array of tragic and horrific ways both at home and abroad, I cannot express in words how much it means to have you and our daughter Clara at my side: may we build a better world for her generation free of gods, masters and self-styled 'prophets'.

Ben Lewis<br>Brighton, April 2022[1]

## Note

1. For more information visit drbenlewis.com.

# Preface

Oswald Spengler (1880–1936) was one of the most important thinkers of the Weimar Republic (1918–33). His work, notably the 1,200-page *Der Untergang des Abendlandes* (*The Decline of the West*, 1918/22), had a profound influence on intellectual discourse in Germany and beyond. In spite of this, his thought has been seriously under-researched. In English, only four major studies have appeared since 1945.

Secondary literature has tended to see Spengler as espousing a theory of world history that is a pessimistic, fatalistic diagnosis of 'the decline of the West' and as defending a gloomy conservative outlook that – as the extension of this overall worldview – is largely backward-looking; that is, reactionary and quietist. Against this view of Spengler as an isolated doomsayer, two things must be stressed: first, that the characterisation of his philosophy as a mere manifestation of *Kulturpessimismus* ignores the optimistic prognosis of a German-led world order in his thought; and, second, that while Spengler can hardly be characterised as a progressive thinker, he is an esteemed and well-connected theorist who does defend an in many ways future-orientated and interventionist political project.

In fact, at different stages in his career, Spengler put forward different political projects. These projects admittedly do not add up to one overarching, holistic programme as the logical outcome of his philosophy of world history, but they all endeavour to shape the fate of Germany and the Western world. This crucial aspect of Spengler's legacy has been almost entirely ignored in the secondary literature and thus it has overlooked a significant aspect of his intellectual output. In part this is due to the success and enduring brilliance of his main work, *The Decline of the West*, which remains the focal point of scholarly discussions of his ideas at the expense of his other copious writings.

This volume, the first of its kind in English, shifts the focus of Spengler scholarship onto his *politics of decline* by foregrounding a contextualisation and analysis of his political activities and writings. It develops a new approach in understanding Spengler the politician by explaining the evolution of his political thought as the outcome of a dynamic interplay between his meta-historical considerations on world history ('the decline of the West') on the one hand, and the practical demands and strategic considerations of *Realpolitik* on the other hand. This novel way of approaching his work brings fresh insights into his intellectual contribution to the complex discourse of German national renewal between the November Revolution of 1918 and the Nazi seizure of power in 1933.

# Introduction

Oswald Spengler's *The Decline of the West: Outlines of a Morphology of World History* (1918/22) exerted a profound influence on intellectual discourse in Germany and across the globe. His ideas were critically received and discussed by Theodor W. Adorno, Ernst Bloch, T.S. Eliot, Georg Lukács, Thomas Mann, Arnold Toynbee and many others. However, despite such wide-ranging influence on twentieth-century intellectual history, Spengler's work has not received the attention it deserves: only four full-length English-language studies have appeared on him in the last seventy years.

Published against the backdrop of social turmoil and revolutionary upheaval, *The Decline of the West* immediately struck a nerve amongst a German population in search of reasons for its own perceived terminal decline following military defeat. Given its length and often difficult style, *The Decline of the West* seemed an unlikely candidate for bestseller status. But a bestseller it became. By 1938, the book had sold a staggering 200,000 copies.

Yet within secondary literature, the success and import of the work with which Spengler has become synonymous have obscured something fundamental about him as a thinker and historical actor. Existing research on him is unduly focused on his magnum opus and the arguments it advances in relation to specialist disciplines such as aesthetics, ancient history, metaphysics and religion.

Moreover, *The Decline of the West* has overwhelmingly been interpreted as a pessimistic and fatalistic text that offers few positive proposals for the last days of the Western world. This *communis opinio* is misleading for two reasons. First, it downplays how Spengler sought not merely to analyse the decline and downfall of the West, but also how he was engaged in sustained attempts to create a political alternative within this process of decline. Specifically, existing research often fails to account for the text's extensive discussion of what Spengler understood as the leadership necessary to navigate the tides of history and ensure that Germany would emerge as the leading power of the declining Western world.

Second, it overlooks how *The Decline of the West* relates to the remainder of Spengler's career as a political activist, networker and publicist; he used the fame he established for himself with this publication to devote his energies to a right-wing nationalist project aimed at overthrowing the Weimar Republic. In so doing, he became a respected and well-connected thinker among the German elite, someone who published extensively on the socio-political issues of his day.

Even a cursory look at Spengler's copious writings, not least his commercially successful political texts such as *Prussianism and Socialism* (1919), *Rebuilding the German Reich* (1924) and *The Hour of Decision. Part I: Germany and World-Historical Evolution* (1933), as well as the various articles, essays and speeches collated in his *Political Writings 1919–1926* (1932) and *Speeches and Essays* (1937), makes clear how there is much more to him than just *The Decline of the West*. Many of his political writings reached circulation numbers in the six figures. His last published work, *The Hour of Decision*, sold even more copies than *The Decline of the West*.

Existing scholarship has done insufficient justice to the breadth, importance and impact of Spengler's political publications and has thus been unable to locate his ideological position within the right-wing nationalist movement (*nationale Bewegung*) against the Weimar Republic. While there has been renewed academic interest in his thought during the past twenty years, this interest has largely been restricted to German-language scholarship, as well as to the potential relevance of *The Decline of the West* in the twenty-first century.

Since the Second World War, there have only been four studies which focus predominantly on the nature of Spengler's political ideas, networks and projects. All are written in German. More importantly, these studies fail to grasp the significance of Spengler the political philosopher in two respects. They tend to view Spengler's political thought as a static and largely unchanging entity that is the logical outcome of his philosophy of history. In other words, instead of exploring in detail his views on democracy, race or socialism across his career, secondary literature often speaks of his *view* of a particular concept in the singular. The few studies that do locate shifts and developments within his political ideas throughout his life either do not explain these amendments with reference to the historical context in which Spengler felt the need to make them, or they do not sufficiently bring out how these amendments relate to central ideas in his thought that he did not feel compelled to modify.

This volume seeks to address this lacuna in Spengler studies. It does so by developing a new way of understanding what I will call his *politics of decline*. It explains the evolution of his thought as the outcome of a dynamic interplay between his metahistorical considerations on world history ('the decline of the West') on the one hand, and the practical difficulties and considerations of *Realpolitik* on the other hand. As we will see, in order to arrive at a more rounded appreciation of Spengler's political thought, it is necessary to consider method alongside motivation, content alongside context, consistency alongside change.

Our discussion will therefore begin with with a biographical chapter, which will serve as a foundation for understanding Spengler's politics of decline by reconstructing the most significant developments in his lifetime and by exploring how these found reflection in his political aims and activities.

Chapter 2 will provide a brief survey of the most significant English- and German-language studies of Spengler over the past eighty years or so. It will identify some of the trends, advances and breakthroughs in Spengler studies. On this basis, it will explain in more detail how this volume attempts to fill the gap in the understanding of his political thought.

An analysis of Spengler's politics of decline presupposes an understanding of what he viewed as the motor of historical change. This is the aim of Chapter 3, which will provide an overview of his theory of history as expressed in *Der Untergang des Abendlandes*. It will show that Spengler's understanding of historical development can be read on two levels: as a largely metaphysical portrayal of the stages through which all historical entities must inevitably pass in their journey from birth to death; and as a more specific socio-political theory purportedly able to predict future developments. Following a critical summary of the general theory, we will discuss why Spengler was convinced that he was able to foresee the future of the West – what he called 'Faustian' culture – and its inexorable decline.

Spengler's theory of the nature of Western decline and his attempts to intervene in this process will be covered in Chapter 4. This chapter will discuss his views on the socio-political challenges and opportunities presented by Western democracies. Following a summary of what *The Decline of the West* highlights as the major features and underlying dynamics of this era, I will demonstrate how – against the common reading of *The Decline of the West* as a fatalist and pessimist text – Spengler understood the decline of the West as a historical process that is both predetermined and to some extent open-ended. The exact arrangement of the Western world's final days is yet to be decided. Above all, it will be influenced by the ideas and actions of powerful individuals in politics, industry, the press and the military. Spengler was convinced that the fate of the world increasingly lies in the hands of a small number of world-historical figures. He referred to this phenomenon as *Caesarism* and felt that his historical method alone could provide these strongmen with the necessary historical consciousness to address successfully the key political questions of the age. This age, as we will discover, is one of industrial warfare and global power politics, not of poetry and painting. Finally, this chapter will outline the basis of Spengler's political alternative, which I will call the project of *Preußentum* (Prussianism). This outlook combined two ideological commitments on his part: his nationalist obligation to Germany as the purported 'last nation of the West'[1] in the latter's final days; and his conviction that a successful modern state must draw on the best of the past. Here he was thinking of the elitist traditions and absolutist politics of the seventeenth and eighteenth centuries, before the French Revolution of 1789 and the rise of mass politics and democracy. However, as we will see, the principles of *Preußentum* outlined in *The Decline of the West* by no means found immediate or consistent reflection in his political writings, but assumed a variety of contours across his career.

A case in point was Spengler's widely read book *Prussianism and Socialism* (1919), which is the subject of Chapter 5. This publication is of central interest to the evolution of his politics of decline because it was written after Volume 1 of *The Decline of the West* in 1918, but before the publication of Volume 2 in 1922, in which his emphasis on the importance of elitist politics and Caesarist authoritarianism is particularly prominent. *Prussianism and Socialism* is significant because it develops the rallying idea of a revitalised German nation inspired not by the ideals of absolutism or Caesarism developed in his main work, but of *Prussian Socialism*. After providing some contextual background, I will discuss exactly what Spengler understood by socialism and explore his captivating, understudied intellectual relationship to the German socialist movement. Close attention will be paid to a discussion of the question of whether Prussian socialism was the concrete manifestation of his philosophy of world history, or whether it was more indicative of an opportunist gamble to exploit the all-pervasive rhetoric of socialism in the early Weimar Republic so as to gain support for his attempts to overthrow that state.

Spengler's activities as a thinker, speaker, organiser and publicist of the *nationale Bewegung* through to the attempted coup against the government in 1923 – the so-called Beer Hall Putsch in Munich – will form the opening section of Chapter 6. These activities provide the backdrop to his most programmatic text, *Rebuilding the German Reich* (1924). After a summary of this largely overlooked work and a comparison of its main arguments with those of *Prussianism and Socialism*, this chapter will make the case that *Rebuilding the German Reich* is not indicative of a conservative theorist who moderated his views on the need to overthrow democracy, rather, it is reflective of a Caesarist thinker who remained committed to a radical overhaul of the Weimar Constitution.

Chapter 7 will explore Spengler's understanding of the force that eventually succeeded in deposing the Weimar Republic: German National

Socialism. It will begin with an overview of Spengler's response to the Nazi rise to power and will discuss his assessment of leading Nazis such as Adolf Hitler, Joseph Goebbels and Gregor Strasser. It will emphasise that Spengler was no Nazi, but that he made various statements on the Nazis that have divided most of the secondary literature between viewing him either as a forerunner of the Hitler regime or as one of its most influential public critics.

The chapter will then discuss Spengler's *The Hour of Decision* (1933) and what it reveals about his understanding of the relationship between Caesarism and National Socialism. In contrast to much of the secondary literature, we will demonstrate how *The Hour of Decision* cannot be viewed as a critique of National Socialism, even though several Nazi thinkers felt compelled to criticise the publication sharply. After surveying some of the Nazi reception of *The Hour of Decision*, I will take a step back from the text in order to analyse Spengler's arguments on race and racism, as well as the so-called Jewish question, across his work as a whole. I will show that Spengler consistently rejected the biological anti-Semitism of many on the German right. At the same time, I will explain how Spengler's historical method proceeded from the assumption of Jewish metaphysical otherness and thus often had recourse to several of the prevalent anti-Semitic prejudices and tropes of his age. This chapter will bring out the ironic and even tragic aspects of Spengler's response to National Socialism. Despite having predicted and agitated for Caesarist dictatorial political institutions in Germany, he was horrified at the reality of dictatorship.

The volume will conclude with some comments on the main arguments it has advanced and the contributions it has made to understanding Spengler's legacy. Moreover, it will provide a synopsis of what the continuities, breaks and shifting emphases in his thought – not least in his changing understanding of socialism and his ideal German state – reveal about the difficulties involved in applying a rigid *Weltanschauung* to the ever-shifting reality of day-to-day politics.

# Notes

1. Spengler, *Der Untergang des Abendlandes. Umrisse einer Morphologie der Weltgeschichte*, 686 (my translation – unless otherwise stated, the translations of German-language citations from Spengler's writings and from the scholarly literature are my own throughout the book).

CHAPTER 1

# Oswald Spengler's Life and Work

## *A Chronological Overview*

Let us begin our discussion of Spengler's politics of decline with an overview of his life and work.[1] There are four main motivations for doing so. First, there are only a handful of extended biographical discussions of his career in English-language scholarship.[2] His unfinished autobiographical notes and aphorisms are yet to be translated, and there has only been one biographical account of his life published in English during this century.[3] Second, this outline of the major events during his life, as well as his publications, will serve as a point of reference to contextualise his political thought and activity. Third, the widespread perception of him as an isolated armchair philosopher who wrote little or nothing of significance beyond *The Decline of the West* is, as will be established here, out of step with the reality of his life and times. This perception has contributed to the neglect of his political writings. By reconstructing his career, it is possible to redress this balance and also to demonstrate that he was in fact one of the best-connected thinkers of his age who gained influence over several of the Weimar Republic's leading lights from politics and industry. Fourth, it can be shown that he was highly conscious of his own legacy and strove to be remembered as a thinker who had not only predicted all the major events during his life, but whose thought formed a coherent and unchanging whole. He claimed that he saw no need to modify his overall outlook in any major way, for he was a historical connoisseur who had established a bird's-eye view of all human history. However, as will be seen below, there is much exaggeration and self-stylisation involved here: such assertions consciously ignored both the failure of many of his predictions to come to fruition and the pragmatic flexibility with which he modified his thought in response to the tumultuous events of his life. This point is of particular significance to the assessment of his legacy, for the handful of studies of his political thought tend to proceed from the assumption that his politics are the immediate and logical reflection of his philosophy of history. With the above points in mind, let me now discuss the life and times of Oswald Spengler.

## Birth and Childhood

Oswald Arnold Gottfried Spengler was born in Blankenburg, in the Harz region of Germany, to Bernhard Spengler, who worked as a postal official, and Pauline Spengler (*née* Grantzow), the sister of the famous ballet dancer Adele Grantzow. Adele's glowing career, during which she performed for such luminaries as Napoleon III, the Russian Tsar, the German Kaiser and Otto von Bismarck, ended in tragedy: she chose death from blood poisoning over the amputation of her infected leg, which would immediately have put an end to her performances. This was not the only tragedy to befall Oswald's extended family during his life.

Oswald had three sisters: Adele, Gertrud and Hilde. Later, he spoke of his 'miserable, joyless youth'.[4] It is evident that he and his siblings came to bear the emotional scars of a stultifying and unloving domestic environment. His parents largely stayed together in order to keep up appearances. Bernhard Spengler was a hardworking postal official who – much to his son's chagrin – eschewed literature and poetry and led a stuffy, *bieder* existence centred on his job. This domestic atmosphere caused Pauline much distress and discomfort. Accustomed to the glitz and glamour of the ballrooms of Moscow and Paris from travelling with her sister on ballet tours, she was, in Oswald's words, 'plunged into a crass reality, into a marriage with a pitiful civil servant ... how my mother must have suffered!'[5]

We do not only learn about the unloving family environment and how his mother often took out her frustration on her children from Oswald's reminiscences. In her diaries, Gertrud Spengler recalled an incident when she was physically attacked by her mother for not having defrosted a chicken. When she defended herself and accidentally scratched her mother, Pauline threatened to take her to court.

In 1887, the family moved to Soest, where Bernhard felt that he had better career prospects. Work dominated the dutiful civil servant's life and he often arranged for his evening meals to be brought to the post office where he worked so that he could avoid the incessant arguing with his wife and keep up with the demands of his career. Apparently, the Spengler household became so untidy that a young Oswald did not dare to invite his classmates to visit. Recalling their childhood in Soest, Oswald's sister Hilde wrote of how the Spengler children attended school in tatty and ill-fitting clothing: 'We somehow always looked dumpy, preposterous and tasteless. Nobody at school was as destitute as we were.'[6]

The young Oswald took refuge from his oppressive family environment in what one of his biographers, Jürgen Naeher, calls his 'aesthetic "alternative worlds"'.⁷ Oswald entertained his sisters with stories of his adventures in fantasy realms with make-believe characters and settings. His imagination was such that he would dream up entire empires, such as Africa-Asia and Greater Germany. In his notebooks, he composed statistical tables for these polities, which outlined population trends and figures for industrial production and trade. He also wrote his own constitution for these imagined empires – the Spengler Code.

Oswald's other way of escaping reality was reading. After the family resettled in Halle in the autumn of 1891, he came to appreciate Nietzsche and Goethe as a grammar-school student at the Latina der Franckeschen Stiftungen. As he could not access such literature at school, he frequented the Halle University library, where he would read for hours on end. Impressed, but perhaps also taken aback, by Oswald's immersion in the world of literature, his uncle, Julius, once joked: 'Well, boy? When you gonna write your famous book?' Or: 'Well? What problems have you bin readin' about now then?'⁸

In 1897, at the tender age of seventeen, Spengler completed his first literary work, entitled *Montezuma*, a verse drama that deals with the Spanish conquest of Mexico. He never published this piece, but the script has now been made available. It is testament to his vivid imagination as an escape from his stifling domestic environment.⁹

Much has been made of Spengler's joyless childhood, his estrangement from his mother and his peers, his troubled relationship with his father, as well as his nervousness and anxiety, which on occasion triggered panic attacks. Indeed, many connections have been drawn – misleadingly, as we will see – between Spengler's glum description of his youth and the isolated intellectual with a pessimistic outlook for which he subsequently became notorious. Naeher suggests that *impotence* – a recurring theme in Spengler's writings on the decadence of late cultures – afflicted Spengler from a relatively early age. This affliction, claims Naeher, is best understood 'in the broadest sense, not solely in a sexual fashion, but rather as a fear of touching and of being touched'.¹⁰ Such deep-seated Angst may account for Spengler's lack of contact with the opposite sex, and many of the anxieties and neuroses that plagued him whenever he found the opportunity to speak to a woman. This fear occasionally found an outlet in several misogynist tropes typical of his surroundings at the time, such as: 'Only morons enjoy a "higher intellectual relationship" with a woman.'¹¹ Others have noted a link between the dominance of the primal feeling of fear or anxiety within Spengler's autobiographical fragments *Eis heauton* and the purported dominance of these moods in his magnum opus.¹²

Samir Osmančević goes even further and claims that the self-pitying and depressing tone of Spengler's autobiographical fragments finds reflection in the language of Spengler's overall outlook. According to Osmančević, these fragments 'speak the same language as the majority of his philosophy: as such, they are not just a necessary feature of a conventional philosophical biography. Often they are this philosophy itself'.[13] This is a most misleading assessment of Spengler the thinker and historical actor in two respects. To begin with, Spengler wrote his gloomy pronouncements on his early life in *Eis heauton* between 1913 and 1919. In other words, they were mostly composed *before* he found his life's '"purpose"'[14] following the fame associated with the success of *The Decline of the West*. So when Spengler claims in these fragments that '*all my life* I preferred to be a spectator from the sidelines than to stand on the stage',[15] it is misleading to infer too much about his supposed ineffectual isolation from this statement. We can certainly not conclude that this nervous seclusion provides the key to understanding *The Decline of the West* or his overall work, as Osmančević implies. As we will establish, it is necessary to distinguish between various stages in Spengler's career. While his statement above might well be an accurate description of his life before he published his major work, it is a world away from the period after 1919, when he became a leading intellectual of the German nationalist movement and had many an occasion to appear centre stage as an active participant in the events of his lifetime.

Moreover, it is necessary to differentiate conceptually between the largely subjective feelings of loneliness on the one hand and social isolation or distance from one's contemporaries on the other. While Spengler certainly suffered from the former, including in the form of lifelong anxiety and depression, these ailments did not translate into the latter for most of his career – quite the opposite, as we will see below.

## From Student to Teacher

Following the successful completion of his *Abitur* and his only episode of drunkenness following an evening of heavy drinking, Spengler headed off into university life. He was exempt from military service due to the heart condition from which he had suffered from birth. He attended the University of Halle to study mathematics and natural sciences alongside the *Lehramt* qualification to become a teacher. He was far from a model student and was not committed to his chosen subjects. After his father's death in 1901, he switched to the University of Munich and then spent the winter semester of 1902–3 at the University of Berlin. He wandered from lecture to lecture on a range of subjects at these three institutions. He showed a keen interest in many of the leading schools of thought of his day, such as socialism and the ideas of Darwin and Haeckel. While in Berlin, he developed a lifelong fascination with August Bebel, the German social-democratic parliamentarian. From time to time, Spengler listened in on some of the Reichstag parliament speeches for which Bebel became renowned.

In 1903, Spengler returned to Halle and completed his doctoral dissertation not in the field of mathematics, but philosophy. The subject was Heraclitus: 'Heraclitus – A Study of the Energetic Foundation of His Philosophy'.[16] The choice of Heraclitus as a subject is significant, not least because his most famous idea of *panta rhei* found prominent expression in Spengler's later conception of historical change. Spengler failed his first doctoral examination due to insufficient citations, but passed the exam on his second attempt in 1904. His *Staatsexamenarbeit*, which he completed in order to qualify as a schoolteacher, was entitled *The Development of the Visual Organs among the Main Groups of the Animal Kingdom*; the manuscript was subsequently lost. This choice of topic is also noteworthy, as Spengler's preoccupation with the metaphysics of sight and depth perception greatly influenced his understanding of historical cultures, as will be explained in Chapter 3.

On his first day of work as a teacher in Lüneburg in 1905, Spengler suffered a nervous breakdown at the very sight of the building in which he was supposed to work. Maybe his collapse resulted from the shock of moving from bohemian intellectual life to waged labour, or perhaps it stemmed from the realisation that he was unwittingly following in the footsteps of his father by becoming a work-focused official. For Spengler's true dream was to have an impact on the world around him: 'practical work in the grand style ... because I do not consider teaching to be "productive activity"'.[17] Despite this inauspicious start to his career, Spengler taught in Hamburg and Düsseldorf between 1905 and 1910. He was a strict but – and this is worth noting – popular teacher, who was known for his immaculate appearance and penchant for the latest clothing fashions.

At the same time, Spengler continued to be drawn by the calling of the arts and by the ambitions of becoming a published author. In 1910, he completed a sketch of a play entitled *The Victor*. Set during the Russo-Japanese War of 1904–5, it depicted a Japanese soldier painting in blood the image of a defeated Russian officer approaching him. Unlike *Montezuma*, it was published in Spengler's lifetime in the *Almanach der Rupprechtpresse auf die Jahre 1923/25*.[18]

## Munich and *The Decline of the West*

Spengler's mother died in 1910 and left him a modest inheritance with which it was possible for him to devote his energies exclusively to writing. He supplemented his income through journalistic pieces and theatre reviews for publications such as *Der Bücherwurm* and the *Neue Preußische Kreuzzeitung*, but was far from content with such employment.[19] In pursuit of his authorial ambitions, he left Hamburg for the more avant-garde Munich, which at the time was a hotbed of intellectual, literary and political creativity.

In 1911, Spengler began to conceive of the work that was to help him flee his solitude. He was prompted to do so by what has become known as the Second Agadir Crisis. This diplomatic emergency entailed a stand-off between Germany and France in Morocco, when Britain took France's side in what was a foreshadowing of the First World War. He drew inspiration for his work from the title of one of the eight volumes of Otto Seeck's *History of the Decline of the Ancient World*[20] he happened upon in a bookshop display window. Inspired by this title, he expanded upon his impression that the real prospect of war heralded by Agadir would mark a radical shift not merely for Germany, but also for the entire Western world. The historical precedent he had in mind was the rise of Rome in the ancient world following the Punic Wars. The book was initially entitled *Conservative and Liberal* to reflect his conviction that a truly conservative Germany could become a new Rome if it could assert itself militarily against 'liberal' France and England. But he increasingly expanded the historical scope of his publication to make the audacious claim that the outbreak of the First World War was no accident, but a necessary phenomenon preordained by the underlying forces of history: 'a historic act. And since this act forms part of a great historical organism, the life of which can be precisely determined, it occupies a predetermined position in the biography of that organism – a position that was fixed centuries ago'.[21]

When the First World War eventually broke out in 1914, several of Spengler's financial securities and investments fell into trouble and no longer bore interest. He consequently lost the relatively solid livelihood he had secured for himself from his mother's inheritance. He was forced to live in extreme financial difficulty, eating in Munich's working-class restaurants and writing *The Decline of the West* by candlelight. He was the embodiment of a night-owl and invariably laboured into the early hours of the morning. Anecdote has it that so as to save money on heating, he even positioned his writing chair on top of his desk in order to work at a higher elevation and stay warm during his marathon writing sessions.[22]

Spengler was horrified at the prospect of being drafted into the German military. Although he described the day when Germany declared war against Russia in August 1914 as the greatest in world history, he was terrified by the prospect of active combat.[23] In his correspondence he fearfully spoke of the 'spectre of conscription'.[24] For all the enthusiasm with which he greeted the war, the conflict was a time of pain and distress for him and those around him. In February 1917, his troubled sister Adele committed suicide. In March 1918, his brother-in-law was killed in battle. Undeterred by all this suffering, Spengler felt that Germany would emerge victorious: 'I would rather die than live in a humiliated Germany. But at the same time, I am certain of victory'.[25]

Spengler continued to labour away at his project, rushing to finish it as soon as possible so that its publication could coincide with the triumphant return of the German army he confidently expected. That victory never came. But, by May 1917, after numerous rejections, Spengler finally managed to find a Viennese publishing house, Wilhelm Braumüller, to print his book. *The Decline of the West. Outlines of a Morphology of World History. Volume I: Form and Actuality*, an obscure work by an obscure author, might have completely passed by an unsuspecting war-torn Germany. However, political events moved at a rapid pace. While Spengler may have been wrong about the outcome of the war, his literary timing could not have been better. The first edition appeared in January 1918 and sold in the tens of thousands because it was overwhelmingly judged by its cover. The population snapped up the book in the search for guidance or solace in a Germany where old truths and certitudes were falling apart. Although he benefited financially from this misreading, Spengler was frustrated by the idea of masses of people purchasing his book in order to read about the catastrophe of the war and its consequences. But the success of this elaborate and demanding tome made him a household name.

By 1919, Volume 1 of *The Decline of the West* had gone through two editions. This feat prompted Spengler to switch to the Munich-based publisher C.H. Beck for subsequent reprints, as well as for the publication of all his later works. The close personal relationship between Spengler and August Albers, one of the publisher's editorial staff, upheld Spengler's links to the Beck publishing house. Following Spengler's death, Albers threw himself in front of a train. Spengler's American publisher, Charles Knopf, claimed that Albers 'was the learned man's devoted slave'.[26]

During one of their many walks together, Albers asked Spengler for his views on socialism and left-wing politics at a time when Germany was in the throes of revolution. This conversation formed the outlines of Spengler's *Prussianism and Socialism* (December 1919), a fiery salvo of radical authoritarian thought that has been largely overlooked in secondary literature. This work, published between Volume 1 and Volume 2 of *The Decline of the West*, provides a fascinating insight into the development of Spengler's political thought. As will be discussed in Chapter 5, it is also reflective of a thinker who is most cognisant of the ideas and factional shades of the German socialist movement. However, it has only been fleetingly discussed in the book-length publications on him: Farrenkopf's is the only English-language study to discuss this text in detail. Other discussions tend to overemphasise the context within which Spengler conceived of the work at the expense of an analysis of how his daring concept of Prussian socialism relates to his political thought as a whole.

Spengler's public profile expanded even further as he became the recipient of the prestigious Nietzsche Foundation Prize and began to increase vastly the number of his personal, intellectual and political ties. The ancient historian Eduard Meyer, the renowned ethnologist Leo Frobenius and the philosopher Hermann Graf Keyserling became intellectual acquaintances and their critical feedback on his work left traces on the further development of his theory of world history. He was also close friends with the poet Ernst Droem (Adolf Weigel) and published an introduction to Droem's collection of poetry in 1920.[27] Spengler's ideas did not exist in an intellectual vacuum, but developed in interaction with these and other thinkers.

There were few thinkers who were not engaged with Spengler's work at this point. A heated dispute – the Spengler Debate – raged over the significance of *The Decline of the West* in a plethora of pamphlets, book reviews and newspaper articles. The German academic world was quick to condemn his ideas as fatalist and factually flawed, and as almost nihilistic in their purported gloominess. Whether out of envy at this academic outsider or out of the conviction that several of his assertions regarding world history, music, architecture, religion and mathematics had done an injustice to their respective specialisms, the reaction of academics was overwhelmingly negative. A special edition of the academic journal *Logos* was even produced, in which experts in several fields highlighted – line by line – Spengler's errors and overly rash conclusions.[28] One critic felt that the only possible effect of Spengler's philosophy could be to reinforce the *Untergangsstimmung* prevalent in Germany at the time – the impression that everything was falling apart. Others maintained that Spengler's claims to uniqueness and originality were rather hollow and that he was simply repackaging arguments already made by other thinkers. Yet Spengler insisted that this criticism was misplaced: he had not even heard of many of his alleged precursors, and the only two thinkers he was drawing on were Goethe, from whom he drew his 'method', and Nietzsche, from whom he developed his 'questions'.[29] Spengler refused to indulge his critics and largely avoided making public statements in response to the various criticisms levelled at him.

One important exception to the snubbing of Spengler's detractors was his polemic entitled 'Pessimism?'. First published in 1921 in the conservative journal *Preußische Jahrbücher*, this article expresses Spengler's dissatisfaction with the 'near universal misunderstanding' and misreading of Volume 1 of his *Der Untergang des Abendlandes* as somehow invoking an aloofness towards the inexorably approaching demise of the Western world.³⁰ Spengler stresses how he had by no means intended to contribute to the atmosphere of despair in Germany. Further, he asserts that his concept of *Untergang* should not be confused 'with the going under of an ocean liner' that one can only observe passively.³¹ Contrary to the claims of much of the later scholarship that Spengler was a prophet of gloom and doom, he adamantly rejected the charge that he was a pessimist: 'No, I am not a pessimist. Pessimism means not seeing any further tasks that need to be completed. I see so many unresolved tasks that I fear we shall have neither sufficient time nor men enough to tackle them.'³²

In Chapter 4, we will discuss exactly what Spengler understood by the unresolved tasks of Western civilisation. Moreover, we will establish how he employed the term *Untergang* both as a way of referring to the unavoidable demise of the Western world in the long term and as a rhetorical device to rally those to the cause of the German nation he was seeking to influence in the short term. This aspect of his thought – a central pillar of his politics of decline – has been seriously under-researched.

In the early 1920s, Spengler certainly had ample opportunity to stress that the Germans should not passively observe the decline of the Western world. He addressed a variety of conservative clubs and student associations committed to the cause of German nationalism and was heavily involved in right-wing plans to overthrow the Weimar Republic. Most notably, he spoke at a meeting alongside the conservative revolutionary Arthur Moeller van den Bruck, at which those present were not driven to pessimistic despair, but pledged their lives to the German nation. Spengler's expanded public profile saw him establish close contacts with German industrial leaders, as is apparent from the various speeches he gave to these circles.

In 1922, he addressed the Rheinisch-westfälische Wirtschaftstagung in Essen on the controversial topic of Russian–German relations. In this speech, entitled 'The Two Faces of Russia and Germany's Eastern Problems',³³ he contends that Russia is grossly misunderstood in Germany because the Russians have been analysed as one would analyse any other 'European' people. Such thinkers, he argues, are misled by the concept of 'Europe'. Real Europe – that is, the *Abendland* – stops at the Vistula. This ensures that the Russian soul is irreconcilably different from that of the West. As the title of Spengler's speech implies, he makes the case for the existence of two contending Russias: one facing towards the West and one towards Asia. This duality is represented by what he views as conflicts between money and simple commodity exchange, industry and agriculture, Petersburg and Moscow, Tolstoy and Dostoevsky, and Western-influenced rationalism and the mystical, believing Russian soul.

Spengler also had contacts in the German military. In 1922, he published the essay 'Modern Warfare' in the weekly army journal *Militär-*

*Wochenblatt: Unabhängige Zeitschrift für die deutsche Wehrmacht.*[34] This short piece expresses Spengler's conviction that the methods and aims of modern warfare are becoming ever more brutal and ruthless. The effectiveness of military tactics and strategy will increasingly depend upon the inventiveness and daring of strong individual leaders. As we will see throughout this volume, such emphasis on the increasing importance of individual leaders in politics, the military and the state bureaucracy is what Spengler refers to as Caesarism. It is a pivotal and often misunderstood aspect of his political alternative.

Volume 2 of *Der Untergang des Abendlandes*, subtitled *Perspectives of World History*, appeared in 1922. In 1923, a revised edition, consisting of Volumes One and Two together, was published. It contained some minor corrections to the previous editions of both volumes. Subsequently, this publication has served as the standard edition. The first English-language translation of Volume One, by Charles F. Atkinson, was published in New York in 1926. It was followed in 1928 by Volume Two. The translated work fared well in the English-speaking world and influenced figures such as the author T.S. Eliot and the historian Arnold Toynbee.[35] However, it was nowhere near as successful as in Germany: by 1926, the Beck publishing house produced a special edition of the work in order to celebrate the book selling 100,000 copies – no mean feat for such a dense theoretical study.

The success of Spengler's first published works established him as a sought-after speaker and influential networker among the German conservative elite. As will be explained in more detail in Chapter 6, he corresponded with and organised alongside such powerful conservatives as the industrialist Paul Reusch, the mining millionaire Hugo Stinnes, the media tycoon Alfred Hugenberg and the steel magnate Gustav Krupp.

## Politics and Publishing

Spengler was an eyewitness to the failed Beer Hall Putsch of November 1923, when Hitler and General von Ludendorff attempted to organise a national uprising against the Berlin government from Munich. Spengler was intricately involved in related efforts to subvert the republican regime. He coordinated plans to establish a secret right-wing press bureau that could serve as a propaganda outlet for the German right and counter what he viewed as the dominant influence of the left-wing press.[36] His aim was the overthrow of the Weimar Constitution and its replacement with a National Directorate (*Direktorium*). This body would dispense with any pretence of democracy and provide the authoritarian regime that Spengler viewed as essential for the rebirth of his beloved country. As will be seen in Chapter 6, the significance of the National Directorate in Spengler's political thought and how it relates to his understanding of Caesarism has either been overlooked or misunderstood in scholarship. However, understanding this institution is an essential aspect of grasping the motivations behind his political activity in this period. In May 1924, he published the most programmatic of all his major political publications, *Rebuilding the German Reich*. This text outlines ambitious and wide-ranging constitutional proposals for a radically overhauled Germany and is thus of immediate interest to understanding Spengler's political thought and the profound impact it had at this time. One of the chapters in the text, 'Public Service and Personality', was even published in a German police journal.[37] To the extent that *Rebuilding the German Reich* has been discussed at all, it has generally been viewed as a text in which Spengler adopted a more pragmatic-conservative outlook that grudgingly came to accept the existence of democracy in Germany. We will show, by contrast, how this interpretation overlooks his continued commitment to dictatorial political forms.

Spengler's heightened political activity and extensive social ties ensured that 1924 was one of his most prolific years as a writer and orator. Alongside short reprints of sections from his earlier works, such as *The Revolution Is Not Over* (taken from *Preußentum und Sozialismus*) and reprints of standalone chapters from Volume 2 of *The Decline of the West*, he wrote a variety of essays and speeches. Some of these were quickly transcribed and readied for publication, whereas others did not appear until the 1930s in his *Political Writings 1919–1926* (1932) or the posthumously published *Speeches and Essays* (1937).

'France and Europe', first published in January 1924 in the *Kölnische Volkszeitung*, is a German-nationalist critique of France's purported revanchism and expansionism.[38] In it, Spengler believes that the ruthlessness of French colonialism has seen it emerge as a leading power with a modern air force funded by the reparations it has seized from Germany.

In February 1924, Spengler gave a speech entitled 'The Political Duties of the German Youth' to the Hochschulring deutscher Art.[39] In this speech, he attempts to warn the young conservatives present that politics is an art form that takes years of patience and sacrifice to master. The youth should therefore not be misled by nationalist movements that offer quick-fix solutions or catchy slogans, such as the racist *völkische Bewegung*, but should learn the necessary statesmanship required for effective political leadership. As we will see throughout this volume, this is one of several occasions when Spengler publicly criticises the plebeian, *völkisch* nationalism of movements such as National Socialism.

At the end of April 1924, Spengler lectured a gathering of wealthy businessmen in Hamburg on 'New Forms of World Politics'. Here he once again emphasises how France has unexpectedly emerged as a leading power and that this has had devastating consequences for Germany, which the French wish to reduce to ruins 'militarily, politically and, if possible, economically too'.[40] After a lengthy discussion of how France is actively pursuing this aim, he concludes the speech with some important observations on what he views as the changing nature of politics. He warns that 'constitutional domestic politics',[41] the stable political order to which all competing political parties are committed, is disintegrating. His prediction for what will come next again relates to the idea of Caesarism: 'high politics increasingly assumes a form of domination [*Herrschaft*] wielded subjectively by unaccountable individual personalities'.[42]

In May 1924, Spengler provided the keynote address at the annual gathering of the German aristocracy (Deutscher Adelstag) in Breslau; it was swiftly transcribed and published as 'Tasks of the German Aristocracy' in the *Deutsches Adelsblatt*. Here he makes the point that the political estate of the aristocracy must be preserved as a 'leading social stratum' in the face of the adversity encountered by Germany.[43]

'Ten Years after the Outbreak of War' was published in August 1924 as part of a special edition of *Süddeutsche Monatshefte*. This short piece places great emphasis on the will of the German people to overcome the defeat of 1918 and, despite the suffering caused by this loss, to achieve greatness. The article's conclusion is noteworthy for somebody who has overwhelmingly been remembered as an incorrigible pessimist:

> In the last instance, we – like all peoples in a similar position – depend on this will. With such a will, there is no historical situation that can destroy all hope. What would really signify the end for us is not our continuing plight [as a result of Germany's military defeat], but rather if this will were to disappear.[44]

In September 1924, he was once again called upon by his contacts in the world of German business to outline his thoughts at a meeting in Duesseldorf of the the Verein zur Wahrung der gemeinsamen wirtschaftlichen Interessen in Rheinland und Westfalen. This address was entitled 'The Relationship between the Economy and Fiscal Policy since 1750'. His main argument in this address is that the decisive difference between the structure of economic and fiscal policy in 1800 and 1900 cannot be explained with reference to capitalism, machinery or factories – all of which could be found already in 1750 – but in the rise of stocks and shares. This has radically undermined the nineteenth-century understanding of taxation as a burden to be borne by the individual, because it is possible for some individuals to obscure their actual wealth using 'the fictitious quantities of monetary speculation'.[45] At a time when the state requires enormous amounts of money from taxation, the rise of finance capital has devastating implications, because the tax burden falls not on 'those who own something, but those who can be seen to own something'.[46] Here Spengler has in mind the Weimar Republic's tax demands on German industry, which he views as a form of fiscal Bolshevism on German soil.

On 2 October 1924, Spengler gave a lecture entitled 'Plan for a New Atlas Antiquus',[47] in which he asserts that historical research urgently needs a cartographical representation of several important periods in the ancient world, such as the Vedic period in India and the Homeric age in Greece. However, in order for these maps to be of use to historical research, they should not only be able to portray the geographical regions of these periods, but should also highlight whether these regions were woodland, flatland or desert and thus how they contributed economically to these past societies. This short speech is a good example of Spengler's immense historical knowledge.

Spengler's last major speech in 1924 was given at the Nietzsche Archive in Weimar to mark what would have been Nietzsche's eightieth birthday on 15 October. In it Spengler flatteringly compares Nietzsche's life to that of Goethe. Whereas Goethe was fortunate to be born during, and to embody, the height of the cultural achievements of the Western *Abendland*, Nietzsche was born a century later. This period was the beginning of the decline of the Western world – what Spengler calls *Zivilisation*. Nietzsche's profound contribution to the understanding of morality and his ability 'to look inside entire cultures as one would living individual beings' is thus all the more astonishing in an age of what Spengler views as shallow rationalism and materialism.[48]

## The Return to Research

By the end of 1924, Spengler drew the conclusion that the opportunity for the advance of the German nationalist right had passed. This realisation ushered in a new chapter in his life. He largely withdrew from his political work to focus on expanding his theory of world history. His political publishing was reduced to a handful of articles published between 1926 and 1928. His 'On the Historical Development of the Press in Germany' draws on his experiences in attempting to set the agenda of the German print media.[49] He notes how modern newspapers are employing cheap correspondents to perform the work once carried out by academics and experts. Moreover, he argues that the regional fragmentation of the German press renders it outdated and unable to keep up with the trends towards centralisation and rationalisation seen in other enterprises and areas of the economy.

'The Relationship between the World Economy and World Politics' was a speech given to the Industrieclub zu Düsseldorf on 9 November 1926.[50] This is a significant lecture as it outlines Spengler's views on the globally connected nature of the world economy and explains why he feels that further military clashes between the leading powers are inevitable. One reason he highlights is that the living standards of the majority of the population are artificially high; there are too many people for the countries of the Western world to feed. The population will therefore have to be reduced or further conflicts over resources will ensue.

'On the German National Character' was published in the annual *Deutschland* in 1927. In it Spengler argues that national character is formed more by suffering and adversity than by prosperity and success. He further claims that if the Germans can unite around a bold and decisive leader, then they might just emerge from the crisis as a stronger people.[51] With hindsight, Spengler's Introduction to Richard Kornherr's essay 'The Declining Birth Rate: An Exhortation to the German People' (1927) proves to be far more controversial. In the Introduction, Spengler emphasises that the 'inner health of the living body of the German people' fundamentally revolves around one factor: that of fertility and birth rates.[52] Kornherr later became an ardent Nazi and in 1943 drew on his studies of changing trends in the German population to deliver the notorious Kornherr Report on the so-called Final Solution to the Jewish question.[53]

The article 'New Forms of Governance', published in the *Bundesjahrbuch* of 1928, is Spengler's last published political piece in the 1920s. It provides a summary of his 'aims ... for the immediate future' in Germany.[54] It does so by emphasising that the parliamentary state forms of the nineteenth century are irrevocably a thing of the past. He proposes that institutions be created, through which 'men of significance' can achieve their full potential and social impact, and out of which hardworking and efficient public servants can emerge to run state affairs.[55] The outcome, he hopes, will be to facilitate the rise of the Caesar figures on whom the future of Germany and the West as a whole hinges. Many of the political proposals in this article can be found his *Rebuilding the German Reich*, which had been published four years earlier.

All the while, Spengler was labouring away on his larger research projects. The two he alluded to at several points during his career were 'a metaphysical book' and a 'world history from the beginning'.[56] He dedicated much of the remainder of his life to both, but never completed either. It is questionable whether such projects could be completed at all within the scope of one career. In any case, his health was gradually deteriorating. A shock stroke in 1927 impaired his ability to work for around three years, and in 1929, he suffered from a severe case of anaemia.

Only returning to something approaching his former working routine in the early 1930s, Spengler began to compile the aphorisms and fragmentary notes for his grander projects that, he felt, could expand upon the understanding of human history as consisting of eight High Cultures, which he had first developed in *The Decline of the West*. The extant fragments of these ambitious projects were not made available until long after his death, when they were collated and published in German under the titles of *Original Questions: Fragments from Spengler's Papers* (1965) and *The Early Period of World History: Fragments from Spengler's Papers* (1966) by Anton Mirko Koktanek.[57] The former deals predominantly with Spengler's metaphysics, whereas the latter outlines four stages of human history (to which Spengler assigns the letters *a*, *b*, *c* and *d*) before the rise of the first of the eight High Cultures in his original schema.[58]

## Later Years

Spengler continued to publish extensively in the 1930s, with *Man and Technics: A Contribution to a Philosophy of Life* (1931) reflecting the results of a career-long fascination with the nature of human existence. This publication was based on a talk he gave at the German Museum on 6 May 1931. Those present expected him to talk about the problems faced by humanity in the age of machinery, but instead he proceeded to discuss anthropology, metaphysics and world history.

In *Man and Technics*, Spengler argues that humans should be viewed both as part of nature and as what he calls anti-nature (*Widernatur*). They possess unique abilities that allow them to transcend a purely animal existence, but in the last instance they are dependent on, and in constant struggle with, the natural world. This leads him to the concept of technics (*Technik*). This term should not be understood in the trite sense of technology or technical innovation. Rather, it encompasses life as a whole: humanity's grand efforts to shape its surroundings in its own image. For Spengler, then: 'Technics is the tactics of all life; it is the inner form of which the process of conflict – the conflict that is synonymous with life itself – is the outward expression.'[59] Human *Technik* is derived from two bodily organs: the eye, which approaches the world theoretically; and the hand, the practical tool with which to implement these theoretical plans. Positioning himself against Darwinism and notions of evolution, Spengler places great importance on *mutations* as being central to the development of humanity. These mutations are best understood as an 'inner transformation … without a "cause", of course, as is the case with everything in the real world'.[60] There are three such mutations in the history of humanity: the discovery of fire, the spoken word and the emergence of the eight High Cultures that he locates at the heart of human development. Looking to the world around him, Spengler concludes that the underlying tragedy of humanity stems from the fact that nature is stronger than humanity, and the struggle against it, while hopeless, will be carried out until the last. The text contains what is perhaps his most famous aphorism: 'Optimism is *cowardice*'[61] (today, it adorns t-shirts of Spengler's grim visage for sale on the internet). However, as will be seen in Chapter 7, this warning about the pitfalls of optimism by no means implies pessimism when it comes to his continued commitment to the reawakening of the German nation.

A case in point was Spengler's reaction to the global economic crisis of 1929 and the dire situation in Germany. Despite his deteriorating health, he was once again drawn towards politics. And with fascism on the march across Europe, in 1932 he sought to clarify his stance on this phenomenon by collating his numerous political works in a single edition entitled *Political Writings 1919–1926*.

In the middle of August 1933, Spengler published his *Jahre der Entscheidung. Erster Teil. Deutschland und die weltgeschichtliche Entwicklung* (translated as *The Hour of Decision. Part I: Germany and World-Historical Evolution*), which was based on the lecture 'Deutschland in Gefahr', delivered to the German Patriotic Society (Patriotische Gesellschaft) in Hamburg on 3 February 1930. As will be explained in Chapter 7, the translation of this title into English as *The Hour of Decision* is most problematic, as it implies that 'the decision' to be made is an urgent one in favour of, or against, fascism, whereas Spengler was in fact thinking more of decisive years or even decades. Moreover, contrary to many claims in the secondary literature, *The Hour of Decision* was not a critique of the National Socialists. True, Spengler was a consistent critic of the biological racialism and plebeian aspects of the racist *völkische Bewegung*. He was also annoyed by Hitler's role in the Beer Hall Putsch of 1923. So while Spengler was personally pleased by the 'national transformation'[62] represented by Hitler's ascension to Chancellor in January 1933, he had a series of fundamental criticisms of National Socialism. However, like so many others at the time, he initially believed that Hitler could perhaps be 'guided' in the right direction to become less of a rabble-rouser and act more like Mussolini, whom Spengler viewed as the true ruler (*Herrscher*) of Italy. Spengler was therefore cautious about making public statements on National Socialism at this point and, as we will show, was equally guarded about being publicly associated with the new regime.

Spengler had a copy of *The Hour of Decision* sent to the Führer, along with the request that the two men should discuss its contents (their first and only meeting took place in July 1933 – see Chapter 7). However, it soon became clear that he could not exert any influence over Hitler.

Moreover, the Nazi regime's consolidation of power had tragic personal consequences for Spengler. The purges conducted during the so-called Night of the Long Knives in June 1934 entailed the brutal liquidation of several of Spengler's closest political allies. These included his friend Gregor Strasser, a Nazi on the 'left' of the party with whom Spengler corresponded and met on several occasions, and Spengler's ally Gustav von Kahr, a leading member of the Bavarian People's Party. To add insult to injury, another close friend, the music critic Willi Schmid, was murdered because of an administrative mix-up: the Nazi Storm Troopers of the Sturmabteilung (SA) were supposed to kill a man by the name of Willi Schmidt. Schmid's body was so gravely mistreated in the process that his family was prevented from accessing his grave. When he heard the tragic news, Spengler had a crying fit.[63]

Spengler provided the eulogy at Schmid's funeral and a year later produced a commemorative volume for him in cooperation with Peter Dörfler.[64] Fearing the consequences of his close ties to some of the SA's targets – the erstwhile influential Gregor Strasser in particular – Spengler burnt many of his papers and letters. Plans for a second volume of *The Hour of Decision* were shelved and the possibilities for him to comment on, let alone shape, developments around him were vanishing rapidly. His final act of protest, in October 1935, saw him step down from the editorial board of the Nietzsche Archive in Munich. This move was a symbolic act of defiance against the distortion of Nietzsche's legacy, spearheaded by Nietzsche's sister, Elisabeth Förster-Nietzsche, for National Socialist purposes.

Although Spengler's political career was now effectively over, his historical research continued to bear fruit in the 1930s. The article 'The Age of the American Cultures' (1933) and the lecture he gave to the Society of the Friends of Asiatic Art and Culture, entitled 'The Chariot's Significance for the Course of World History' (1934), both attested to this.[65] The former outlines some tentative suggestions about how his understanding of history could contribute to reconstructing the lost history of Ancient America. The latter is a novel way of approaching the study of history by suggesting that the best way to arrive at an impression of the ethos and mentality of those living in the second millennium BC is not to be found in the analysis of ceramics, but in thinking about what Spengler calls the first sophisticated weapon: the chariot.

In 1935, Spengler published a long treatise under the title 'On the World History of the Second Millennium BC' in the journal *Die Welt als Geschichte*.[66] This piece summarised some of the observations he had made when attempting to compose his history of humanity. He had come to the conclusion that the second millennium BC was central to the subsequent development of humanity, for this was a time when two of the historical cultures he highlights in *The Decline of the West* – the southern cultures of Egypt and Babylon – were coming to an end. In the north, from Western

Europe through to East Asia, new kinds of peoples were beginning to emerge who were fundamentally different from those in the south. This, then, was the period when the peoples of three of Spengler's historical cultures – the ancient Greek, the Chinese and the Indian – came into being.

Spengler's final published article – 'Is World Peace Possible?' – took the form of a cable telegram. It was written three years before the outbreak of the Second World War in response to a survey produced by the American publication *Hearst's International Cosmopolitan*.[67] Its readers were asked whether world peace was a realistic prospect. Spengler answers this in the negative, claiming that pacifism was a mere expression of a tired and forlorn populace of a degenerate Western world.

Spengler died from a heart attack in 1936 at the age of fifty-five. His poor diet and penchant for beer and cigars probably compounded the heart complaints from which he had suffered from a young age. In light of the horror that was to be unleashed on the Western world to which he had devoted his intellectual energy, his passing could be described – slightly modifying the words of former German Chancellor Helmut Kohl – as 'the blessing of an early death'.[68] His early departure from this world freed him from the burden of having to make difficult moral and political choices.

On his insistence, Spengler's sisters Gertrud and Hilde arranged for a humble burial and requested that expressions of sympathy, which one would expect to be rather numerous, should not be sent.[69] Spengler saw to it that copies of his two most coveted books, Goethe's *Faust* and Nietzsche's *Thus Spoke Zarathustra*, were placed alongside him in his coffin.

John F. Fennelly reflects the general consensus on Spengler when he writes that Spengler 'died, as he had lived most of his life, in relative isolation'.[70] Spengler was no longer the well-connected and well-travelled political figure he had once been, and his only close contacts were his sister Hilde and her daughter, Spengler's niece (rather confusingly also called Hildegard), who together had taken care of his household since the mid-1920s. Fennelly's statement nonetheless belies the enduring impact Spengler's thought exerted on German society. The German edition of *The Hour of Decision* sold an estimated 150,000 copies in 1933 alone, and two volumes edited and published posthumously by his niece – *Speeches and Essays* (1937) and a collection of aphorisms (*Thoughts*, 1941)[71] – both sold well.

## Image and Reality

We have seen above how prolific Spengler was, what a huge impact he exerted on those around him and how he enjoyed connections in German politics, industry, the military and even the police. Yet in the secondary literature he has overwhelmingly been remembered as a prophetic loner.

In their portrayals of Spengler, some of the most important researchers of his life have argued that he should be seen as 'our Cassandra',[72] 'the foreseer',[73] a man whose 'personality reminds one strongly of the Old Testament prophets',[74] a 'prophet of decline',[75] a figure who was 'able to see the future like Cassandra and who was just as outrageous and lonely'[76] or a thinker whose literary success with *The Decline of the West* 'really verges on clairvoyant abilities'.[77]

The understanding of Spengler as an isolated prophet does not, as we have seen, reflect the reality of the various stages of his career. However, it must be stressed that Spengler himself bears some responsibility for this state of affairs. Particularly towards the end of his life, he had a propensity to portray himself as an all-seeing thinker who was alone in having foreseen the major events in recent German history. In the Foreword to his *Political Writings 1919–1926* in 1932, for instance, he claims to have predicted the German November Revolution of 1918: 'the unavoidable revolution, which both Metternich and Bismarck had seen clearly, which had to come, and not only to Germany, regardless of whether we returned home as victors or as the vanquished'.[78] In reality, he had been shocked by the revolutionary events of November 1918 and by the German military defeat that fed into this upheaval. As he wrote in the Preface to the first German edition of *The Decline of the West*: 'I only wish to add the desire that this book might not be entirely unworthy alongside Germany's military achievements.'[79]

Moreover, Spengler misleadingly sought to create the impression that he was unable to establish any lasting or meaningful connections with his contemporaries, either because of their inability to break with the prevailing modes of thought he viewed as outdated or because they were blinded by the kind of narrow party-political affiliations and prejudices that his method purported to stand above. He considered himself to be 'made for *seeing*' and felt that to possess 'this vision is the real philosophical gift'.[80] Safe in the knowledge that he had developed such an ability, he wrote towards the end of his career:

> I see more clearly than others because I think independently – free from parties, schools of thought and interests. I have foreseen how things developed organically, according to fate [*schicksalhaft*] and how they will continue to develop. I am able to foresee things even more, but feel lonelier, than ever before.[81]

The pictures and busts of himself that Spengler commissioned fit precisely into this mould in their portrayal of the visage of an intense, austere man with a stern, fixated gaze. However, a contrasting image of Spengler to that of the lonesome theorist is that of the man who ate in cheap restaurants, drank beer, smoked and ate voraciously among the 'taxi-drivers and similar patrons',[82] visited auctions and travelled extensively to an array of meetings, gatherings and social occasions. This Spengler was also recalled by several of his contemporaries. On a visit to Munich, Spengler's American publisher Charles Knopf and his wife felt that Spengler's self-projected image did not coincide with the reality of him as a human being. Mrs Knopf recalls: 'He struck me as being an extremely human and considerate person – enormous in bulk, very forceful-looking, and – for a man of his stature – exceedingly easy to talk to.'[83] Elements of the neurotic, or even the bizarre, were doubtless present in Spengler's personality: his insistence on placing a sign with 'On holiday!' on his front door (which he duly removed when actually holidaying) or his penchant for showing his watch to friends and colleagues when meeting them in order to demonstrate that he had shown up exactly on time. Such quirks and idiosyncrasies – often found among people who devote their lives to ambitious political and intellectual aims – should not obscure the fact that he was one of the best-connected thinkers of his time.

To point out the discrepancies between Spengler's life and Spengler as he sought to portray himself to posterity is not to deny his frequent feelings of loneliness and depression. But by highlighting the gulf between Spengler the man and Spengler as he subsequently came to be understood, we can assess his legacy based not on what he said of himself, but what he actually did – on the activities and interventions of this important thinker seeking to achieve his dream of German world hegemony. Only then will we be able to understand how his *politics of decline* took shape in response to the immense social changes that unfolded during his lifetime.

## Notes

1. This synopsis of Spengler's life builds upon his correspondence: Spengler, *Briefe 1913–36*; his biographical fragment *Eis heauton*, named after the diaries of the Roman Emperor Marcus Aurelius; Spengler, *'Ich beneide jeden, der lebt'. Die Aufzeichnungen 'Eis heauton' aus dem Nachlaß*; life sketches written by several of his close contemporaries such as Dakin (ed.), *Today and Destiny: Vital Excerpts from the 'Decline of the West' of Oswald Spengler*, 353–64; Drascher, 'Begegnungen mit Oswald Spengler', in Koktanek (ed.), *Spengler-Studien. Festgabe für Manfred Schröter zum 85. Geburtstag*, 9–31; subsequent German-language scholarship, particularly Conte, *Oswald Spengler. Eine Einführung*; Felken, *Oswald Spengler. Konservativer Denker zwischen Kaiserreich und Diktatur*; Henkel, *Nationalkonservative Politik und mediale Repräsentation. Oswald Spenglers politische Philosophie und Programmatik im Netzwerk der Oligarchen (1910–1925)*; Koktanek, *Oswald Spengler in seiner Zeit*; Naeher, *Oswald Spengler*; and Tartsch, *Denn der Mensch ist ein Raubtier. Eine Einführung in die politischen Schriften und Theorien Oswald Spenglers*, 9–92, as well as some of the observations of the English-language studies cited in footnotes 2 and 3 below.
2. Fennelly, *Twilight of the Evening Lands: Oswald Spengler – A Half Century Later*; Fischer, *History and Prophecy: Oswald Spengler and the Decline of the West*; Hughes, *Oswald Spengler: A Critical Estimate*. All contain a chapter on Spengler's life.

3. Spengler, *'Ich beneide jeden, der lebt'. Die Aufzeichnungen 'Eis heauton' aus dem Nachlaß*. Spengler's notes, often headed 'Ego' or 'Eis heauton', were typewritten by his sister Hilde. They are arranged in no particular order and are for the most part undated. In total, Spengler's reflections comprise 145 typewritten fragments. The only chapter in English that deals with Spengler's life in this century is in Farrenkopf, *Prophet of Decline: Spengler on World History and Politics*, 5–16.
4. Spengler, *'Ich beneide jeden, der lebt'. Die Aufzeichnungen 'Eis heauton' aus dem Nachlaß*, 21.
5. Ibid., 41.
6. This entry is from her unpublished diaries, which form part of Spengler's private papers. Cited in Tartsch, *Denn der Mensch ist ein Raubtier*, 10.
7. Naeher, *Oswald Spengler*, 15.
8. Cf. ibid., 18.
9. See Birkenmaier, *Versionen Montezumas. Lateinamerika in der historischen Imagination des 19. Jahrhunderts. Mit dem vollständigen Manuskript von Oswald Spenglers 'Montezuma. Ein Trauerspiel' (1897)*.
10. Naeher, *Oswald Spengler*, 50.
11. Spengler, *'Ich beneide jeden, der lebt'. Die Aufzeichnungen 'Eis heauton' aus dem Nachlaß*, 64.
12. Merlio, 'Urgefühl Angst', in ibid., 89–123. See also Wagner, '"Weltmacht oder Niedergang". Wilhelmische Mentalität, extreme Emotionen und Bilder des Kommenden am Beispiel Oswald Spenglers' in particular. Markus Henkel's study is the only one in the secondary literature to highlight the excessive importance attached to the notion of Angst in Spengler's work: Henkel, *Nationalkonservative Politik*, 50, fn. 138.
13. Osmančević, *Oswald Spengler und das Ende der Geschichte*, 87.
14. Spengler, *Eis heauton*, 14.
15. Ibid., 10–11 (emphasis added).
16. Spengler, 'Heraklit', in *Reden und Aufsätze*, 4–44.
17. Spengler, *'Ich beneide jeden, der lebt'. Die Aufzeichnungen 'Eis heauton' aus dem Nachlaß*, 75.
18. Spengler, 'Der Sieger', in *Reden und Aufsätze*, 45–49.
19. Hardly any of these journalistic pieces have been published. For some rare examples, see Spengler, 'Zum Problem der modernen christlichen Kunst', in Falck (ed.), *Zyklen und Cäsaren. Mosaiksteine einer Philosophie des Schicksals*, 155–60; Spengler, 'Krieg, Drama und Roman', in ibid., 161–67.
20. Seeck, *Geschichte des Untergangs der antiken Welt*, 8 vols.
21. Spengler, *Der Untergang des Abendlandes. Umrisse einer Morphologie der Weltgeschichte*, 1167.
22. Farrenkopf, *Prophet of Decline*, 13. However, there are other versions of this anecdote. One is Tartsch's claim that Spengler's desk consisted of a small ironing board: Tartsch, *Denn der Mensch ist ein Raubtier*, 30.
23. 'Today, the 1 August 1914, is the greatest day in world history, which falls in *my* life and which is so powerfully bound up with the *idea* for which I was *born*. I am sitting at home alone. Nobody is thinking of me'; Spengler, *'Ich beneide jeden, der lebt'. Die Aufzeichnungen 'Eis heauton' aus dem Nachlaß*, 50.
24. Spengler to Hans Klöres, 3 November 1915, in Spengler, *Briefe 1913–36*, 49.
25. Spengler, *'Ich beneide jeden, der lebt'. Die Aufzeichnungen 'Eis heauton' aus dem Nachlaß*, 23.
26. Dakin (ed.), *Today and Destiny*, 358.
27. Spengler, 'Einführung zu Ernst Droems *Gesängen*', in *Reden und Aufsätze*, 50–57.
28. Kroner and Mehlis (eds), *Logos. Internationale Zeitschrift für Philosophie der Kultur*, 9.2 (1921).
29. Spengler, *Der Untergang des Abendlandes*, IX.
30. Spengler, 'Pessimismus?', in *Reden und Aufsätze*, 58–71.
31. Ibid., 58.
32. Ibid., 68.
33. Spengler, 'Das Doppelantlitz Rußlands und die deutschen Ostprobleme', in *Politische Schriften 1919–1926*, 112–28.

34. Spengler, 'Moderne Kriegsführung', in Falck (ed.), *Zyklen und Cäsaren*, 258–60.
35. On the influence of Spengler on Eliot's *The Waste Land*, see Barry, 'The "Waste Land": A Possible German Source', 429–42. On Spengler and Toynbee, see Joll, 'Two Prophets of the Twentieth Century: Spengler and Toynbee', 91–104. For a good overview of the reception of Spengler's work across Europe, see Gasimov and Lemke Duque (eds), *Oswald Spengler als europäisches Phänomen. Der Transfer der Kultur- und Geschichtsmorphologie im Europa der Zwischenkriegszeit 1919–1939*.
36. On this initiative, see Hoser, 'Ein Philosoph im Irrgarten der Politik. Oswald Spenglers Pläne für eine geheime Lenkung der nationalen Presse', 435–58.
37. Spengler, 'Staatsdienst und Persönlichkeit', 276–79.
38. Spengler, 'Frankreich und Europa', in *Reden und Aufsätze*, 72–78.
39. Spengler, 'Politische Pflichten der deutschen Jugend', in *Politische Schriften 1919–1926*, 128–54.
40. Spengler, 'Neue Formen der Weltpolitik', in ibid., 160.
41. Ibid., 312.
42. Ibid., 313.
43. Spengler, 'Aufgaben des Adels', in *Reden und Aufsätze*, 79.
44. Spengler, 'Zehn Jahre nach Kriegsausbruch', in Falck (ed.), *Zyklen und Cäsaren*, 321.
45. Spengler, 'Das Verhältnis von Wirtschaft und Steuerpolitik seit 1750', in *Politische Schriften 1919–1926*, 289.
46. Ibid.
47. Spengler, 'Plan eines neuen Atlas antiquus', in *Reden und Aufsätze*, 85–92.
48. Spengler, 'Nietzsche und sein Jahrhundert', in ibid., 105.
49. Spengler, 'Zur Entwicklungsgeschichte der deutschen Presse', in ibid., 111–13.
50. Spengler, 'Das heutige Verhältnis zwischen Weltwirtschaft und Weltpolitik', in *Politische Schriften 1919–1926*, 295–319.
51. Spengler, 'Vom deutschen Volkscharakter', in ibid., 116–19.
52. Spengler, 'Einführung zu einem Aufsatz Richard Korherrs über den Geburtenrückgang', in *Reden und Aufsätze*, 120.
53. On the Kornherr Report, see Hilberg, *Die Vernichtung der europäischen Juden*, 1283.
54. Spengler, 'Neue Regierungsformen', in Falck (ed.), *Zyklen und Cäsaren*, 271.
55. Ibid.
56. Cf. Conte, *Oswald Spengler*, 67.
57. Spengler, *Urfragen. Fragmente aus dem Nachlaß*; Spengler, *Aus der Frühzeit der Weltgeschichte. Fragmente aus dem Nachlaß*.
58. For an excellent summary of these insights, see Osmančević, *Oswald Spengler und das Ende der Geschichte*, 125–34.
59. Spengler, 'Der Mensch und die Technik. Beitrag zu einer Philosophie des Lebens', in Falck (ed.), *Zyklen und Cäsaren*, 371.
60. Ibid., 380.
61. Ibid., 406.
62. Spengler, *Jahre der Entscheidung. Erster Teil. Deutschland und die weltgeschichtliche Entwicklung*, 4.
63. Cf. Falck (ed.), *Zyklen und Cäsaren*, 119.
64. Schmid, Spengler and Dörfler (eds), *Unvollendete Symphonie. Gedanken und Dichtung von Willi Schmid*.
65. Spengler, 'Das Alter der amerikanischen Kulturen', in *Reden und Aufsätze*, 120–21; Spengler, 'Der Streitwagen und seine Bedeutung für den Gang der Weltgeschichte', in ibid., 122–130.
66. Spengler, 'Zur Weltgeschichte des zweiten vorchristlichen Jahrtausends', in *Reden und Aufsätze*, 139–258.
67. Spengler, 'Ist Weltfriede möglich?', in *Reden und Aufsätze*, 259–60.
68. Kohl first used the phrase 'the blessing of a late birth' ('Die Gnade der späten Geburt') on German television in 1983; see Fischer and Lorenz (eds), *Lexikon der 'Vergangenheitsbewältigung' in Deutschland. Debatten und Diskursgeschichte des Nationalsozialismus nach 1945*, 247.

69. Henkel claims that many letters of condolence were in fact sent to Spengler's sister and his friend Albers in the weeks following the funeral; Henkel, *Nationalkonservative Politik*, 19, fn. 24.
70. Fennelly, *Twilight of the Evening Lands*, 27.
71. Spengler, *Gedanken*.
72. Farrenkopf, 'The Transformation of Spengler's Political Philosophy', 481.
73. The title of a section in Martin Falck's discussion of Spengler; see Falck (ed.), *Zyklen und Cäsaren*, 124–45.
74. Fennelly, *Twilight of the Evening Lands*, 27.
75. The title of Kurt Breysig's review of *The Decline of the West*: Breysig, 'Der Prophet des Untergangs', 261–70, which Farrenkopf drew on for the title of his own study eighty years later, *Prophet of Decline*.
76. Koktanek, 'Spenglers Verhältnis zum Nationalsozialismus in geschichtlicher Entwicklung', 55.
77. Osmančević, *Oswald Spengler und das Ende der Geschichte*, 94.
78. Spengler, 'Vorwort', in *Politische Schriften 1919–1926*, 8.
79. Spengler, *Der Untergang des Abendlandes*, xi.
80. Spengler, '*Ich beneide jeden, der lebt*'. *Die Aufzeichnungen 'Eis heauton' aus dem Nachlaß*, 9, 11.
81. Spengler, 'Vorwort', in *Politische Schriften 1919–1926*, 14.
82. The words of Mrs Knopf; cf. Dakin (ed.), *Today and Destiny*, 360.
83. Cf. ibid., 359.

CHAPTER 2

# Spengler Reception and Research

In order to trace historically how scholarship has engaged with Spengler's thought, let us now proceed to discuss the literature written on him. Over the past one hundred years, Spengler's work has prompted numerous writers from across the globe to engage with his ideas that they find most provocative or illuminating. What follows is a brief overview of the main developments and trends in the English- and German-language reception and research of his thought. We will proceed chronologically and will largely postpone a critical engagement with the arguments advanced within the secondary literature until later in the book.

We will begin with the immediate reception of Spengler's work through to the end of the Second World War. This overview will be followed by a summary of the four English-language book-length studies of Spengler. We will then discuss the most significant German-language publications on Spengler since the Second World War through to the end of the twentieth century. Subsequently, we will take a closer look at the small renaissance in Spengler studies in German-language scholarship during the past twenty years. Let us begin with the immediate reception of Spengler in the 1920s and 1930s.

## Early Reception

The 'Spengler Debate' that raged over *The Decline of the West* prompted what Manfred Schröter calls a 'chaos' of responses as part of Germany's attempts to process the implications of military defeat in the First World War.[1] In total, the immediate reception of Spengler's main work is estimated to amount to over 400 articles, publications and scholarly treatises, including by some of Germany's most celebrated thinkers.

Thomas Mann, for instance, was initially stirred by Spengler's richly metaphoric account of human history. In notes written between 1919 and 1920, he described *The Decline of the West* as a compelling 'intellectual novel', the power of which the calculating criticism of the historical specialists could not match.[2] However, as Barbara Beßlich has shown, such admiration did not last for long. Later, Mann scornfully referred to Spengler as 'Nietzsche's clever ape', 'a defeatist of humanity' and the 'hyena'.[3]

For Georg Lukács, Spengler's denial of progress across human history was symptomatic of a desperate German imperialist bourgeoisie following the Russian October Revolution of 1917. Lukács argued that Spengler's method typified how pronounced this class's eschewal of rational thought had become. Spengler was abusing age-old notions concerning the law-like emergence, blossoming and decline of cultures – found amongst thinkers such as Giambattista Vico and Hegel – to invent arbitrary historical analogies.[4]

Ernst Bloch was similarly unimpressed by Spengler's historical method. Spengler treated past societies as exhibition pieces in a museum and lacked 'any feeling for living reality' or for 'the reality of nascent development'.[5] The outcome of such a simplistic treatment of the past was an affront to the ever-changing complexity of human development. As we will see in Chapter 4, what is significant about Bloch's engagement with Spengler is that it targeted both Spengler's theory of history and his political project. Such analysis of Spengler's politics is rare both in the immediate reception of him and in subsequent studies.

Spengler also faced much criticism from the German right. Following the success of his *Jahre der Entscheidung* in 1933, there was a campaign to undermine this book headed by Reich Minister for Propaganda Joseph Goebbels, who had become exasperated by his failure to win over Spengler to express support for the National Socialist regime. The Nazi response to Spengler at this point in time deserves a more detailed discussion, so we will return to this question in Chapter 7.

Following the catastrophe of the Second World War, Theodor W. Adorno discussed Spengler's thought in an extended essay, 'Spengler after the Decline'.[6] He claimed that many of Spengler's critics had failed to engage with his ideas on any meaningful level. Looking back to the 1920s, Adorno claimed that it was apparent 'how much the German mind collapsed when confronted with an opponent who seemed to have inherited all the historical force of its own past'.[7] He further felt that the technical coordination of the world predicted by Spengler had become a shocking reality in the form of the Holocaust.[8]

It appears that Adorno's criticism of the pedantic academic discussion of Spengler's ideas helped to bring about a rediscovery of his work in German scholarship. Yet, before we turn to this rediscovery, let us discuss the English-language publications on Spengler, all of which have been written by American scholars.

## Spengler in English

The Princeton academic H. Stuart Hughes's *Oswald Spengler: A Critical Estimate* (1958) mainly focuses on the intellectual context within which Spengler's theory of history was formed.[9] Just three of the book's ten chapters relate to Spengler's views directly or to his response to the events unfolding around him. This approach leads to two shortcomings in Hughes's analysis. First, he views Spengler's magnum opus and his writings from the 1920s or early 1930s as largely pursuing the same aims with the same means. Second, he approaches Spengler's political thought as a mere phase in his career. This is all the more disappointing as Hughes is unable to explore the distinction he draws between the qualified short-term optimism and longer-term pessimism he locates in Spengler's outlook.

By contrast, neither John F. Fennelly's *Twilight of the Evening Lands: Oswald Spengler – A Half Century Later* (1972) nor Klaus P. Fischer's *History and Prophecy: Oswald Spengler and the Decline of the West* (1988) even countenances the possibility that Spengler developed positive or interventionist ideas. Fischer views Spengler as an 'unconditional pessimist' and devotes just one short chapter to his political thought and activities.[10] He also argues that Spengler's only response to the declining Western world is a stance of 'manly pessimism'.[11] After all, how could Spengler 'move men when he knew that the West was doomed'?[12] Fennelly devotes exactly three pages to Spengler's political career, as the 'primary emphasis' of his study is the relevance of *The Decline of the West* to America in the 1970s.[13] Fennelly exemplifies a recurrent understanding of Spengler that has led to the neglect of his political career in the secondary literature. He claims that politics was not central to Spengler's outlook, but a short-lived embarrassment:

> when we come to a consideration of Spengler's postwar political activities it must be admitted candidly that he made something of a fool of himself. It was the old story of the philosopher turned statesman; a mistake made by Plato at Syracuse, but one which Goethe scrupulously avoided in his ministerial duties for the tiny Duchy of Weimar.[14]

The neglect of Spengler's political career in English-language research is only partially redressed by John Farrenkopf in his *Prophet of Decline: Spengler on World History and Politics* (2001).[15] This study does include a discussion of several of Spengler's political writings, but the central concern of Farrenkopf's study is what he views as a transformation in Spengler's philosophy of history throughout his life. In making this case, Farrenkopf usefully contrasts Spengler's arguments in *The Decline of the West* with the posthumously published works *Original Questions* and *The Early Period of World History*.

## Spengler in German

With few exceptions, the predominant focus on Spengler's rich theory of history at the expense of a comprehensive engagement with his politics has been characteristic of German-language scholarship too. Armin Baltzer's *Untergang 'oder' Vollendung. Spenglers bleibende Bedeutung* (1956) argues that a superficial reading of Spengler's *The Decline of the West* misled his German readership into viewing the desperate situation in Germany after the First World War as an unavoidable catastrophe.[16] For Baltzer, this view of Spengler ignored how Spengler felt that decline could be mitigated through political action – what Baltzer calls Spengler's 'constructive ideas'.[17] But Baltzer does not expand on this idea. He does not engage with Spengler's political writings and claims that Spengler never managed to articulate clearly how strong political leadership might offset the most harmful consequences of Western decline.

Ernst Stutz's *Die philosophische und politische Kritik Oswald Spenglers* (1958) is the first and only study in the twentieth century to outline in detail what Stutz calls Spengler's conception of politics as 'the exquisite form of human existence'.[18] Although long out of print, Stutz's book set something of a precedent in the study of Spengler's politics by claiming that: 'Spengler's political and philosophical writings bear the same handwriting, are an expression of the same personality and they ultimately both pursue the same aims.'[19] The result of this approach is that Spengler's political thought is not given the attention it deserves, with his various political writings relegated to the status of a mere echo of his – more significant – philosophy of history. As we will see, this approach is stubbornly persistent in the secondary literature up to the present day.

Edited by Anton Mirko Koktanek, the *Festgabe* for Manfred Schröter entitled *Spengler-Studien. Festgabe für Manfred Schröter zum 85. Geburtstag* (1965) is illustrative of postwar German scholarship's overwhelming focus on Spengler the historian.[20] With the exception of one illuminating autobiographical essay by Wahrhold Drascher ('Encounters with Oswald Spengler') and Bodo Herzog's essay on Spengler's relationship with one of his closest political allies, the industrialist Paul Reusch, this volume revolves exclusively around various tenets of Spengler's theory of history.

Koktanek was involved in a number of other publications and has contributed most to Spengler studies in the twentieth century. As the director of Spengler's literary archive, he presided over the publication of Spengler's notes and fragments under the titles of *Original Questions: Fragments from Spengler's Papers* (1965) and *The Early Period of World History: Fragments from Spengler's Papers* (1966).[21] Moreover, Koktanek's *Oswald Spengler in seiner Zeit* (1968) meticulously reconstructs the events of Spengler's life and discusses the people with whom he was in contact as well as the political and intellectual climate in which his thought developed.[22] Koktanek's biography also incorporates an analysis of Spengler's correspondence, which Koktanek had collated, edited and published in 1963.[23] These publications laid the basis for a critical appreciation of Spengler's German-nationalist mission by demonstrating how well connected he was. However, Koktanek's biography does not itself attempt to provide this analysis. As he puts it: 'This biography provides an overview of Spengler's life, not an interpretation of it.'[24] He hoped to write such a critical overview of Spengler's life and work, but never completed it.

*Spengler heute*, edited by Peter Christian Ludz to mark the centenary of Spengler's birth in 1980, marks a slight shift in twentieth-century scholarship on Spengler that is built on the biographical insights provided by Koktanek. The volume is reflective of endeavours to analyse Spengler not simply as a philosopher of decline, but – in the words of Hermann Lübbe – as 'the rare case of a German philosopher who reached a mainstream audience'.[25] Yet the political publications with which Spengler gained the ear of a mass audience are not deemed worthy of closer analysis in their own right. For instance, Horst Möller follows Stutz in dismissing these publications as tantamount to 'updated paraphrases of his main work that caused such an enormous stir'.[26]

Jürgen Naeher's short biography *Oswald Spengler* (1987) seeks to demonstrate Spengler's purported 'projection' of his troubled personal situation onto the historical period as a whole.[27] This psychobiographical approach ensures that Spengler's public life is almost entirely overlooked. Naeher's Spengler is a lonely and isolated independent scholar who, 'for all his political "activity", remained a philosopher'.[28]

Detlef Felken's *Oswald Spengler. Konservativer Denker zwischen Kaiserreich und Diktatur* (1988) comes close to the kind of judgement on Spengler's life that Koktanek had hoped to complete. Felken attempts to show how 'above all Spengler's political activities are of considerable significance to understanding him as a thinker'.[29] Yet despite the wealth of biographical material on which he bases his study, Felken has a tendency to reduce Spengler's thought to a product of the general period between the Wilhelmine Empire and Nazi Germany. Referring to Spengler's *Hour of Decision*, he contends that the text provides a 'comprehensive image of the period, which in retrospect appears as a balance sheet of his political thought'.[30] Felken's study ultimately remains stuck within the interpretation that Spengler's politics are largely the immutable manifestation of his philosophy of history.

Frits Boterman's *Oswald Spengler und sein 'Untergang des Abendlandes'* (2000) was first published in Dutch as *Oswald Spengler en 'Der Untergang des Abendlandes'. Cultuurpessimist en politiek activist* in 1992.[31] The Dutch title is a more accurate summary of the study, which explores Spengler's public impact by looking at the seeming paradox of how a purported cultural pessimist could emerge as a leading political thinker of the German right. This involves a useful discussion of some of Spengler's most important political writings and concepts, even if these are mainly viewed through the prism of *The Decline of the West*.

Additional indications of an assessment of Spengler the politician in the secondary literature came with the publication of the collection of essays *Der Fall Spengler* (1994), edited by Farrenkopf and Alexander Demandt.[32] Three of the nine essays in this volume analyse the impact and reception of Spengler's political ideas. In his contribution, Farrenkopf argues that Spengler aimed, in line with Machiavelli's concept of *raison d'état*, at providing the political toolkit with which the next generation of statesmen could bring about German hegemony. This point is explored further in Hermann Lübbe's essay, which compares the aims and rhetoric of *Prussianism and Socialism* with Ernst Jünger's *The Worker: Dominion and Form* (1932). Finally, Clemens Vollnhals's essay provides an overview of some of Spengler's political and journalistic activities.

## Spengler in the Twenty-First Century

Spengler scholarship since the turn of the millennium falls into three partly overlapping trends. First, there are the new editions of his writings and speeches following his works going out of copyright. Second, there have been a number of publications that seek to explain his thought with reference to the context of his life and times. Finally, other studies have recently appeared that use his ideas as a foil with which to explain the modern world and the issues it faces. Let us now look at these categories in turn.

After Spengler's works went out of copyright in the early 2000s, three publications made his political writings and speeches available to a modern audience. Two reprints of his works first published in the 1930s – *Politische Schriften 1919–1926* (2009) and *Reden und Aufsätze* (2014) – were joined by *Zyklen und Cäsaren. Mosaiksteine einer Philosophie des Schicksals*, edited by Martin Falck.[33] This study reprints a variety of Spengler's largely overlooked writings and speeches dating from between 1914 and 1936. In addition, Falck provides a 145-page introduction to this material, which outlines Spengler's main ideas and uses them as a metaphor with which to understand modern-day political controversies. In so doing, he makes some questionable claims. He argues, for instance, that Spengler's political thought is not characterised by 'blinkered nationalism',[34] because Spengler's historical point of departure – one that supposedly finds immediate reflection in his politics – is not the German nation, but Faustian culture, the supranational *West*. As we will see below, this soft-pedalling of Spengler's ardent nationalism in some of the recent studies that make the case for Spengler's relevance in today's world has not been without controversy. However, before we discuss these studies, let us look at recent publications that focus on the historical context in which Spengler developed his ideas and how they were received by his contemporaries.

Samir Osmančević's *Oswald Spengler und das Ende der Geschichte* (2007) draws on Spengler's concept of *Zivilisation* to address one of the central questions posed by *post-histoire*: namely, 'how is it possible to still conceive of history in a theoretical environment that is replete with discourses and paradigms?'[35] The insightful discussion of Spengler as a philosopher of history who pre-empts the theoretical concerns of *post-histoire* is the central concern of the study; there is little discussion of Spengler's political career. To the extent that conclusions are drawn on this aspect of Spengler's legacy, Osmančević remains within the twentieth-century interpretive framework discussed above. He claims that Spengler's political thought was 'uniquely and exclusively purely the *consequence* of his philosophy of history, a kind of concrete, day-to-day political exemplification and local application of his historical vision to the conditions in Germany of the time and the problems following defeat in the war, which Spengler had not foreseen'.[36]

The historian Alexander Demandt has established himself as one of the leading authorities on Spengler's philosophy of world history. This is reflected in his essays collated in *Untergänge des Abendlandes. Studien zu Oswald Spengler* (2017).[37] Yet the chapter on Spengler's 'Political Practice' is a short and selective summary of several of Spengler's ideas with no differentiation across his career.

Recent Spengler scholarship has seen examples of scholars cooperating on an international basis to develop new perspectives on his work and to explore his reception beyond Germany. The collections of essays *Oswald Spengler als europäisches Phänomen* (2013) and *Spengler ohne Ende. Ein Rezeptionsphänomen im internationalen Kontext* (2014) both explore his cultural and intellectual impact internationally.[38] Michael Thöndl's *Oswald Spengler in Italien. Kulturexport politischer Ideen der 'Konservativen Revolution'* (2010) is an informative account of Spengler's influence on Mussolini and of how Italian fascist thinkers responded to Spengler's work.[39]

*Spengler. Ein Denker der Zeitenwende* (2009)[40] provides a wide range of essays seeking to establish the place of Spengler's theory of history in German thought, while *Tektonik der Systeme. Neulektüren von Oswald Spengler* (2016) brings together writers from various countries and disciplines attempting to explore 'the complex and ambivalent genealogy the intellectual and inter-discursive history of the reception of Spengler'.[41] Neither volume contains much by way of new readings of Spengler's political impact or reception. *Oswald Spenglers Kulturmorphologie – eine multiperspektive Annäherung* (2018) is an impressive volume of collected essays on Spengler's anthropology, cultural morphology and the relevance of his ideas on topics such as the decline of the American hegemon, finance capital and money.[42]

Thomas Tartsch's *Denn der Mensch ist ein Raubtier. Eine Einführung in die politischen Schriften und Theorien Oswald Spenglers* (2008) is the only recent study to provide a critical overview of all of Spengler's main political publications. However, Tartsch is unable to locate important shifts and developments across these writings. He makes the odd claim, for instance, that a text such as *Rebuilding the German Reich* does not contain anything novel or different from the ideas Spengler first developed in *Prussianism and Socialism*.[43]

It is only with Domenico Conte's *Oswald Spengler. Eine Einführung* (2004) that the understanding of Spengler's political thought as the static embodiment of his theory of history is challenged directly.[44] In contrast to Stutz and Felken, Conte refuses to treat Spengler's politics as a coherent and unchanging body of thought, and instead identifies three distinct periods within Spengler's career. Conte argues that, in the immediate aftermath of the German revolution, Spengler should be viewed as a thinker of the Conservative Revolution; by contrast, during the Weimar Republic's major tests of strength in the early 1920s, his ideas assume more of a 'classically conservative dimension'; in the latter stages of his life, he becomes an isolated thinker who can genuinely be described as a pessimist, as embodied in the rhetorical question he poses in his *Hour of Decision*: 'If I call man a predator, who have I insulted, man or beast?'[45] This book will challenge Conte's periodisation of Spengler's political output, but the fact that Conte makes such distinctions marks a milestone in Spengler studies.

Published in 2012, Markus Henkel's *Nationalkonservative Politik und mediale Repräsentation. Oswald Spenglers politische Philosophie und Programmatik im Netzwerk der Oligarchen (1910–1925)*[46] develops Conte's insights by highlighting the 'dialectic of political and philosophical thought',[47] the 'interplay between historical-sociological determinism and political activism'[48] in Spengler's career as a politician. Yet despite highlighting and explaining how these two facets of Spengler's thought combine to create a variety of shifts of emphasis and nuance within his political project, Henkel nonetheless treats his political thought through to 1925 essentially statically.

## Spengler Today

We now arrive at recent publications that predominantly use Spengler as a tool with which to understand the twenty-first-century world. Wolfgang Krebs's *Die imperiale Endzeit. Oswald Spengler und die Zukunft der abendländischen Zivilisation* (2008) represents an attempt to update Spengler's theory of history in response to the controversy surrounding Francis Fukuyama's *The End of History and the Last Man* (1992) and Samuel Huntington's *The Clash of Civilizations and the Remaking of World Order* (1996).[49]

Sebastian Maaß's *Spengler. Eine politische Biographie* (2013)[50] may have only been published ten years ago, but has quickly been consigned to oblivion. It was hastily pulped by the publisher Duncker & Humblot soon after its appearance.[51] The immediate catalyst for this decision was a highly critical book review, written in 2013 by Volker Weiß of the *Historisches Seminar der Universität Hamburg* and published on the popular German academic website *H-Soz-Kult*.[52] Weiß accused Maaß of pursuing an extremist ideological agenda that downplayed Spengler's role in the rise of German National Socialism. Consequently, the publisher recalled the book. Almost all online traces of its existence have been eradicated and Maaß has withdrawn the doctoral thesis on which the book is based[53] (Weiß's accusation is certainly justified, but whether censorship is the most effective form of combating the ideology of a regime characterised by extreme censorship is another matter).

Maaß's short political biography devotes just ten of its hundred pages to a discussion of *The Decline of the West*, whereas works such as *Prussianism and Socialism* receive thirty pages of analysis. Maaß views Spengler as a thinker of heroic realism, which Maaß describes as: 'A course of action that adapts to the new conditions of *Zivilisation* and does not try desperately to cling on to a past age.'[54] For Maaß, Spengler has been unfairly tainted with the heritage of the Nazi past. Maaß essentially rejects outright any connection between Spengler's nationalism and Hitler's National Socialism, arguing instead that the ideas of Spengler and other theorists of the Conservative Revolution is best 'understood as a school of thought that must be strictly separated from National Socialism'.[55] The fate of Maaß's study underlines how Spengler's legacy continues to be a sensitive issue in modern German political discourse.

David Engels's *Auf dem Weg ins Imperium. Die Krise der Europäischen Union und der Untergang der römischen Republik. Historische Parallelen* (2014) is motivated by the idea that understanding Spengler provides the key to addressing the problems of today's world. It builds on Spengler's method of historical analogy by likening the unfolding demographic, social, political and military issues faced by the current European Union to those in the Roman Republic as described by Spengler.[56]

Engels was instrumental in a collection of essays to mark the centenary of Spengler's *The Decline of the West* entitled *Der lange Schatten Oswald Spenglers* (2018). This was published by the recently established Oswald Spengler Society for the Study of World History under the editorship of Engels, Michael Thöndl and Max Otte.[57] Plans for a society of this nature had first been made by Baltzer and others in the 1950s, but failed to come to fruition back then.[58] This collection brings together many of the leading Spengler scholars at this moment in time. It reflects the work conducted by Spenglerian historians to attempt to complete Spengler's morphology of world history by applying his method to the societies that he was not in a position to analyse. Nonetheless, the only section of the publication in which there is a reference to Spengler's politics comes in the Introduction, written jointly by Engels, Otte and Thöndl. The authors make the case for Spengler's continued socio-political relevance due to his purportedly visionary insights, but in so doing make some slightly questionable claims, such as the idea that Spengler the prophet 'was the first to thematize the destruction of the environment as a new and fundamental problem of humanity'.[59]

Peter Strasser's *Spenglers Visionen. Hundert Jahre Untergang des Abendlandes* (2018) is another publication that commemorates one hundred years since the publication of *Der Untergang des Abendlandes*.[60] For Strasser, Spengler remains relevant to the modern age only in a negative sense. He claims that Spengler possesses a 'relevance that flows precisely from the fact that again more and more despisers of humanity are entering the fray in order to make the case for the rights of "blood", the "people" and the "homeland"'.[61]

## Spengler's Politics of Decline

Our overview of the trends in research on Spengler over the past one hundred years has demonstrated how much of the twentieth-century secondary literature – particularly in the English-speaking world – proceeded from the assumption that Spengler was an isolated thinker who developed a fascinating, albeit fatalist and determinist, understanding of historical development. Only following the research by Koktanek in the 1960s was there a wider understanding that Spengler was, alongside his work as a prolific historian, a leading thinker and activist of the German conservative movement who wrote extensively on the political issues of his time. Despite this realisation, it remains the case that scholarship has not sufficiently researched Spengler's political career.

Instead of discussing how Spengler's political activism and publications relate to and differ from his underlying diagnosis of Western decline, scholarship has either ignored these writings altogether or – in the case of the few studies that focus on these writings – has claimed that they amount to little more than the direct practical application of the theoretical arguments in Spengler's magnum opus. This approach belies the complexity and fluidity of Spengler's political thought.

This book will provide a new understanding of Spengler by analysing how and why his political ideas evolved across the entirety of his career. The focus on the output of Spengler the political activist, networker and theoretician in the convulsive period between 1918 and 1936 will contribute to scholarship in three main ways.

First, through a contextualisation and analysis of Spengler's political writings, speeches and correspondence with influential figures from the German elite, I will demonstrate how even a text such as *The Decline of the West* is an inherently political treatise. Although Spengler ultimately failed in his endeavours, his politics should be treated seriously against the backdrop of the unfolding socio-historical changes he lived through, and not simply dismissed as the project of a thinker who was out of his depth in the world of politics.

Second, my approach will facilitate an analysis of the positive or 'optimistic' aspects of Spengler's prognosis for the future of the Western world. This will be predominantly achieved by a critical engagement with Spengler's socio-political alternative of authoritarian German nationalism (*Preußentum*) and how he attempts to realise this aim with different methods at different points in his career. In contrast to the handful of studies that foreground Spengler's political activity, I will closely link developments within his thought to concrete socio-political changes and to his personal and intellectual relations with numerous political actors – party leaders, influential industrialists, press magnates, military generals and others.

Third, my contextualisation of the shifts in Spengler's thought will illustrate concretely why it is necessary to break with the understanding of Spengler's politics as the immediate outgrowth of his philosophy of world history. By contrast, this volume will make the case that an understanding of the various manifestations of Spengler's political thought across his career are the outcome of Spengler the philosopher of world history on the one hand and Spengler the *Realpolitiker* of German nationalism on the other hand. While the latter is clearly informed by the former, I will show that the two aspects of Spengler's thought are in constant tension, creating a fascinating to and fro in Spengler between his all-encompassing historical narrative and his more detailed, day-to-day political judgements. I will discuss how a largely determinist thinker such as Spengler could on occasion become a voluntarist political actor who engaged with and embraces a variety of ideological causes and movements across his career. While Farrenkopf is correct to characterise Spengler's thought as 'a kind of unconventional manual for the philosophy of international politics',[62] as a guide for leading statesmen in the halls of power, this book will demonstrate how Spengler had no compunction in throwing that textbook out of the window if he considered such a move to be favourable to his goal of rearming the German nation with a new leadership.

## Notes

1. Schröter, *Der Streit um Spengler. Kritik seiner Kritiker*, v.
2. Cited in Beßlich, 'Untergangs-Mißverständnisse. Spenglers literarische Provoktationen und Deutungen der Zeitgenossen', 29.
3. Ibid., 33.
4. Lukács, *Die Zerstörung der Vernunft*, 318–432 (373).
5. Bloch, 'Spengler als Optimist', in *Philosophische Aufsätze zur objektiven Phantasie*, 193.
6. Adorno, 'Spengler nach dem Untergang'.
7. Ibid., 116.
8. Dina Gusejnova makes a strong case that Spengler's influence on Adorno continues to be underestimated and that Adorno's discussion of Spengler is not a 'negation of his work, but a critical appropriation'; Gusejnova, 'Der Prophet als Parfum. Das Spenglersche am europäischen und amerikanischen Modernismus'.
9. Hughes, *Oswald Spengler: A Critical Estimate*.
10. Fischer, *History and Prophecy: Oswald Spengler and the Decline of the West*, 21.
11. Ibid., 78.
12. Ibid., 199.
13. Fennelly, *Twilight of the Evening Lands: Oswald Spengler – A Half Century Later*, 3.
14. Ibid., 18.
15. Farrenkopf, *Prophet of Decline: Spengler on World History and Politics*.
16. Baltzer, *Untergang 'oder' Vollendung. Spenglers bleibende Bedeutung*.
17. Ibid., 26.
18. Stutz, *Die philosophische und politische Kritik Oswald Spenglers*, 239.
19. Ibid., 1.
20. Koktanek (ed.), *Spengler-Studien. Festgabe für Manfred Schröter*.
21. Spengler, *Urfragen. Fragmente aus dem Nachlaß*; Spengler, *Frühzeit der Weltgeschichte. Fragmente aus dem Nachlaß*.
22. Koktanek, *Oswald Spengler in seiner Zeit*.
23. Spengler, *Briefe 1913–36*.
24. Koktanek (ed.), *Spengler in seiner Zeit*, xv.
25. Ludz (ed.), *Spengler heute. Sechs Essays mit einem Vorwort von Hermann Lübbe*, viii.
26. Ibid., 51. As we will see in Chapter 4, Detlef Felken also employs this misleading term to describe the relationship between *The Decline of the West* and Spengler's political activity.
27. Naeher, *Oswald Spengler*, 10.
28. Ibid., 101.
29. Felken, *Oswald Spengler. Konservativer Denker zwischen Kaiserreich und Diktatur*, 9.
30. Ibid., 195.
31. Boterman, *Oswald Spengler und sein 'Untergang des Abendlandes'*; Boterman, *Oswald Spengler en 'Der Untergang des Abendlandes'. Cultuurpessimist en politiek activist*.
32. Demandt and Farrenkopf (eds), *Der Fall Spengler. Eine kritische Bilanz*.
33. Spengler, *Politische Schriften 1919-1926*; Spengler, *Reden und Aufsätze*; Falck (ed.), *Zyklen und Cäsaren. Mosaiksteine einer Philosophie des Schicksals. Reden und Schriften Oswald Spenglers*.
34. Ibid., 130–31.
35. Osmančević, *Oswald Spengler und das Ende der Geschichte*, 199.
36. Ibid., 108.
37. Demandt, *Untergänge des Abendlandes. Studien zu Oswald Spengler*.
38. Gasimov and Duque (eds), *Oswald Spengler als europäisches Phänomen. Der Transfer der Kultur- und Geschichtsmorphologie im Europa der Zwischenkriegszeit 1919–1939*; Merlio and Meyer (eds), *Spengler ohne Ende. Ein Rezeptionsphänomen im internationalen Kontext*.
39. Thöndl, *Oswald Spengler in Italien: Kulturexport politischer Ideen der 'Konservativen Revolution'*.
40. Gangl, Merlio and Orphälders (eds), *Spengler. Ein Denker der Zeitenwende*.

41. De Winde, Fabré, Maes and Philipsen, 'Geschichtete Geschichten. Spengler zur Einführung', in de Winde et al. (eds), *Tektonik der Systeme. Neulektüren von Oswald Spengler*, 11.
42. Rollinger and Fink (eds), *Oswald Spenglers Kulturmorphologie – eine multiperspektive Annäherung*.
43. Tartsch, *Denn der Mensch ist ein Raubtier. Eine Einführung in die politischen Schriften und Theorien Oswald Spenglers*, 147.
44. Conte, *Oswald Spengler. Eine Einführung*.
45. Cf. ibid., 63.
46. Henkel, *Nationalkonservative Politik und mediale Repräsentation. Oswald Spenglers politische Philosophie und Programmatik im Netzwerk der Oligarchen (1910–1925)*.
47. Ibid., 15, fn. 7.
48. Ibid., 180.
49. Krebs, *Die imperiale Endzeit – Oswald Spengler und die Zukunft der abendländischen Zivilisation*.
50. Maaß, *Oswald Spengler. Eine politische Biographie*.
51. Fortunately, my doctoral supervisor Henk de Berg had retained his copy.
52. Weiß, 'Rezenzion zu Sebastian Maaß, *Oswald Spengler. Eine politische Biographie*'. Weiß has also written an informative study of the German *neue Rechte* and its intellectual inspirations; Weiß, *Die autoritäre Revolte. Die Neue Rechte und der Untergang des Abendlandes*.
53. There are no longer any references to the book on Amazon.
54. Maaß, *Oswald Spengler*, 23.
55. Ibid., 9, 10.
56. Engels, *Auf dem Weg ins Imperium. Die Krise der Europäischen Union und der Untergang der römischen Republik. Historische Parallelen*. Engels explains his work in a two-part interview with Henk de Berg entitled 'Is the EU Doomed to Fail?' It is available at: https://www.sheffield.ac.uk/prokhorov-centre/news/eu-doomed-fail-historian-david-engels-1.711246 (retrieved 4 February 2022).
57. Engels, Otte and Thöndl (eds), *Der lange Schatten Oswald Spenglers. Einhundert Jahre Untergang des Abendlandes*.
58. On this, see Henkel, *Nationalkonservative Politik*, 29.
59. Engels, Otte and Thöndl, 'Einhundert Jahre *Untergang des Abendlandes* (1918–2018)', in Engels, Otte and Thöndl (eds), *Der lange Schatten Oswald Spenglers*, 9, emphasis added.
60. Strasser, *Spenglers Visionen. Hundert Jahre Untergang des Abendlandes*. Braumüller is the Viennese publisher that originally brought Spengler's magnum opus to the market.
61. Ibid., 12.
62. Farrenkopf, 'Klio und Cäsar. Spenglers Philosophie der Weltgeschichte im Dienste der Staatskunst', 46.

CHAPTER 3

# Decline, Determinism and Development

In order to determine how Spengler's underlying theory of history relates to his politics of decline, let us now familiarise ourselves with his arguments in *The Decline of the West*. This two-volume study is his best-known work. It can be read on two levels. It offers both a general theory of history, underpinned by an (as we will see, not always very clear or convincing) metaphysics, and a more specific social and political theory. Let us explore the general theory first.

*The Decline of the West* represents an explicit attempt to overhaul traditional 'Western' historiography (as Spengler sees it). This standard approach to history, Spengler maintains, tends to project 'Western' preconceptions and prejudices onto the past and is thus more a reflection of our own historical condition than an impartial attempt at understanding past societies. Specifically, the conventional approach does two things. First, it falls victim to a Eurocentric focus on the development of the West, around which the histories of all other countries are then centred. This produces a teleological and simplified view of world history with the triad of *Classical antiquity – Middle Ages – Modernity* at its core. In order to avoid this approach of viewing modern Europe as the zenith of world history, Spengler calls for a 'Copernican Revolution' in historiography.[1] Second, the traditional view remains stuck at the surface level of individual events, which it then links together as a pseudo-scientific causal chain. As a result, it overlooks the deeper realities that, in his opinion, underlie these events.

## Cultures, Symbols and Souls

What does Spengler replace the standard view of history with? Instead of an approach centred on major events in the history of the West, he favours an approach based on *cultures* as overarching entities, of which various individual events, and indeed even larger historical formations – 'French history' or 'German history', for example – are merely surface manifestations. These are what Spengler calls expressions of life (*Lebensäußerungen*) of a culture's essence. This is not easy to understand, but let us try and get as good a picture of these ideas as we can: one that does justice to Spengler's approach, which, as we will see, is deliberately unanalytical or even anti-analytical.

What, then, does Spengler mean when he talks about cultures; how does he view the development of each individual culture and how does he conceptualise their relation? Spengler distinguishes the following eight cultures: Babylonian, Egyptian (ca. 2500 BC–1500 BC),[2] Chinese (ca. 1300 BC–220 AD), Indian (ca. 1500 BC–500 AD), Greco-Roman or 'Apollonian' (ca. 1100 BC–200 AD), Arabian or 'Magian' (ca. 0–1000 AD), Mexican, and Western or 'Faustian' (ca. 900 AD–today).[3]

A culture consists of people and peoples linked as societies that cohere as one *Kultur* because they are bound together by a shared, albeit largely unconscious, understanding of space and time that is unique to each culture and that becomes the guiding principle behind its birth, growth, decay and demise. Before we explore this idea in more detail, let us look at an initial example.

Spengler contends, for instance, that Apollonian culture and modern Western 'Faustian' culture are informed by diametrically opposed understandings of depth and distance. Apollonian culture is fixated upon the static and the corporeal. By contrast, Faustian culture is obsessed with the infinite and the intangible. Spengler illustrates this disjuncture with reference to the artistic output of the two cultures. He views the Greek sculpture of Discobolus of Myron (4 BC) as a typical expression of the Apollonian cultural outlook, since it depicts *stasis* and focuses on the final moment before the discus is thrown (336). Faustian culture's guiding principle of unlimited space, by contrast, is expressed in an artistic output which seeks to sweep its audience away from the immediate towards the ethereal and the immeasurable. He thus views the incorporeal melodies and polyphonies of contrapuntal music as the purest expression of Faustian culture. The fundamental difference between the Faustian and the Apollonian conception of the world, he adds, becomes most apparent in the contrast between how an Athenian sculptor and a Faustian musician understand figures, lines and shapes (112).

The above distinction is one of many of the insightful observations Spengler makes about the nature of history in *The Decline of the West*, but it does not explain why he feels that each culture is informed by a distinct, all-encompassing idea of space and time. In order to understand why he believes this, let us now look at his concept of the prime symbol of each culture (*Ursymbol*). This idea is pivotal to understanding how Spengler tries to give his theory of history a metaphysical underpinning. It is not always convincing or coherent and is difficult to follow in a systematic fashion. Nonetheless, as we will see, his profound contributions to the understanding of world history are not at all dependent on his metaphysics.

The inspiration for Spengler's *Ursymbol* is Goethe's postulation of a primal, original form (*Urgestalt*), of which all living forms (*Gestalten*) are an expression, and to which they can be traced back. As will become evident in the course of our discussion, Spengler aims to apply Goethe's study of the development of organic forms – *die Gestaltenlehre* – to the realm of human history in the form of the eight cultures mentioned above. Spengler refers to this method as the morphology of world history, as expressed in the subtitle of his main work: *Outlines of a Morphology of World History*. But what does Spengler mean when he claims that the original form historians should be looking to in order to understand the essence of a historical culture is a prime *symbol*?

As we saw in our overview of Spengler's life and work, a recurring feature of his thought is an emphasis on the metaphysics of light, distance and sight.[4] For him, the variety of ways in which human beings see – how they perceive and explain space and time in their surrounding environment – underpins the entirety of their behaviour and actions. He considers the existence of such an epistemological framework to be a precondition for the emergence of human society and culture. This idea is highly abstract, so let us try and explain it in more detail with reference to the question why Spengler places so much emphasis on symbolism and sight in his culture-based conception of history.

The example of the Greek sculptor and the Faustian musician cited above underlines Spengler's conviction that historical inquiry should break with the assumption that all peoples subjectively grasp space and time in a transhistorical or commonly 'human' fashion. By contrast, he insists, there are a near-infinite number of ways in which a world-outlook (*Weltanschauung*) can be formed. He views this process of grasping the surrounding environment as a highly symbolic one, with the panoply of objects we see around us forming a kind of metaphysical bridge between the world as it is and the world as we understand it: 'Everything that is, is also a symbol' (212). The precise manner in which these symbols are placed alongside each other and arranged within a framework of depth and space in order to form a coherent view is culturally determined: one's understanding of the world is dictated by the culture's underlying *Ursymbol*. At various points, Spengler refers to this determinant prime symbol as a culturally specific 'kind of extension' (226) or a culture's 'experience of depth, through which the world becomes' (233). This *Ursymbol* is so all-encompassing and innate to each member of a culture that it can be found in that culture's socio-political entities, religious myths, ethics, aesthetics and so on. The *Ursymbol* is thus:

operative through the form-sense [*Formgefühl*] of every man, every community, period of time and epoch and dictates the style of every expression of life. It is inherent in the form of the state, the religious myths and cults, the ethical ideals, the forms of painting and music and poetry, the fundamental notions of all the sciences. (226)

Moreover, Spengler claims that each of the eight cultures possesses, and is organised around, its own distinct *Ursymbol*, which cannot be transferred to or understood by another culture. Each historical culture has established its own secret language that alone can express this: what Spengler calls the unique world-feeling of a culture's soul (251).

Let us try and flesh out this idea by taking a closer look at Spengler's explanation for how all members of a given culture come to share this secret world-feeling. He argues that a distinct perception of space and time is instinctively assimilated by each of a culture's adherents. This perception is both congenital and socially reinforced:

> This prime form of the world is *innate* insofar as it is an original possession of the soul of that culture which is expressed by our life as a whole, and *acquired* in so far that every individual soul re-enacts for itself that creative act, and unfolds in early childhood the symbol of depth to which its existence is predestined, just as the emerging butterfly unfolds its wings. (225–26)

In order to explain this, Spengler likens the acquisition of a culture's soul (*Seele*) to a child gradually becoming conscious of its environment. At first, the child has no sense of depth and will, for example, reach out to grasp the moon in its hand (225). However, as soon as the child has stopped doing this, it has developed a distinct worldview that – the point bears repeating – is conditioned by the prime symbol of the culture in which this process occurs. There is no escaping the influence of this prime symbol, whether it be that of Apollonian, Faustian, Chinese or Egyptian culture:

> And it is only with the awakening of the soul that direction also reaches living expression – in the Classical world in a steady adherence to the near-present and an exclusion of the distant and future; in Faustian culture in direction-energy which has an eye only for the most distant horizons; in Chinese culture in freely wandering here and there that nevertheless eventually leads to the goal; in Egyptian culture in a resolute march down the path once taken. (225)

Spengler asserts that historians can only begin to understand these world cultures on their own terms and locate the true significance of their rise and fall within world history by understanding the overarching idea that informs their fate (*Schicksal*). Indeed, the history of every such culture can be summarised as the attempt to realise, or to put into practice, that culture's guiding idea. Once all possibilities for doing so have been exhausted, the culture itself begins to go into decline and will eventually return to a formless state of existence (*Urseelentum*), in which there is no longer a worldview as the basis of social, political, religious and artistic life: a culture 'dies when this soul has realised the full sum of its possibilities in the shape of peoples, languages, doctrines, arts, states, sciences, and reverts to a child-like state of existence (*Urseelentum*)' (143).

## Goethe

This brings us to our second question: how does Spengler see the *development* of each individual culture? Our explanation above has already made it clear that by building on Goethe's concept of the primal form (*Urgestalt*), Spengler is convinced that cultures are entelechies. In other words, they are organisms that emerge from a primal form, flourish, decline and die. In order to explore further the connection between Goethe's study of forms and Spengler's historical morphology, let us first take a closer look at the former's approach and how it finds reflection in *The Decline of the West*.

One of Goethe's various intellectual projects is to formulate a morphology of plants, as outlined in his essay *The Metamorphosis of Plants* (*Der Versuch die Metamorphose der Pflanzen zu erklären*) (1790).[5] Here, he seeks to establish the exact relationship between all plants, as well as their leaves, fruits and blossom and so forth that develop from each other. Ultimately, Goethe feels that it is possible to posit the existence of an original or archetypal plant (*Urpflanze*), from which the variety of all plant life can be morphologically derived and explained.[6] Moreover, on the basis of what one of his biographers has called 'pursuing the spectre' of such a plant, Goethe is convinced that his ideas on the metamorphosis of plants can be applied to the animal world.[7] According to one of his biographers, Nicholas Boyle, Goethe infers that 'animal nature ... showed not only multiplicity, but unity', with the bones 'at least of all mammals' displaying 'a single unchanging arrangement'.[8] From this assumption, Goethe draws conclusions about past stages of animal evolution for which there exists no recorded evidence. Boyle continues: 'different though the femur may look in a horse and a monkey, it never proceeds from the head, and between the bones of the upper jaw there will always be found at least the traces of the *os intermaxillare* [the intermaxillary bone]'.[9] According to Boyle, Goethe even seeks to establish an 'osteological type' or 'a standard skeleton for all vertebrates, not derived from any particular species, in which position, form, and function of every bone would be defined ... and their characteristic variations described. Animal metamorphosis could thus be more precisely defined and the way prepared for an understanding of the laws which govern it'.[10] The contrast between the evidence-based methods of biology and those of Goethe becomes strikingly apparent here. Despite the lack of existence of any recorded 'proof' of a human intermaxillary bone at a previous stage of human evolution, Goethe confidently postulates that, at some point in our past, a human intermaxillary bone *must have existed*. He feels justified in making this claim from the methodological assumptions outlined above. If it is supposed that everything stems from a primal form, and if it is possible to compare and contrast these forms on the basis of their function and position within an organism, then it logically follows that conclusions can be drawn on the essence of evolution that the objective methods of science are simply incapable of drawing, insofar as their reasoning is limited – or even imprisoned – by a fixation on observable and recorded phenomena. It thus comes as little surprise that Goethe's unconventional approach is opposed by those thinkers defending the methods of the natural sciences that are taking shape in his time. This is particularly the case for his much-discredited *Theory of Colours* (*Farbenlehre*) (1810), in which he rejects Newton's suggestion that the visible world can be traced back to invisible physical connections. In the words of one of his contemporaries, Goethe's 'experiments on colour and refraction are the occasion for much shrugging of shoulders among the experts … and many witticisms among the mockers'.[11]

For Spengler, by contrast, Goethe's comparative approach is groundbreaking. It represents the key to understanding the past in all its richness and complexity. For just as Goethe seeks to trace the biological destiny of plants and animals via a comparison of their various manifestations of life (as expressed in its fruits, leave shapes, colours and so on), Spengler will, as we will now discuss, do the same by approaching his historical cultures in similar terms and by comparing their expressions of life (*Lebensäußerungen*). As he puts it: 'Just as the plant's being is brought to expression in the form, dress and carriage by leaves, blossoms, twigs and fruit, so too is the being of a culture manifested by its religious, intellectual, political and economic formations' (148).

In order to explain the cyclical, repetitive nature of the organic process through which all cultures must pass, Spengler likens each stage of development to the four seasons with quintessential, distinctive characteristics in intellectual, religious, artistic and political life. He also deploys further metaphors to explain the development of cultures: they grow, blossom and wither; they are born, grow up, become old and frail, and die. In less metaphorical terms, this means for Spengler that each culture goes through at least three phases: *prehistory*, *culture* (in a narrow sense) and *civilisation* (*Zivilisation*). Below we will discuss in more detail Spengler's –

somewhat nebulous – understanding of how a culture is born, but before we do, let us look at how Spengler uses historical events, ideas and movements to elucidate his seasonal metaphors – spring, summer, autumn and winter – for past cultures, as well as how these seasons map onto his use of the terms *Kultur* and *Zivilisation*.

According to Spengler, the early *Kultur* phase through which all his historical cultures pass – their springtime – is predominantly rural and agricultural in nature. He notes that this period is one of dynamism, imagination and intuitive attempts to realise in practice the culture's newly established *Ursymbol*. Hence, he refers to this season as one of birth and expansion, which expresses itself in an explosion of artistic forms. These, he argues, are not consciously planned or theorised, but spontaneous expressions of the dominant rural spirit of a young and energetic culture. He cites the Doric columns of the Apollonian world and the Gothic cathedrals of Faustian culture as examples. These aesthetic achievements are impulsive realisations of the prime symbols of proximity and infinite space, respectively. At the intellectual level, Spengler notes the emergence of an all-encompassing myth, which is ushered in by a new understanding of god and the divine along with the birth of a culture. Here he has in mind the rise of the Olympian gods and goddesses in the Apollonian world ca. 1000–800 BC and the rise of Germanic Catholicism from ca. 900 AD. In what he views as the latter stages of a culture's spring, he identifies the first attempts to provide a theoretical basis for these new religious forms, as in the writings of Thomas Aquinas.

## *Kultur* and *Zivilisation*

Spengler argues that the spirit of the countryside dominates the political and social life of a culture's springtime. Cities and large towns, to the extent that one can speak of them at all, revolve solely around the market or the castles and palaces, whose rulers and armies are imbued with knightly ideals. For Spengler, the expansionist Crusades (1096–1291) were a particularly Faustian – as we have seen, a culture defined by its tendency to the infinite – manifestation of this knightly outlook.

Spengler argues that there are two primal estates (*Urstände*) that drive forward a culture's development: the aristocracy and the priesthood. He describes them as 'symbols in flesh and blood' (969) and claims that they form the two estates that are in a position to lead others in society:

> Those who inwardly belong to these estates – and not just in name – are really something quite different to the rest; their lives are, in contrast to those of the bourgeois or the peasants, underpinned through and through by a symbolic dignity. These people do not exist merely in order to live, but to have meaning. (971).

Spengler views the nobility as a living symbol of time. This estate seeks to realise the culture's guiding idea in the realm of political action. Here he is thinking of the medieval state forms created in the Middle Ages or, as in the example above, the Crusades. The priesthood plays an opposite but equally important role. Spengler sees this estate as a living symbol of space. This estate revolves around metaphysical and religious reflection, with priests and theologians pursuing a life defined not by action and intervention, but by thought and contemplation. They provide a religious framework within which the culture's soul finds early expression. For example, Spengler views Germanic Catholicism in the spring of Faustian culture (ca. 1000 AD) not as the continuation of earlier Christian doctrines, practices and outlooks, which were developed ca. 0–300 AD in Arabian (or Magian) culture, but as a novel manifestation of the Christian faith that is reflective of the newly established Faustian world outlook. We will return to this example in more detail below.

The *Kultur* phase continues with the emergence of summer. It is a period of scholarly output and philosophical reflection in which there are the first signs of a transition to an urban way of life. In addition, the first criticisms of the ideas and political practices established by the two *Urstände* can be observed. At the beginning of the summer period, Spengler claims, we find the beginnings of a 'reformation' in all cultures. Whether this takes the form of the Dionysus cult in Classical antiquity, the figure of Augustine in Magian culture, or Martin Luther and John Calvin in Faustian culture, what unites all these phenomena is a popular rebellion against the dominant religious practices and outlooks that emerged in the culture's spring. Spengler notes that all these rebellions occur *within* the framework of the culture's central religious feeling and thus serve to reaffirm rather than overhaul the religious foundations of that culture. Here Spengler has in mind the Protestant Reformation's claims to uphold the values of Christianity against the perceived anti-Christian values and excesses of the Catholic Church. During the latter stages of their summer periods, Spengler finds, all cultures exhibit a tendency towards puritanism. For all their differences, Pythagoras, Muhammad and the English Puritans are expressions of this tendency in Apollonian, Magian and Faustian culture.

Alongside this, Spengler views summer as marking the early stages of a purely philosophical expression of the culture's world-feeling that, until this point, has been mainly expressed through the framework of religion. He contends that the pre-Socratic thinkers in the Apollonian world and those such as Francis Bacon, Galileo Galilei and Descartes in sixteenth- and seventeenth-century Europe are illustrative of these philosophical endeavours.

A culture's autumn marks the zenith of the *Kultur* phase. It is primarily characterised by the emergence of an urban, bourgeois intelligentsia and a focus on reason and rational inquiry – as opposed to faith and devotion – as the basis for understanding, and giving expression to, the world-feeling of that culture. One of the most innovative, anti-Eurocentric arguments Spengler advances regarding this period of cultural development is his contention that what is seen as the 'Age of Enlightenment' in eighteenth-century Western Europe is no singular, unique period in the history of humanity, but a necessary stage through which *all* historical cultures must pass. He claims that the Sophists, Socrates and Democritus are to Apollonian culture what Locke, Voltaire and Rousseau are to Faustian culture. As with the above example of Pythagoras, Muhammad and Cromwell, they are what Spengler calls *simultaneous* phenomena across cultures (*Gleichzeitigkeit*). We will discuss his use of this term in more detail below.

Spengler asserts that a given culture's autumnal emphasis on reason culminates in the advent of ambitious and all-encompassing thought systems, or what he calls in his historical tables 'the great conclusive systems'. These schema attempt to provide a rational basis for the world and the story of humanity, but invariably they reflect the outlooks and prejudices of the culture in which they are developed. Autumnal thinkers challenge blind faith in the authority of the Church, but remain embedded within a religious framework by contending that reason, not faith, represents the path towards a true understanding of the divine. Here, Spengler mentions the ideas of Plato and Aristotle as well as the work of Goethe, Kant and Hegel.

Politically, the autumn period of all cultures represents for Spengler the most perfectly developed state form: absolutism. For him, this system embodies a functioning unity between the city and the countryside, between the state and society, and between the three estates: the nobility, the Church and the estate of the commoners, which has emerged in the towns and countries. Spengler's point of reference here is the *ancien régime* and figures such as Louis XIV and Frederick the Great. As we will see in the following chapters, Spengler views such leaders, and the absolutist politics they embody, as the highest form of political representation achievable within the life-cycle of a culture. This pinnacle of a culture's development also finds reflection in artistic and cultural terms. In Faustian culture, it represents the age stretching from Bach, Mozart and the Rococo through to Beethoven from ca. 1700 to the middle of the nineteenth century. Simultaneously, however, this cultural output is the first outward expression of the manifestations of that culture's decline. As with the absolutist state form, it is the most complete expression of a rational understanding of musical and artistic forms.

Thus we arrive at a culture's final stage. This is what Spengler refers to as the end of the phase of *Kultur* and the emergence of *Zivilisation*. This stage corresponds to the last of the four seasons, winter, and is defined by the rise of the metropolis, the dominance of money and materialism over metaphysics, thinking-in-money (*das Denken in Geld*) and artistic forms that are no longer able to give aesthetic form to the culture's guiding idea, but are conceived solely in terms of titillation and triviality. As Spengler puts it, 'art itself becomes a sport – that is the meaning of *l'art pour l'art*' (49). Whereas the previous seasons of a culture involve attempts to express that culture's soul, in the age of *Zivilisation* the metaphysical bonds that were once self-evident are disappearing. What was once an organic entity of harmoniously interacting estates is dissolving into a formless and diffuse mass. Spengler describes this process of disintegration as one in which 'life itself becomes problematic'.[12]

Now that all possibilities for the expression of the culture's founding principles have been exhausted, Spengler argues, a cult of science, utilitarianism and happiness emerges. Whether in the form of the communist, atheist sects that emerged in the Abassid caliphate of Magian culture, or in the ideas of Feuerbach and Marx in Faustian culture, vital religious matters regarding the nature of human have, in Spengler's eyes, been reduced to social issues and campaign slogans.

Politically, a culture's winter phase is dominated by the rule of money, and which Spengler equates with 'democracy'. He argues that this period falls between 1800 and 2000 in Faustian culture and that there are parallels with the period of political Hellenism (ca. 300–100 BC) in Apollonian culture and the Warring States Period in Ancient China (ca. 475–221 BC). However, he adds that the dominance of money over politics will not endure. Democracy has an inbuilt tendency towards dictatorship, in that it concentrates power among an ever-smaller and more powerful elite. These tendencies will culminate in the overthrow of democracy by great individuals who mobilise the masses not for the sake of votes, but for the sake of seizing political power. In the forefront of Spengler's mind here is Caesar's overthrow of the Roman Republic. For Spengler, the modern Faustian incarnation of the figure of Caesar will emerge between ca. 2000 and 2200. However, as we will see later on, Spengler is tempted to see Benito Mussolini as such a figure. Moreover, Spengler's political thought has as its aim the creation of the socio-political conditions in which a Caesar figure can emerge in Germany.

The strongmen Spengler has in mind will not be able to prevent the further degeneration of social life into a primitive and unorganised collective of individuals and families: 'a gradual emergence of primordial conditions'.[13] Here Spengler seems to be suggesting that the final phase of a culture's development is similar to that of its prehistory. There is no cohering force to drive forward expansion and development, and the world has become little more than bounty pursued by the small number of sovereign rulers (*Einzelherrscher*). This is the third and final phase of a culture's winter. Spengler locates this period in Apollonian culture between 100 and 200 AD – from Troy to Marcus Aurelius – and expects a similar disintegration of the modern Western world to set in after ca. 2200. Just as the Classical world and ancient Egypt passed through these stages of development and lived their lives to their ultimate, preordained conclusion, so too will modern Western culture. This approach entails Faustian culture moving towards its own inexorable end: the *decline* of the Western world is simultaneously its fulfilment or completion (*Vollendung*).

## Analogy and Homology

Now that we have outlined Spengler's views on the development of cultures, let us take a closer look at how he attempts to compare and contrast them, as well as some of the conclusions he draws when doing so. Since Spengler treats his eight cultures as organisms lasting for around a thousand years that must, as a matter of biological necessity, pass through the preordained stages of development described above, he feels that it is possible to compare and contrast the historical fruits that they must inevitably bring forth at certain stages in their lifespan.[14] Again, the model is Goethe's principles of natural inquiry, not the logic of cause and effect:

> And just as he [Goethe] traced the development of the plant form from the leaf, the emergence of the vertebrate type, the development of the geological strata – *the destiny of nature, not its causality* – so here we shall develop the form-language of human history, its periodic structure, its *organic* logic out of the plethora of all evident details. (35)

In order to see exactly how Spengler attempts to trace the organic development of historical cultures as Goethe sought to discover the evolution of biological forms, let us now look at three of the most significant concepts in Spengler's method, namely *Homologie*, *Analogie* and *Gleichzeitigkeit* – homology, analogy and simultaneousness.

*Homologie* refers to what Spengler calls the morphological equivalence of phenomena across different cultures. It is best understood in terms of the four seasons of each culture described above. Since, as we have seen, Doric columns and Germanic Catholicism are two features of the spring period of Apollonian and Faustian culture, they can be described as homologous phenomena since they occupy the same morphological *position* within the life-cycle of two different cultures. They are characteristic expressions of a culture in its early phase of development.

*Analogie*, by contrast, refers not to the relative *location* of two or more phenomena across cultures, but to their *function*. Since, in our example above, Doric columns reflect developments in the world of architecture and Germanic Catholicism pertains to the religious expression of the Faustian soul, these two phenomena are not analogous, but homologous. Before we outline some of Spengler's historical examples of these phenomena, let us first look at how he uses a biological comparison of land animals and fish to explain the distinction between analogy and homology.

Spengler asserts that the lungs of land animals are comparable to two organs within fish: the swim bladder and the gills. The lungs and the gills carry out the same biological role within the two different species (the ability to breathe). They are thus analogous phenomena. However, they are not homologous phenomena because they are situated in different parts of each organism (the gills on the head of the fish and the lungs at the heart of land animals). Therefore, in terms of their relative morphological position, Spengler argues that the lungs of a land animal are analogous with the swim bladder of a fish, which is found at the centre of the fish, but the function of which is to facilitate the fish's buoyancy in the water (149–50).

Spengler contends that the application of these biological insights to the study of history has revolutionary implications. It allows the historian to locate, for the first time, two historical facts that appear in the same relative stage of a culture's development and thus to arrive at a rounded appreciation of their historical significance. This is what Spengler means by the term *Gleichzeitigkeit*, or simultaneousness: two historical facts that, existing in completely different cultures or times, appear in exactly the same – relative – position in a culture's life. In Spenglerian terms, Archimedes and Carl Friedrich Gauss, Polygnotus and Rembrandt, as well as Alexander the Great and Napoleon, are contemporaries. What distinguishes these contemporaneous phenomena from each other and what marks them out as exceptional historical occurrences is the unique *Ursymbol* of the culture from which they emerge. Therefore, it is the prime symbol that make thinkers such as Pythagoras and Descartes or artists such as Polygnotus and Rembrandt uniquely different from each other, even though they appear in the same relative position in the life-cycle of their respective cultures and thus, as Spengler puts it, can be 'characterised as *simultaneous*' (151) or as morphological equivalents.

So central is the concept of *Gleichzeitigkeit* to Spengler that he commences his magnum opus with extensive tables listing other such 'simultaneous' intellectual epochs, political developments and aesthetic trends across his historical cultures. In addition to the example of Muhammad and the Puritans discussed above, he lists ancient Greek sculpture, Nordic instrumental music, the pyramids of the fourth Egyptian dynasty and Gothic cathedrals as further examples of homologous phenomena. He adds that while Christianity and Buddhism share a wide following and historical significance, they are neither homologous nor analogous. Moreover, returning to our example of the cult of Dionysus above, he claims that this phenomenon is analogous with the Reformation of Faustian culture, but homologous to the Renaissance.

By illustrating how there is no historical phenomenon without an exact counterpart in another culture, Spengler feels that historians can move beyond the surface of history and draw informed historical parallels that are no longer based on mere whims or arbitrary constructions. For instance, he claims that widespread comparisons between Alexander the Great and Caesar (53–54), given the deceptive similarity between their personalities, outlooks and achievements, are an illusion; they are not homologous phenomena. As we saw above, a figure such as Alexander the Great is a typical manifestation of a culture's *transition* from *Kultur* to *Zivilisation*, whereas the emergence of a Caesar-type figure is characteristic of *Zivilisation* itself.

Spengler is not the first historian to deploy historical analogy as a way of facilitating historical understanding. There is an overlap between his method and other schools of historical research, such as German historicism. This school seeks to understand history through looking at 'what actually happened' (Leopold von Ranke) by exploring what a historical entity's politics, art, ethics and so on can reveal about the nature of the era and how this is similar to, and differs from, similar output from another epoch. Gilbert Merlio convincingly shows that Spengler is influenced by German historicism and the attempts of those such as von Ranke and Wilhelm Dilthey to understand past societies on their own terms. However, adds Merlio, Spengler rejects German historicism's conviction that, in so doing, their exploration of the plurality of historical phenomena can reveal the *continuity* of human experience across these varied societies. As we will see below in more detail, Spengler's view of history precludes any notion of genuine historical transmission across or between cultures.[15]

Spengler is critical of German historicism for another reason. He describes von Ranke, for instance, as a master of drawing elaborate historical analogies from historical sources, but dismisses most of von Ranke's parallels – his comparison of King Cyaxares and Henry I, for instance – as morphologically meaningless. What Spengler means by this is that von Ranke's comparisons are not integrated into an overall comparative understanding of cultures as organically changing forms. Von Ranke treats history as a series of events supposedly linked by cause and effect (*Kausalität*) rather than a living entity (*Schicksal*). Von Ranke is thus dismissed as an empiricist who collects, arranges and compares purportedly objective data in the search for a group of facts (*Tatsachen*) as the explanation for the emergence of another group of facts. The outcome of this approach, Spengler contends, is that von Ranke's comparisons are often misleading and invariably impressionistic. Even when his comparisons happen to be historically accurate – as in his analogy between Alcibiades and Napoleon – they are correct deductions from an incorrect method and thus are unable to depict the underlying significance of either man's place in history. Therefore, Spengler's comparative method does not amount to a radical departure from the established methods of historical research: analogies and parallels are not misleading per se, but they must break with the dominant conception of causality in rationalist historiography (*rationale Geschichtsschreibung*). In opposition to the futile 'hunt for causal relations' (140, fn. 2) inherent in this approach, Spengler's method relies on the historian's impressions, inferences and imagination when establishing the organic logic of past organisms. Spengler refers to this historical instinct as physiognomic tact (172). For just as a gifted judge of character (*Menschenkenner*) is able to detect the underlying emotions, habits or even ideas of people through their mannerisms and facial expressions, so can the morphological historian infer what historical forms reveal about the reality of cultural development: 'What concerns us is not what the historical facts which appear at this or that time *are*, per se, but what they signify, what they point to, through their appearance' (8). Spengler summarises this deliberately anti-analytical approach by claiming that the study and writing of history has more in common with poetry than with science: 'Nature should be dealt with scientifically, history should be approached poetically' (129). But this novel, nonscientific method should not obscure the fact that Spengler views his own morphology of world history as holding the key to grasping fully the *objective truth* of past events for the first time: 'at last, we see in the words youth, growth, maturity and decay, which until now, and today more than ever, have been used to express subjective evaluations and entirely personal preferences in sociology, ethics and aesthetics, as objective descriptions of organic states' (36).

This claim represents a methodological problem in Spengler's view of history. Let us briefly outline this issue before looking at how cultures follow on from each other.

One of Spengler's major shortcomings as a historian is simultaneously one of his main strengths: his ability to compress a wealth of human experience into a creative and powerful overarching narrative. The historical analogies and comparisons he develops often captivate his audience and offer original insights into the study of the nature and function of past events, ideas and outlooks. Not for nothing has he, in the apt phrase of Samir Osmančević, been called the 'Proust of the philosophy of history'.[16] However, in Spengler's moving story of the rise and fall of cultures, he permits himself a generous amount of poetic licence, and instrumentalises the diversity and uniqueness of past events in order to buttress his overall narrative. *The Decline of the West* reveals Spengler to be a most creative historian in both a positive and a negative sense. He tells a spellbinding tale, but his arguments can never be invalidated. It is not that his approach is verifiably false, but that it can never be proved wrong – at least on its own terms. This becomes evident in the example of the Greek sculpture of Discobolus of Myron in Apollonian culture discussed above. We recall that Spengler views this sculpture as a typical form of Apollonian culture's emphasis on the immediate and the *static*: 'an art of proximity, of the tangible, the timeless. It therefore loves motifs of the brief, the briefest possible calm between two movements, the last instant before the discus is thrown' (336). However, it is equally possible to interpret such a statue in a completely opposite manner – that is, that the statue is reflective of a distilled moment of change and transition, motion and target-orientated focus: his body is wound tightly and prepared to unwind so as to hurl the discus as far as possible into the distance and outdo the competition. Is it not possible that there were contending conceptions of the dangers and thrills of the distant and the limitless within the Classical world, as the myth of Icarus might suggest? Spengler's schema must answer this question in the negative, or at least suggest that any deviations from his conclusions regarding the omnipotence of stasis and proximity in this culture were mere surface phenomena on the part of those who were out of step with their time. There are no universal or scientific criteria by which an ancient Greek sculpture can be interpreted. Nor are there such criteria by which the works of an author published in what Spengler views as the late, culturally decadent days of a culture (Brecht, Hauptmann or Kafka) can be deemed inferior to those published during that culture's ostensible zenith (Goethe, Schiller or Shakespeare). Interpretation is in the eye of the historical morphologist, and the fact that Spengler views the latter writers as superior therefore reveals as much about his ideological-intellectual framework as it does about the logical coherence of his overall scheme. One historian's 'decline' is another's 'progress'. In this light, Demandt notes that Spengler's choice of the fall of the Roman Republic as the *decline* of the ancient world is a spurious one due to the subsequent 'Golden Age' of Rome, which Demandt sees as coming into being with Augustus.[17] More generally, falling birth rates, alongside the decline of traditional family life and rural existence, can also be viewed as signs of progress, with the rise of women's rights, sexual enlightenment, and the social and cultural opportunities presented by urban life. This methodological bias in Spengler is amplified by his robust and occasionally dogmatic argumentation – what he calls writing in the concise style of Hindenburg – and his continued disdain for references and footnotes.[18]

On closer inspection, several of Spengler's historical assertions seem most baffling. He shoehorns a wide range of phenomena into his argument that there are similar phenomena *between* cultures, as well as his claim that the entirety of phenomena *within* a single culture can ultimately be traced back to that culture's soul. For instance, he argues that since it was informed by the guiding symbol of the immediate, Roman imperialism lacked a modern Faustian thirst for expansion and that its wars were conducted solely to secure what the Romans already owned (433). This may have been difficult to explain to large swathes of the Western European population, irrespective of their *Ursymbol*.

Despite this bias, Spengler correctly notes that all historical writing requires striking a balance between faithfulness to the historical record – Hegel's 'facts'[19] – and the maintenance of a self-sustaining (and readable) argument. *The Decline of the West* is a rewarding read and, particularly in times of social disarray and confusion such as our own, Spengler's reminder that nothing lasts forever assumes a particular poignancy.

We are now in a position to answer our third question: how do cultures follow on from each other? According to Spengler, there are no causal relations here because each culture is like a windowless monad that follows the same predetermined (in Leibniz's phrase, 'pre-established') quasi-biological pattern. It simply and automatically goes through the same phases as the other cultures – it emerges, realises its innate potential, and then withers away and dies. But why, according to Spengler, do cultures emerge in the first place and why in the form that they do? Further, how is it possible for cultures to coexist simultaneously? These are the questions to which we will now turn.

## Birth and Coexistence

As we saw above, Spengler views the birth of a culture as a deeply metaphysical process resulting from the development of a unique sense of depth-perception, which in turn flows from that culture's *Ursymbol*. He claims that this insight into the true nature of historical cultures marks him out as a thinker.

Spengler highlights two stages in the emergence of a culture. The first, which we will explain below, is what we have already referred to as its prehistory (*Vorzeit*). The second is the 'spring' phase of a culture after its birth, when it begins to assert itself and develop.

Spengler argues that modern Western (Faustian) culture has its origins in the tenth century, but that this formation – like all of his cultures – has a prehistory of around 200–400 years. For Faustian culture, this period begins ca. 500. He sees this period as one where it is impossible to speak meaningfully of politics or the state; society is organised along the lines of primitive groupings and small clans that cannot organise themselves into a coherent social structure as they lack an all-encompassing view of the world to unite them. Here Spengler is thinking of the state of a primitive ahistorical human condition (*Urmenschentum*), to which dying cultures will eventually return. Politically he associates this period with the reign of Charlemagne, whose gradual establishment of an empire in Western Europe began to overcome the fragmentation of the various peoples there at that time. But there is no causal link between Charlemagne and the birth of Faustian culture: Spengler views Charlemagne as a fleeting phenomenon who exerts no impact on Faustian culture at all. It is only in 900, long after Charlemagne, that *something new* emerges in Western Europe. Spengler refers to this sudden awakening of a new spirit and outlook on several occasions, but his description lacks any reference to historical events or turning points. He abstractly refers to various *forms* of the new soul emerging: 'In the tenth century the Faustian soul suddenly awakens and manifests itself in countless forms' (*Gestalten*) (760).

There are two reasons why Spengler avoids a detailed discussion of the birth of a culture. First, he claims that the *Ursymbol*, the glue around which a new culture suddenly coheres, can never be fully understood or described, even by those who were witness to this process. Concepts and ideas which attempt to describe the significance of the *Ursymbol* as the profound metaphysical basis of a culture can only create an *impression* of its meaning and importance:

> If, as we will henceforth claim that it is, the prime symbol of the Classical soul is the material and the individual body, and that of Western culture is pure infinite space, we must not overlook how concepts do not represent things that can never be conceived: the sound of words can only evoke a significative impression of it. (227)

Second, we have seen that Spengler rejects the supposedly rational and 'scientific' explanation of causality. He asserts that the beginning of a culture cannot be *explained*, but must be intuitively perceived or inferred. His account of the origins of Faustian culture thus has nothing of the detail or specificity of his historical tables, and it implies that the form assumed by each historical culture is a metaphysical accident: 'Between the time of Charlemagne and that of Conrad II *something took shape in the stream of existence* [*Strom des Daseins*] that cannot be explained, but must be felt if we are to understand the dawn of a new culture' (972, emphasis added).

This unconvincing description of the origins of Faustian culture represents a significant lacuna in Spengler's method and undermines some of his other – convincing – explanations for the rise and fall of cultures, as well as how this process maps onto concrete historical phenomena. Spengler's efforts to embed his theory of history within a metaphysical framework, which even encompasses the relationship between sexual organs and blood circulation, are often exasperating and add little of value to his insights.

But let us return to Spengler's description of historical cultures. What about his contention that cultures can coexist temporally? To explain this, it is helpful to draw on Spengler's likening of his cultures to flowers in a field. Each culture will grow within a distinct soil and will remain attached to it for the entirety of its existence. A culture 'blossoms on the soil of a precisely delimitable landscape, to which it remains bound like a plant' (143).[20] Cultures, then, are distinct plants, emerging from a particular seed within a distinct set of soil in a given field. This explains the uniqueness of each culture. And while the germination period of Faustian culture, for instance, overlaps with the latter stages of Magian culture's life, both cultures remain spatially restricted to the soil on which their existence and predetermined development depends. But how does Spengler account for phenomena which can be found in both? To continue with the metaphor, Spengler concedes that while it is possible for the leaves and fruits of one culture to be blown from one field to another, there is no possibility of genuine cross-fertilisation between two cultures. In order to understand this, let us recall the example of Christianity within the Faustian world discussed above. The early Christian movement (*Urchristentum*), ca. 0–300 AD, is a product of the spring period of Magian culture, but Christianity can also be found during the emergence of Faustian culture towards the end of the first millennium AD. Spengler argues that this Christianity is worlds apart from that of Magian culture. It may *appear* that there is historical transmission between the two cultures, but we are dealing with two mutually incompatible and incomprehensible phenomena: the Christianity of the morning lands (the East) and that of the evening lands (the West). However, Spengler is far from consistent on this score. In the first, unrevised edition of *The Decline of the West*, for instance, he cites the fifth Benedictine Abbot of Cluny, St Odilo (ca. 962–1049 AD), as having transformed early Christianity (*morgenländisches Christentum*) into a religion befitting of the soul of the emerging *Abendland* by combining it with ancient Germanic paganism and the latter's propensity for the infinite, which lay dormant in the Nordic landscape long before the first Christian set foot on it.[21] This passage was removed from subsequent editions, but the question of whether and how cultures can impact upon each other continues to exercise Spengler's thought, with the problem of cross-cultural transfer becoming a leitmotif of his later endeavours to compose a truly comprehensive account of world history.[22] Although he never admits to it, he later appears to recognise that his main contention regarding the monad-like separation of cultures from each other is erroneous.[23]

In *The Decline of the West*, however, Spengler makes the case that his culture-centred morphology of world history enables him to do two things that other methods simply cannot. On the one hand, he is convinced – as we saw earlier – that his approach can enable the historian to postulate the existence of certain past phenomena, as expressions of a particular stage in the development of their soul, even if there is an absence of sufficient documentary evidence or historical records that would, at least using more traditional methods of historical inquiry, be required in order to *prove* their existence. On this basis, Spengler is able to make a number of claims about cultures for which there is little by way of source material, such as ancient China, just as Goethe was able to postulate the existence of the human intermaxillary bone. With regard to the 'reformation' that Spengler locates in the summer of each culture, for instance, he infers that such a movement is present in every culture, regardless of whether we have historical evidence of it (as in ancient Egypt) or not (as in China). Spengler thus considers his method to be capable of filling in the morphological gaps of human written history, of grasping intuitively the exact outlines of so-called lost or missing Civilisations and thus of postulating their position within the jigsaw puzzle of history. Turning his ire against von Ranke again, Spengler pointedly wonders whether a past event has ceased to be history merely because the historian has no written 'evidence' of its existence thousands of years later: 'Does life only become a fact when it is mentioned in books?' (611).

More importantly, on the other hand, Spengler contends that his method can shed light on the future. This is one of his central claims. Indeed, it is the assertion he makes in the very first sentence of *The Decline of the West*: 'In this book an attempt is made to predetermine history for the first time' (3). The *history* he is thinking of here is that of what he considers today's most important and most powerful culture, the *Abendland* – that is, the West. The book thus sets itself the task of 'following the yet to be travelled stages in the destiny of a culture, and specifically of the only culture of our time and on our planet which is actually in its phase of fulfilment [*Vollendung*] – the Western-European-American' (ibid.).

With this attempt at prediction, we have arrived at the second level at which Spengler's magnum opus can be read – as a theory of contemporary society and politics. This theory proceeds from the conviction that Faustian culture has entered into its own period of civilisation. Spengler feels that his comparative historical method makes it possible to determine the exact socio-political challenges posed in the final days of the Faustian world and to provide an intellectual framework for addressing them. We will explore exactly how he does so in Chapter 4.

## Problems

Before turning to Spengler's view of Faustian civilisation, however, let us have yet another look at some of the problems that his historiographical morphology throws up. We will examine these issues in detail in the following chapters, but it seems useful to provide at least an initial indication of them here.

First of all, Spengler's use of the term 'decline' (*Untergang*) is neither clear nor consistent in *The Decline of the West*. He deploys it in a variety of ways, with several implications. One use of *Untergang* is Spengler's attempt to portray the 'terminal crisis' of Western culture and the inevitability of it going under. This is the dominant reading of Spengler's *Untergang* and is usually cited as evidence of his pessimist and fatalist understanding of history. The West is doomed to perish because, like all organisms, it is destined to do so. It can do no other.

However, on other occasions, it is unclear whether Spengler's concept of *Untergang* in the Faustian world refers to a culture's transition from *Kultur* to *Zivilisation*, which has already taken place, or whether it is a reference to the final, winter days of a culture itself, with much to be decided before then.[24] This ambiguity is compounded by Spengler's lack of clarity on whether, and how, cultures eventually disappear: his account of the demise of cultures is often as vague as his explanation of their birth. He even suggests that a culture may not disappear at all, but may remain in its phase of *Zivilisation* for hundreds or thousands of years. It is internally dead, but retains the outward appearance of life: 'As such, like a worn-out giant of the primeval forest, it [*Zivilisation*] might thrust its decaying branches towards the sky for hundreds or thousands of years, as we see in China, in India, in the Islamic world' (143).

The vagueness in relation to whether Faustian culture's *Untergang* is already in the past (ca. 1800), in the future (ca. 2200) or a process of transition encompassing both finds reflection in Spengler's lack of consistency in making predictions as to how long Faustian culture will last. The historical tables in *The Decline of the West* state that the *ultimate* demise of the Faustian world will set in around 2200 and that what he calls the Caesarism of Faustian culture (*the formation of Caesarism*, which we will analyse in the following chapters) will not emerge until ca. 2000. However, in his political writings and activities, he not only maintains that the great struggles over the precise nature and form of Faustian Caesarism have *already begun*, but he also seeks to intervene in them.

This leads us to yet another way in which the term *Untergang* can be interpreted. Recent developments in Weimar historiography highlight the need to distinguish between *terminal crisis* as a social condition and the *evocation of crisis* as a rhetorical device – as a way to disqualify the status quo and prepare the ground for something new. Seen in this light, Spengler's deployment of the term *Untergang* is not a call to a passive acceptance of one's historical fate, but to historically informed political action. This significant insight has not yet been applied to the importance of the political in Spengler's thought, so we will take a closer look at its implications in Chapter 4.

A second problem in Spengler's morphology of world history is his provocative belief in the incompatibility of the modern *Abendland* with peoples, religions and races from other historical cultures. This is a particularly significant issue, as it has fed into the dominant perception of Spengler as a racialist thinker or even a (proto-)Nazi.

On the one hand, Spengler explicitly distances himself from biological understandings of race that were popular in Europe during his time. For instance, he is scathing of the pseudo-science of examining and comparing skulls from various 'races' in order to establish the supposed superiority of the Aryan people. His understanding of different races and nations flows not from biological categories, but metaphysical ones, with different peoples viewed as embodying something significant about the essence of the culture within which they emerge. As we have seen, for him, it is *cultures*, not *races* that are decisive. This foregrounding of the soul and living out one's destiny is integral to the German tradition of the philosophy of life (*Lebensphilosophie*) in which Spengler stands, emphasising the non-'scientific' or irrational basis of human behaviour.[25] Moreover, despite Spengler's claims regarding the incompatibility of historical cultures, his perceptive critique of Eurocentrism foregrounds the *equality* of all historical cultures and peoples. He notes, for example, how even the most erudite scholars find it difficult to explain concepts and ideas from Arabic or Japanese, which makes it difficult to do justice to the significance and uniqueness of such societies.

On the other hand, Spengler's view of cultures is decidedly essentialist. His understanding of non-Western cultures involves a de facto Eurocentrism in its overreliance on the typecasting of non-European cultures. He repeatedly makes homogenising claims about non-European cultures, not least because his method must trace the multifarious events of past societies back to one holistic principle. So it is that we find references to 'Indian man', 'the Egyptian' or 'the Chinese' *as such*: 'Indian man forgot everything, the Egyptian could not forget *anything*' (16). While Spengler insists that terms such as race or blood – commonplace within his political writings in particular – are metaphysically informed, this is not immediately apparent from his work. Against the racially charged backdrop within which he is writing, the preponderance of such terminology is at best misleading and at worst dovetails with the rhetoric of racial hierarchies. In Chapter 7, we will see how Spengler's views on the so-called Jewish question in Germany often blur the distinction he claims to have established between metaphysical and biological conceptions of *Rasse*.

A third shortcoming within Spengler's methodology is the apparent paradox at the heart of his sweeping claims on history: to wit, if there is no genuine historical transmission between cultures, if cultures cannot influence each other in any meaningful sense, then why does he claim to be the first who can provide the framework for a biography of all of the previous seven cultures, as well as to provide informed prognoses for the last stages of his own?

For Spengler, there is no paradox at the heart of his outlook because the Faustian *Ursymbol* of infinite space frees critical thought from a focus on the here and now: it is thus innately historical. Instead of focusing, as previous cultures had, on the nature of what the scientists can see in front of their eyes, as in Apollonian culture, he argues that modern Faustian culture looks beneath the surface to understand and implement the invisible driving forces of change and *development*: 'The Greek asked, what is the essence of visible being? We ask, what is the possibility of mastering the invisible driving forces of becoming?' (490). Therefore, for the first time, it is possible to conceive of history as a process within which the infinite possibilities of the future are linked to the present and, in turn, to the endless horizon of the past: 'Will links the future to the present, thought links the boundless to the here. *The historic future is distance-becoming, the boundless world-horizon distance-become*: this is the meaning of the Faustian depth-experience' (394).

Foremost in Spengler's mind when it comes to this unprecedented Faustian view of history is the teleological triad of *Antiquity – Middle Ages – Modernity*, which itself is a product of Faustian culture: 'the image of a world history in the Faustian style' (465). *The Decline of the West* – itself a tremendous expression of what Spengler views as the Faustian passion for the historical – develops a critique of this teleological triad not because of this approach's claim to understand the past, but, as we have seen, because of its blinkered perspective in seeking to do so.

However, Spengler's reasoning cannot account for the paradox. Although his culture-centred approach rejects the idea of historical transmission, he is clearly of the view that there is a unique, *qualitatively different* historical consciousness latent in Faustian culture, even if, as he claims, this consciousness is the result of historical accident rather than historical transmission: 'We men of Western European culture are, with our sense for history, the exception, not the rule' (20). He criticises thinkers such as Hegel and Marx for their view that bourgeois society brings with it a historically unprecedented basis for human freedom: 'Why, *from the mor-*

*phological point of view*, should the eighteenth century be more important than any of the sixty that preceded it?' (23). But a similar problem applies to Spengler's own method: if Faustian culture is the exception and not the rule, why is it so important to focus on the *eleventh* century as representing the key to genuine historical understanding? In short, there is a contradiction between his critique of Eurocentrism on the one hand and his hypostatisation of Faustian culture on the other.

A final problem with Spengler's morphology of world history is the tension between his conception of historical development as an organic, determined and cyclical process, and his conviction that there is much to play for between those peoples who will experience the final two to three centuries of the Faustian world. There are – historically determined and outlined – problems to be solved and possibilities to be embraced: the '*possibilities* of the West-European mind in its next stages' (6–7).

This is a particularly significant point because it has not really been discussed in the secondary literature and is central to understanding the interplay between the determined and the voluntaristic aspects of Spengler's political thought. It is misleading for critics such as Ernst Bloch to argue that *The Decline of the West* lacks any 'connection to the process of becoming, to the question of the new' within the final stages of Faustian civilisation.[26] Indeed, as we will see in the following chapters, it is by no means the case that *The Decline of the West* views the precise outlines of the decline of the West as an already decided affair. Spengler expects the Western world to go out with a bang, not a whimper, in an age of global imperialism, wars and uprisings. Nations will compete to be the last, victorious people of the Faustian world that can emerge as 'the last race in form' (1128–29).[27] Spengler's historical framework is thus geared towards understanding and mastering the remaining challenges presented by Faustian civilisation. For him, these challenges and clashes are *both* historically predetermined *and* open-ended, contingent events, the outcome of which depends on the ideas and actions of historical actors involved in them.

This tension between Spengler's claims to predict the future and his recognition that there is a need for active intervention in the events and processes that will *shape* that future has important implications for his method. As we will see, despite his pretensions at viewing history in a nonpartisan or ideological fashion – 'from timeless heights … not with the eyes of a party man or an ideologue' (47) – his prognosis for the future of the West cannot always be seen as the logical outcome of his purportedly objective method, nor can this prognosis be abstracted from his own subjective aims and affiliations, such as his passionate German nationalism and his conviction that Germany can and must emerge victorious in the battles that will define the final years of the West.

# Notes

1. Spengler, *Der Untergang des Abendlandes. Umrisse einer Morphologie der Weltgeschichte*, 24. All subsequent references to this version of the text in this chapter will be placed in parentheses in the main text. The philosophical proclamation of a 'Copernican revolution' is a recurring feature among German thinkers. Both Kant and Freud made similar claims regarding their own theories; cf. De Berg and Large (eds), *Modern German Thought from Kant to Habermas: An Annotated German-Language Reader*, 3, 43–44; cf. also Henk de Berg, *Freud's Theory and Its Use in Literary and Cultural Studies*, 62.
2. Hilde Kornhardt makes clear in her short preface to the historical tables at the beginning of *Der Untergang des Abendlandes* that the chronology of Egyptian culture has been updated to reflect the latest developments in historical research; Spengler, *Der Untergang des Abendlandes*, 71.
3. Spengler does not specify dates for the lifespan of the Babylonian or Mexican cultures in *Der Untergang des Abendlandes*, nor does he incorporate them into the historical tables in this work.
4. For instance, we need only recall the *Staatsexamensarbeit* that Spengler wrote in order to qualify as a teacher, entitled *The Development of the Visual Organs among the Main Groups of the Animal Kingdom*.
5. Goethe, *Der Versuch die Metamorphose der Pflanzen zu erklären*.
6. As Nicholas Boyle has argued, the idea of 'botanical structure' and the formation (*Bildung*) of organic life-forms finds reflection in the development of the main protagonist in Goethe's *Wilhelm Meisters Lehrjahre*, the 'internal structure' of which is 'involuted and encapsulated, like that of a seed, and it begins by presenting us with a moment in which all of Wilhelm's previous existence … is implied'; Boyle, *Goethe: The Poet and the Age. Volume II: Revolution and Renunciation*, 412.
7. Graham, *Goethe: Portrait of the Artist*, 204.
8. Boyle, *Goethe: The Poet and the Age*, 81.
9. Ibid.
10. Ibid., 256.
11. Cf. ibid., 104.
12. This quote is taken from the table for 'Winter' in the 'Tafel "gleichzeitiger Geistesepochen' ('Table of "simultaneous" intellectual epochs') in Spengler, *Der Untergang des Abendlandes* (no page reference).
13. See his 'Tafel "gleichzeitiger" politischer Epochen' in ibid.
14. Spengler sees each culture typically lasting for about a millennium in the way that a human life, at least in his time, usually lasts seventy years: Spengler, *Der Untergang des Abendlandes*, 148.
15. Merlio, 'Spenglers Geschichtsmorphologie im Kontext des Historismus und seiner Krise', 134–36.
16. Osmančević, *Oswald Spengler und das Ende der Geschichte*, 130.
17. 'A peculiar "decline"! How we would welcome such a "decline"!'; Demandt, *Untergänge des Abendlandes. Studien zu Oswald Spengler*, 57.
18. A description of his desired form of writing 'in Hindenburg style', which is 'concise, clear, Roman, *natural* above all … far removed from Nietzsche's snobbery'; Spengler to Klöres, 14 July 1915, in Spengler, *Briefe 1913–1936*, 45. Otto Neurath claims that Spengler's approach can 'force the reader into submission', for 'Who can check all the fields that Spengler touches on, especially since there are no references to sources?'; Neurath, 'Anti-Spengler', in Neurath and Cohen (eds), *Otto Neurath: Empiricism and Sociology*, 161.
19. Hegel supposedly informed one of his students that: 'If the facts contradict the theory, then all the worse for the facts.' Interestingly, Spengler points out how: 'When Hegel claimed, with such naivety, that he would ignore those people that did not fit into his historical schema, he was simply being honest and admitting the methodological premises required by all historians if they are to achieve their aims'; Spengler, *Untergang des Abendlandes*, 30.

20. In the original 'unrevised edition' of *The Decline of the West* published by Beck, Spengler explicitly claims that 'cultures are plants'. This passage was struck from subsequent versions, but he continued to treat cultures as plants in these editions too; Spengler, *Untergang des Abendlandes. Umrisse einer Morphologie der Weltgeschichte. Erster Band: Gestalt und Wirklichkeit*, 199.
21. Ibid., 254.
22. In Volume 2 of *The Decline of the West*, for instance, Spengler develops the concept of historical pseudomorphosis (*historische Pseudomorphosen*) to describe cases where an older, more established culture can hinder the development of another culture or even alter the course of its predetermined development as an organism. We must leave aside a discussion of this idea and its implications for Spengler's theory of history.
23. On this, see Conte, *Oswald Spengler. Eine Einführung*, 74–76.
24. Thöndl, '"Wie oft stirbt das Abendland?" Oswald Spenglers These vom zweifachen Untergang', in Gangl, Merlio and Orphälders (eds), *Spengler. Ein Denker der Zeitenwende*, 251–72.
25. For an introductory overview of this tradition and some of its thinkers, see Herf, *Reactionary Modernism: Technology, Culture and Politics in Weimar and the Third Reich*, 26–30.
26. Bloch, 'Spenglers Raubtiere und relative Kulturgärten', in *Erbschaft dieser Zeit*. Werkausgabe, Vol. 4, 318–29 (324).
27. We will return to his precise use of this term race (*Rasse*) with reference to his ideas on the Germans and the British in Chapter 5.

CHAPTER 4

# Faustian *Zivilisation*
## *Prognosis and Perspectives*

Now that we have summarised Spengler's morphology of world history and indicated several of the shortcomings and tensions within his conception of historical change, we can proceed to discuss why he thinks that his theory of history can predict what lies ahead for the Faustian world, and why – as a consequence – he believes that he can contribute to shaping its future. Specifically, we will analyse what *The Decline of the West* outlines as the central features of, and dynamics behind, Faustian *Zivilisation*, or the winter period of Faustian culture's life-cycle. We will then explain how this text conceives of the remaining opportunities for socio-political change within the process of Western decline.

At first sight, our continued focus on *The Decline of the West* may appear out of step with one of the central contentions of this study – to wit, that the secondary literature's overemphasis on Spengler's main work has come at the expense of an engagement with his major political writings and has skewed the dominant understanding of him. Already in 1940, Edwin D. Franken claimed that: 'As happens with many men, he [Spengler] had one great work in him, and all the rest was residue and froth.'[1] This notion is still dominant today. Joe Paul Kroll, for instance, claims that, aside from *The Decline of the West*, the 'remainder of Spengler's *oeuvre* remained *short* or *fragmentary*'.[2] This volume is, it should be recalled, a direct challenge to these and similar appropriations of Spengler's legacy and aims to shift the scholarly focus onto his other works. Far from being short, fragmentary or frothy, these writings are, as we will see in the following chapters, some of the most influential conservative interventions into public life in the Weimar Republic. So why is it necessary to include another chapter on *The Decline of the West*, the dominant point of reference for Spengler scholarship? Two points must be emphasised here.

First, as variegated as the scholarly reception of Spengler's magnum opus has become over the past century, this work's extensive discussion of the need for political leadership to navigate the historical tide of Western *Zivilisation* has been overshadowed by its interpretation as an example of German *Kulturpessimismus*.[3] For instance, the claim that *The Decline of the West* provides a 'post-mortem'[4] of Western society overlooks the interventionist, positive or even optimistic features of this text. This particularly applies to the work's repeated calls to historically informed political action, which we will discuss below. In so doing, this chapter will challenge the dominant reading of the main work of this supposed 'prophet of doom and gloom'[5] by making the case that it provides not only a diagnosis of the decline and ultimate demise of the Western world, but also a prognosis. Further, I will demonstrate the principles behind Spengler's emphasis on the need for the political leadership he believes is required to address the political and economic challenges posed by Faustian *Zivilisation* most effectively, and thus to assist his beloved Germany in becoming a global hegemon *before* the life cycle of Faustian culture reaches its conclusion.

Second, the few studies that do engage with the conception of politics in Western *Zivilisation* in *The Decline of the West* all too often proceed from the assumption that the ideas contained in this text find practical reflection in the entirety of Spengler's political actions across his career. As we saw in Chapter 2, Ernst Stutz claims that 'Spengler's philosophical and political work … bear the same handwriting, are an expression of the same personality and ultimately pursue the same aims'.[6] Similarly, the Spengler biographer Detlef Felken contends that the ideas outlined in Spengler's later political writings tend to be little more than '"updated paraphrases" of his main philosophical work', while Samir Osmančević claims that Spengler's politics are 'solely and exclusively the *consequence* of his philosophy of history'.[7]

In order to prevent our study from falling into the conceptual trap of approaching Spengler's politics of decline as a static body of thought that grows directly out of his main work and finds immediate and unadulterated reflection in his political oeuvre, this chapter will outline how *The Decline of the West* understands the need for, and possibility of, a political *alternative* developing within the framework of social dissolution and decline. This analysis will serve as a foil against which we can trace the tensions and developments in Spengler's move from the realm of theory to the realm of political practice, which is the focus of the remaining chapters in this book. As a result, the developments and shifts in emphasis within Spengler's politics of decline will be contextualised and explained in a manner that the secondary literature has hitherto failed to do. Before we take a closer look at the book's discussion of the need for alternative political leadership within Western *Zivilisation*, however, let us first provide a summary of what Spengler views as the driving forces of the winter period of Faustian culture.

## Winter

Unlike English-language philosophy, German thought tends to distinguish rigorously between the concepts of culture and civilisation (*Kultur* and *Zivilisation*),[8] with the former having positive implications of high intellectual and artistic output and an association with a golden age of reflection, philosophy and poetry, as well as a more harmonious religious, social and economic order. *Zivilisation*, by contrast, refers to the supposed baleful influence of money, urbanism and rationalism on intellectual culture, which has contributed to the rise of mechanistic, instrumentalist and short-termist thought in all areas of life.[9] In Germany, this distinction long pre-dates Spengler's philosophy and finds particularly salient reflection in Nietzsche's ideas on decadence.[10] It becomes prominent among intellectuals on the German right during and after the First World War. Spengler asserts, for instance, that *Zivilisation* represents the stage of a culture in which tradition is no longer valid and in which each and every idea must be rearticulated in monetary terms if is to be realised successfully.[11] He thus views *Faustian* or *Western Zivilisation* – analogously to all hitherto existing periods of *civilisation* – as predominantly characterised by urbanism, the triumph of money over metaphysics, democracy, the rise of the masses (*Masse*) as opposed to the people (*Volk*), *panem et circences* and the levelling of social hierarchy.

What does Spengler mean by the distinction between the masses and the people? We may recall from the previous chapter that he considers the nobility and the priesthood as the two prime estates that drive forward the development of a culture, and also that the absolutist state embodies a harmonious unity between these estates and the commoners. This is how Spengler understands the term *people*: as a living entity with (metaphysical) ties to the cultural soul that underpins them all. Similarly, the rise of the masses in modern cities is not merely a sociological, but also a metaphysical phenomenon – the breaking apart of society's inner bonds by the 'negating and disintegrating' (1120) implications of the need to pursue a life defined by money. For this reason, Spengler contends that the mass has its roots in the bourgeoisie or – as he puts it in a possible reference to Emmanuel-Joseph Sieyès – the first non-estate (*Nichtstand*, 1120).[12] This development has irreversible consequences for the fate of the culture as an organism, with individuals becoming rootless and estranged from their own essence: money has become a 'form of active wakefulness ... which no longer has any roots in being' (672). In these and similar comments on the alienated nature of city life, there is an unmistakeable veneration of the peasantry and an idealisation of the rural way of life. For instance, he views the peasantry as the only self-supporting grouping in society and claims that it is the basis of all higher forms of economic activity (1152–53).

However, as was discussed in the previous chapter, Spengler is convinced that it is impossible to turn back the clock of history to a previous stage of a culture: those seeking to influence events must begin with the world as it is and as it will be, not as it once was or how one might like it to be in the future. We will return to this paradoxical idea further below, but let us first look at what *The Decline of the West* describes as the other central features of Western *Zivilisation*.

Spengler argues that Faustian *Zivilisation* came into existence around 1800, to the emergence of modernity (a term he does not use) in the wake of the emergence of capitalism and the French Revolution. He insists that this transition from *Kultur* to *Zivilisation* ensures that the 'Western' beliefs and ideals once championed as the zenith of human achievement and enlightenment – the victory of reason and systematic thinking, the possibility of peaceful coexistence and a stable world order through trade and negotiation, democracy, the emancipatory power of art and literature and so on – now reveal themselves as mere illusions. The unbound optimism of the Faustian world's autumnal Enlightenment ushered in by 'city man' (942) has inevitably morphed into cynical scepticism or even nihilism.

So, for instance, Spengler denies the possibility of genuine religious belief in our times. Here it is worth stressing how both religious conviction and atheist commitment possess a metaphysical significance in Spengler's thought. He views atheism not as irreligion, but as indicative of a soul that has exhausted the entirety of its possibilities of looking at the world: living experience has atrophied to the extent that nothing is left. Within this framework, even irreligious people are religious in the time of a flourishing culture. The converse is true of believers in the period of *Zivilisation*. In this period, he claims, the only true belief is in atoms and numbers, but this requires intellectual 'hocus pocus' if it is to be tolerable in the longer term (941). This futile search for metaphysical meaning is necessarily shallow and dishonest during a time when materialist thought – which he calls shallow and honest – reigns supreme. A 'second religiousness' (ibid.) therefore emerges in the age of *Zivilisation*. Whether it amounts to a most attenuated Christianity or a faith in tarot cards and healing crystals, Spengler is convinced that it is but a watery image of the bold action to realise the Faustian spirit of the infinite and the boundless once so intuitively pursued by its leading subjects.

In similar terms, Spengler claims that the age of *Zivilisation* is one in which there is no longer any possibility of genuine artistic production or expression. Talk of new and exciting artistic forms merely represents the recycling of old ideas, trends and materials – indicative of a society that has exhausted the possibilities for fulfilment in an 'ossification' (686) of these forms: 'Culture and Civilisation – the living body of a soul and a mummy of it' (450). The age of art is irrevocably over within Faustian civiliation.

Indeed, one of Spengler's stated objectives in composing *The Decline of the West* is to turn the youth away from art and towards technology, imperialism and political statesmanship: 'And I can only hope that men of the new generation may be moved by this book to devote themselves to technics instead of lyrics, the navy instead of the paint-brush, and politics instead of epistemology' (57).

Spengler's description of *Zivilisation*, his explanation of its origins and his assessment of this phenomenon's purportedly harmful impact on all areas of life is not unique.[13] Nonetheless, his analysis of *Zivilisation* is novel in two key respects. First, the concept is integrated into his philosophy of world history insofar as *Zivilisation* is not viewed as a historically unprecedented or distinctly 'modern' crisis, but rather as a cyclically recurring spectacle within each of his historical *cultures*. He thus claims to have placed the established intellectual distinction between *Culture* and *Civilisation* on a historical-philosophical footing:

> For every Culture has its own Civilization. In this work, for the first time the two words, hitherto used to express an indefinite, more or less ethical, distinction, are used in a periodic sense, to express a strict and necessary organic succession. Civilization is a Culture's inescapable fate. (43)

Seen in this light, the decline of the West means nothing less than 'the problem of *Civilisation*' insofar as this decline is best understood as the inevitable outcome of the West's organic development, just as birth presupposes death (ibid.). It is therefore a predetermined and inescapable phenomenon for all cultures:

> the inevitable destiny of the Culture, and with this principle we arrive at the viewpoint from which the deepest and gravest problems of historical, morphology can be solved. Civilizations are the most external and artificial states of which a species of developed humanity is capable. They are a conclusion, the thing-become succeeding the thing becoming, death following life, rigidity following expansion, intellectual age and the stone-built, petrifying world-city following mother-earth and the spiritual childhood of Doric and Gothic. They are an end, irrevocable, yet by inward necessity reached over and again. (Ibid.)

Second, Spengler claims that his choice of the nineteenth century as marking the rise of the winter of Faustian culture flows not from an arbitrary assessment or moral judgement of late-Faustian culture, but precisely from his method of comparing historical cultures in their journey from birth to death. This allows him to claim that the First World War in Western culture has heralded an age that is 'contemporary' with the 'transition from the Hellenistic to the Roman age' (36). What Spengler has in mind here is that the last phase of Western culture will look similar to the period of the Roman Republic between ca. 300 BC and its overthrow by Caesar in 27 BC. Moreover, as we saw in the previous chapter, this statement is no mere comparison or analogy, but in Spengler's eyes represents an *objective truth* on which any analysis of the Western *Zivilisation* must be based. How does Spengler believe that this development will express itself in the politics of his time? Does this idea of history repeating imply a glum and passive fatalism, as the secondary literature often implies? These are the questions to which we must now turn.

## Parliament and the Press

The most important parallel Spengler finds between Apollonian and Faustian *Zivilisation* is that both are characterised by the existence of *democracy* as a state form. For him, elections, parliaments and parties are not historically novel pheonema, but rather the inevitable expression of life of a money-centred, urban *Zivilisation*. He claims that the notions of popular sovereignty and influence over the functioning of the state – whether sincerely held by voters or cynically exploited by party leaders running election campaigns – are mere illusions. Democracy is little more than a façade behind which the forces of finance and moneyed speculation can exercise their control – the best democracy money can buy in what he calls a 'dictatorship of money' (1134). Politics has become subsumed by the bourgeoisie and its thinking in money (*Gelddenken*, 950). The triumph of this class, Spengler adds, is embodied in the rise of parliaments across Western Europe: 'the appearance of a party of the nobility in a parliament is inwardly just as artificial as that of a proletarian one. Only the bourgeoisie is at home here' (1124).

For Spengler, the illusions of the masses in democracy are garnered and sustained by the mass media in the form of the press. He ascribes to this medium an almost demonic control over the outlook and agency of the rootless urban masses: 'Three weeks of work by the press, and everybody has realised the truth' [i.e. the so-called truth] (1139). This manufactured common sense will only be called into question if another, better-resourced, press outlet appears and uses its funds to proclaim an alternative opinion in an even noisier and more relentless fashion:

> What is truth? For the majority, it is what they constantly read and hear ... today, the public opinion of the current moment, which is the only thing that counts in the world of facts [*Tatsachenwelt*], of impact and success, is a product of the press. What is wants to be true is true. Its commanders create, transform and reverse truths. (1139)

With reference to his historical morphology, Spengler claims that the modern press is to Faustian *Zivilisation* what rhetoric was to the corresponding period of Apollonian culture. Both fulfil a function that revolves primarily around the immediate impression and not the actual content (1139). Nonetheless, in keeping with the Classical *Ursymbol* of proximity, the impact of ancient rhetoric was limited to those present during the speech, whereas the modern press possesses a Faustian dynamism that aims at *'lasting* effects' (ibid.). The impact of the latter is all the more profound. Spengler argues that those who are able to buy the press can mobilise and exert command over the people just as a general leads an army (1140).[14]

Yet Spengler is convinced that the days of democracy are numbered. In spite of its noble claims about representation and equality, the democratic system can only concentrate real political decision-making in the hands of an ever smaller number of plutocrats. The outcome of this is that Faustian democracy will follow in the footsteps of its 'alter ego' (37) in Apollonian culture and be overthrown by strongmen who will dispense with the pretence of democracy and take power into their own hands (1143). The figures who emerge from this process will rule with an iron hand and usher in the end of democracy. This phenomenon is referred to in *The Decline of the West* as Caesarism.

Spengler views this prediction – the inevitable death of democracy and the historically determined emergence of dictators presiding over formless masses of people – not as pessimistic or fatalistic in nature. We have seen above how *The Decline of the West* continues to be interpreted in such a fashion. A further example of this interpretation can be found in the work of one of Spengler's biographers, Jürgen Naeher. Naeher considers *The Decline of the West* to be the work of an outsider who assesses the world around him, but whose feelings of his own 'deficiencies, limitations and vacuity'[15] ensure that he remains largely incapable of intervening in the events around him. This is a seriously mistaken view of Spengler and his work. Moreover, one of the reasons why the secondary literature has overlooked or downplayed Spengler the historical actor as opposed to Spengler the historian is that it has not engaged with the concrete ideological-rhetorical context in which Spengler uses the term *Untergang*. In order to address this shortcoming, let us take a closer look at Spengler's motivations for heralding the decline of the Western world.

## *Untergang* and the State

A defining feature of Spengler's politically charged age is the abundance of a rhetoric of *crisis* across the political spectrum. In his groundbreaking study of political rhetoric in the early Weimar period, Rüdiger Graf has convincingly shown how the abundance of the rhetoric of crisis, decline and decay had little to do with pessimism or dystopian pronouncements on the unavoidably gloomy days ahead.[16] Rather, the invocation of crisis serves to disqualify certain ideas and prepare the ground for an alternative approach: during the Weimar Republic – a period of self-proclaimed prophets and saviours – the term *Untergang* is used to refer to the end of obsolete institutions in society or to key turning points in a (perceived) social crisis. It is a way of grasping and coming to terms with the critical junctures (*Entscheidungssituationen*) on the horizon and of intensifying the crisis in the imagination of those living at the time.[17] However, this important insight has not been applied to Spengler's ideas and rhetoric. By doing so, we can render visible the explicitly political and positive thrust of *The Decline of the West* and thus address a significant lacuna in Spengler scholarship.

We noted in the previous chapter how Spengler's use of the concept *Untergang* in the context of the Faustian West is not entirely consistent. Sometimes it describes the West's transition from *Kultur* to *Zivilisation*, which has already taken place, while sometimes it is a reference to the final, winter days of a culture itself, with much to be decided before then. We now arrive at another pivotal way in which Spengler uses the term: as a call to arms that underlines the historical condition of those to whom his book is addressed, as a way of preparing them for the many pivotal events taking place both within and between the nations of the West in its final days. We will discuss the decisive moments Spengler describes in our discussion on Caesarism below, but here it is worth stressing that his evocation of the decline of the West serves to emphasise how the *Abendland*'s final chapter is yet to be written. It is therefore misleading to claim, as the prominent Spengler scholar Alexander Demandt does, that there is a 'split within Spengler's theory' or that 'a rupture separates prognosis and programme', since '[t]hose who know what is going to happen do not say what should be done'.[18] Let us now proceed, then, to outline the relationship between prognosis and programme, between Spengler's historical morphology and his politics of decline, by taking a closer look at what Spengler understands by Caesarism.

Spengler's concept of Caesarism is best understood on two levels. On the one hand, it is a *prognosis* – purportedly drawn from his theory of history – of what lies ahead for Faustian *Zivilisation*. As the historical tables at the beginning of *The Decline of the West* underline, Spengler foresees the – vaguely expressed – *emergence of Caesarism* as setting in in ca. 2000 and lasting for roughly two centuries, before Faustian culture disappears altogether. This period is therefore a 'general stage of development, lasting for two centuries, which can be established in all historical cultures' (1081). On the other hand, Spengler portrays Caesarism as a core value that must underpin any political alternative (or *programme*) seeking to influence the events and struggles of his time – that is, long before 2000. Let us begin by looking at the emergence of Caesarism as historical prognosis.

In *The Decline of the West*, Spengler defines the period in which he is writing as the transition from the age of Napoleon to the age of Caesarism: the 'final political constitution of late Civilisations' (942). What Spengler understands by this is what we discussed above: the gradual decay of parties, parliaments and elections ushered in by the French Revolution and their eventual overthrow by power-driven individuals. This process is historically determined and thus inevitable, but Spengler by no means wishes to imply that this will be a straightforward, let alone peaceful, procedure. He expects the final stages of the Western world to be characterised by struggles *within* the nations of the Western world for the reins of state power, but also *between* them for world supremacy. Spengler calls this 'an age of giant battles' (1081), a period of wars and uprisings across the globe. What will ultimately seal the fate of the peoples and nations caught up in these dramatic events is might, not right, action, not theory. At the forefront of his mind is the age of global imperialism, the struggle for colonial power and the brutality of the First World War. These phenomena are unavoidable features of the age: a necessary product of all civilisations (1089). Where Faustian *Zivilisation* differs from its predecessor in ancient Rome is that the assassinations, coups, uprisings and wars that characterised Apollonian *Zivilisation* were not truly global in nature. By contrast, the Faustian drive towards the boundless and infinite means that gargantuan struggles over genuine world power will ensue, with the lives of millions of people on the line. Spengler notes: 'We are dealing with the most difficult period in the history of all cultures' (1101), in which masses of people will be 'trampled in the battles between those seeking to conquer power' (1107).

Spengler, then, is convinced that the world has fundamentally changed and that the age of *Kultur* is over. What lies ahead is therefore not a period of reflection, philosophical output and poetry, but one of industrial warfare, in which politics is gradually becoming more authoritarian. This is the era of the engineer and the entrepreneur, not the painter or the poet: 'In the shareholders' meeting of any limited company, or in the technical staff of any first-rate engineering works there is more intelligence, taste, character and capacity than in all of the music and painting of present-day Europe' (378).

Such disdain for the artistic output of the age is of course a trope of German *Kulturpessimismus*. But Spengler's recognition that the age of Goethe is irrevocably a thing of the past is not straightforwardly pessimistic in nature. Following the idea that everything is always in flux and that nothing ever remains (cf. the concept of *panta rhei* put forward by

Heraclitus, on whom Spengler wrote his doctoral dissertation, 'Heraclitus – A Study of the Energetic Foundation of His Philosophy'), Spengler is simply stressing the inevitability of historical change. Moreover, in a stance that combines Bismarckian notions of *Realpolitik* with Nietzsche's *amor fati*, Spengler contends that a true understanding of, and hence a real influence on, Faustian *Zivilisation* is only possible if one proceeds not from despair at the state of affairs in this era, but rather from an acknowledgement of the world as it is, warts and all. Those nations that do not grasp the inevitability of imperialism and warfare, for instance, will cease to be the subjects of history and will be swept aside. Spengler therefore contends that it is necessary for aspiring statesmen to avoid what he calls two forms of political *idealism* within Faustian *Zivilisation*: the belief that the course of history can be reversed, and the conviction that the historical process has an ultimate *telos* from which political principles and methods should be derived.

For Spengler, beginning with the world as it is means recognising the inexorable process of disintegration that all nation-states undergo during *Zivilisation*. He refers to this development as the gradual *formlessness* of the state. This is best understood with reference to two aspects of Spengler's philosophy of history in *The Decline of the West*. First, the dissolution of society's metaphysical bonds – a dissolution he locates at the core of all atomised *civilisations* – has unalterable implications for the political process. The organic solidity of the absolutist state or the limited social coherence provided by political parties is no longer a possibility when these metaphysical bonds become gradually more meaningless. Second, Spengler believes, as we saw in the previous chapter, that dying cultures will eventually return to the ahistorical human condition, the *Urmenschentum* that characterises the primitive origins of all cultures. The outcome of these two developments is the need for formless – that is, brutish and direct – institutions of political power: 'I use the term "Caesarism" to denote that kind of government which, irrespective of any constitutional formulation that it may have, is in its inward self a return to thorough formlessness … It is the return of a form-fulfilled world into primitivism' (1101). The objective necessity of authoritarian political forms paves the way for those seeking to rule in a more direct and forceful manner: 'To the extent that nations cease to be politically in "condition" (in Verfassung), to that same extent *possibilities* open up for the energetic private person who means to be politically creative, who wants power at all costs, and who as a phenomenon of force becomes the destiny of an entire people or culture' (1083, emphasis added).

Spengler's description of Caesarism as historical prediction is rather abstract. This has led some scholars to claim that Spengler never explained in concrete terms what modern-day Caesarism would look like. Thomas

Tartsch, for instance, asserts that 'even if today Spengler's name is always mentioned alongside Caesarism, he never explicitly outlined what it would look like'.[19] This statement overlooks the other sense in which Spengler uses the term: as a central aspect of his political alternative. Before we take a closer look at what Spengler understands by Caesarism as a political principle, let us clarify what he means by states being 'in condition' (*in Verfassung*) politically. This is a particularly important aspect of his politics of decline. In spite of his insistence – in opposition to more traditional conservative strands of thought – that it is impossible to return to the *Kultur* phase of Faustian culture, in *The Decline of the West* the underlying view of the ideal state form is, in fact, a classically conservative one. Politics is the natural preserve of an assiduous, enlightened and selfless nobility (*Dienstadel*), whereas parliaments, elections and political parties are mere manifestations of the corrupting influence of the masses on state life.[20] Indeed, for Spengler, the true nobility and the true state are essentially synonymous:

> But a genuine old nobility assimilates itself to the state, and cares for all as it would for its own property. This care, in fact, is one of its grandest duties and one of which it is most deeply conscious; it feels it, indeed, an innate privilege and regards service in the army and the administration as its special calling. (1014)

Spengler's political commitment to the nobility – 'man as history' (976) – and its supposed values of chivalry, discipline, honour, self-denial and tradition is a stable feature of his political philosophy. Nonetheless, this commitment assumes a variety of forms in his political writings and plans throughout his career. Although his own background is petty bourgeois, not aristocratic, he claimed to have always felt part of the latter: 'I have *always* been an aristocrat. Nietzsche was self-evident to me before I read anything he wrote.'[21] In *The Decline of the West*, the existence of this layer is the *conditio sine qua non* of a strong and stable state: 'Politically gifted peoples do not exist. There are only peoples that are firmly in the hands of a ruling minority and as such feel that they are in good condition' (1111). Indeed, politics should not be understood in terms of how the individual relates to the state or how social classes struggle for influence over it. Rather, politics is *war*, and a functioning state – one that is 'in condition' – is prepared for the unescapable reality of conflict, which for Spengler is the prime foundation of politics in all living beings (1109). In the coming battles, nations will hold their own not through the ideals of democratic legitimacy or accountability, but through the authority, certainty and superiority of their political leadership (1015).

But how does this understanding of the indispensability of the nobility to a war-ready state square with Spengler's contention that the era of the nobility actually lies in the past? There is clearly a tension, perhaps even a contradiction, between *The Decline of the West*'s historical-philosophical prognosis of political formlessness during *Zivilisation* and the claim that it is nonetheless possible for political leadership to draw on the best aspects of earlier aristocratic attitudes and outlooks in order to influence the final events of the Western world. One concrete manifestation of this paradox in Spengler's politics is his attitude towards the monarchy in *The Decline of the West*. We will have occasion to discuss this question at several points in this volume, but it seems helpful to examine it briefly here. Spengler views the monarchy as the embodiment of many of the various aristocratic values discussed above. Moreover, he is mortified by the abdication of the German Kaiser in 1918 and worries that the fall of the Hohenzollern dynasty may herald difficulties for the German nation in the years to come.[22] Nonetheless, in his main work, it is unclear whether he considers the reinstatement of the German monarchy to be an example of the kind of aristocratic political leadership required in his times or whether it should be seen as a proud blossom of the past. As we will see in the forthcoming chapters, the public approach Spengler takes in relation to the monarchy in Germany varies across his career; as a consequence, it does not do justice to the complex and evolving nature of his thought to suggest either that Spengler 'was a man of the old pre-war order who wanted to see the re-establishment of the Hohenzollern monarchy' (Fischer) or that the 'restoration of the Hohenzollerns never formed the core of his proposals' (Struve).[23] By contrast, we will demonstrate how *both* these statements can hold true when it comes to Spengler's politics, but only at certain stages of his political career.

Spengler is convinced that the values of the nobility can thrive in an age of money, materialism and democracy, providing that those seeking to uphold honour and tradition in Faustian *Zivilisation* work 'with, and within, the existing historical form' (1118). This even applies to two of his most resented phenomena in the modern world: elections and the press: 'The means of the present are, and will be for many years, parliamentary elections and the press. Whether we respect or despise them, we must *master* them' (1119). To do so is to recognise that these forms are currently driven by money, but that their influence can be used to promote the values of tradition. As he puts it: 'Caesarism grows on the soil of democracy, but its roots reach deeply into the substrates of blood and of tradition' (1142).[24]

Therefore, Spengler is not necessarily bemoaning the fact that Faustian *Zivilisation* is characterised by thinking in money; his point is that money should be used in such a way that one can win elections, wars and global influence. And if democracy is a sham in the hands of an oligopoly of press barons and agenda-setters, this should not dampen the spirits of those commited to the knightly virtues of earlier centuries either: gaining the ear of these invididuals will enhance the control that a small group of influential figures can exert over the formless masses. And while democracy and elections are increasingly unpopular and irrelevant – 'a fixed game that is dressed up as the self-determination of the people' (1141) – those who recognise why this is the case can exploit the democratic process to gain support and facilitate its overthrow. This steering of historically given forms is exactly what Spengler has in mind when he talks of *mastering* the socio-political forms of Faustian *Zivilisation*.

Spengler predicts that the party form of politics will eventually be replaced by what he calls an allegiance to individuals (1125). These individuals gather around them circles of influential supporters who, regardless of the existing consitutional forms, preside over real power and social weight. Moreover, they are able to call on the riotous mob when needed. Spengler predicts that these individuals will be able to do so by exploiting – whether through bread and circuses or through the press – the political disenchantment of the masses in modern democracies. The result will be a violent uprising against democracy to usher in the primitive forms of state power discussed above, with people '"elect[ing]"' their 'destiny again using the primitive methods of bloody violence when the politics of money become intolerable' (1143).

Fundamentally, Spengler argues that this Caesarist rebellion embodies the triumph of politics over the dominance of money: 'The age of Caesar in every Culture alike signifies the end of the politics of mind and money' (1102). He speaks of a 'final battle between *economics and politics*, in which the latter reconquers its realm' (1144). As the term 'Caesarism' implies, Spengler's point of reference lies in the past, particularly the shifting alliances of the private circles of the Roman Triumvirates. The wealth, military support and social connections of figures such as Caesar, Pompey and Crassus ensured that they formed the true centre of power in the Roman Republic, with Caesar eventually emerging as dictator. However, the Caesar figure in *The Decline of the West* is not merely a historical point of reference or a general prediction of things to come, but an ideal type of leader to appear from the organised forces of *tradition* and *personality* in the struggle against the dictatorship of money that Spengler calls 'democracy'. The kind of Caesar figure Spengler has in mind in *The Decline of the West* is the British colonialist Cecil Rhodes: 'the energy of the men of culture is directed inwards, whereas that of the man of civilisation is directed outwards' (51).

Rhodes' combination of aristocratic assertiveness, a veneration of empire and a grasp of modern technology is characteristic of the kind of leader Spengler sees as emerging: a figure who will embody the noble virtues of past political forms, while possessing a sense of the tasks of the hour – 'a Caesar of machine warfare', in Ernst Bloch's sardonic phrase.[25]

## Caesarist Consciousness

It is with the speculation surrounding potential Caesar figures that we arrive at the second way in which *The Decline of the West* uses the term 'Caesarism': as the basis of Spengler's political alternative in this period. After all, Spengler's concept of Caesarism should not only be viewed as a description of a supposedly objective, predetermined historical process, but also as a rhetorical device with which he can organise the socio-political forces that, he believes, can become the true subjects of Faustian *Zivilisation* and take their place in history alongside their 'contemporaries' from previous declining *cultures*. As with his historical method, Spengler's political assertions regarding the looming death of democracy as an objective outcome of cultural development cannot be separated from his own subjective opposition to democracy, his veneration of the so-called great men of history, or from his desire to see Germany emerge as a world hegemon. Therefore, let us now take a closer look at how he views his own role in contributing to the rise of Caesarism.

The precise *form* that Caesarism will assume in the *Abendland* is 'dependent on the *contigency* [*Zufall*] of great individuals' (977, emphasis added). This statement by no means implies waiting with folded arms for a man on a white horse – leaving matters to historical chance. Rather, political forms and institutions must be instituted, within which 'great men who base themselves on the facts' (*große Tatsachenmenschen*, 1083) can emerge. These men will possess the true virtues of selfless and bold statesmanship. Such leadership is fundamental, since 'political talent in a people is nothing but confidence in its leadership. But that confidence has to be acquired; it will ripen only in its own good time, and success will stabilise it and establish it as a tradition' (1112).

Spengler's philosophy is thus geared towards advising such men who, by combining the political culture of the nobility with a morphological understanding of historical development, can provide the necessary political leadership at a time when one wrong decision could lead to the disappearance of entire peoples and nations.

Spengler's use of the term *Zufall*, then, is best understood not as 'chance' or 'accident', as it is often translated, but 'contingency'. It is Faustian *Zivilisation* itself – one's historical fate – that poses the possibility of Caesar figures emerging, but the precise nature of these figures, where and when they will emerge, and the exact configuration of the politics informing their actions are *contingent* upon the outcomes of the battles ahead. Those who can understand these conflicts, as Spengler claims to, can potentially exert a real influence on them. For while the historical tables in *The Decline of the West* predict that Caesar-type rulers will not emerge until ca. 2000, his own political career aims at ensuring that those opposed to parliamentary democracy organise in such a way that the best leaders can emerge from within their ranks. As Spengler's reference to Cecil Rhodes as a potential Caesarist leader show, Spengler believes that the great battles over the soul of Caesarism have already begun. As we will see in Chapter 6 in particular, Spengler's project in the 1920s aims to *facilitate* the rise of what he views as the leader required by his cherished Germany in particular – despite claims to the contrary in the secondary literature.[26]

Spengler's political programme, then, is premised on the certainty that the decline of the West presents new opportunities, in particular for those individuals and nations that are able to read the sign of the times and act accordingly. His aim is for such individuals – arising from an elite of landowners, statesmen, generals, industrialists, press barons and others – to become what he calls 'history in person, its directedness as individual will, its organic logic as individual character' (1113). Here there are clear echoes of Hegel's concept of the world-historic individual and Marx's understanding of a historically self-liberating class gaining *insight into necessity*. Indeed, Spengler distinguishes between '*historically necessary* and *superfluous* politics' (976–77), as well as between organising on the understanding that Caesarism is inevitable and seeking to defend an increasingly anachronistic democracy. 'The necessary', he adds, 'should be done at the right time' (1118).

Spengler draws an analogy between the situation facing the *Abendland* of his times to a walker atop a perilous mountain, and warns that there are two options available: 'Either stand firm or perish – there is no third option' (1100). Similarly to a thinker such as Albrecht Erich Günther, a conservative revolutionary and member of the Juni-Klub, the 'most active center of neo-conservatism', in the early 1920s,[27] Spengler is convinced of the impossibility of upholding 'what existed yesterday'.[28] Where Spengler differs from others in and around the Conservative Revolution is that he rejects what Günther deems 'a life consisting of that which remains true eternally'.[29] For Spengler, nothing lasts forever and the tides of history are in constant flux. His understanding of historically informed political action is thus not dissimilar to how his hero Bismarck defined the business of politics: seeking to listen to God's footsteps across the stage of world history so as to judge instinctively when is the appropriate time to leap and grab hold of His coattails before He has passed by for good.[30] The logic behind Spengler's conception of political leadership is reminiscent of Brutus's exhortation to Cassius in *Julius Caesar*:

> There is a tide in the affairs of men,
> Which, taken at the flood, leads on to fortune;
> Omitted, all the voyage of their life
> Is bound in shallows and in miseries.

On such a full sea are we now afloat,
And we must take the current when it serves,
Or lose our ventures.[31]

Here we grasp the fundamental import of the Stoic philosopher Seneca's words that conclude *Der Untergang des Abendlandes* – 'Ducunt fata volentem, nolentem trahunt' (1195). This statement represents the logical conclusion of the work's endeavour to 'understand the *era*, for which you are born' (1113). So while Spengler can certainly be criticised for being oblivious to notions of change and development *between* cultures, it is quite misplaced to argue that *The Decline of the West*, as Otto Neurath puts it, 'excludes the appearance of anything new'.[32]

The era of Faustian *Zivilisation*, then, is unique in Spengler's overall historical schema, in that he is not merely an analyst of it, but also an active participant within it. This dual role as observer and historical actor has fascinating implications for his deterministic, culture-centred conception of history. The strictly determinist outlook allows for a highly limited *freedom*, a certain amount of wiggle room, a 'degree of elasticity' (1117) for those seeking to influence the remaining stages of the Faustian odyssey. However, the precondition for doing so is precisely the ability to grasp the limited possibilities for change: there can be no return to the past, nor can one base political action on the notion – however selective – that the world will one day be different: 'We do not have the freedom to achieve this or that, but the freedom to do what is necessary or to do nothing. And a task that historic necessity has established will be resolved with the individual or against him' (1195).

In the Faustian age of war and revolution, a range of authoritarian figures with varying agendas and ideologies will step forward, and Spengler is not indifferent to the question of who will emerge victorious. For example, he cites the Russian revolutionary leader Lenin as one such possible ruler of that country. Yet, his veneration of Lenin's leadership qualities notwithstanding, Spengler is an intransigently anti-Bolshevik thinker and, in terms of his own politics, would much prefer a leader along the lines of Cecil Rhodes or Mussolini (we will discuss his thoughts on the latter in Chapter 7). Such an ideal figure will not only be able to lead the struggle against democracy in Spengler's Germany, but will also successfully wage its campaign against other nations in the battle for global dominance.

Here we arrive at the other core value of Spengler's politics of decline: his nationalist commitment to Germany. Germany, a nation whose essence is that of Faustian *Zivilisation* itself but who has never had the chance to fight for her ideas in any meaningful way, can finally become what she was always destined to be – the leading Faustian nation, the driver of the end-phase of the modern world. This subjective commitment to Germany is not accidental or tangential to Spengler's schema. When preparing his main work, Spengler writes a letter to a close friend outlining how the demise of the *Abendland* will be preceded not only by the emergence of Caesarism, but also that of the German nation itself. He countenances the possibility of a new culture emerging in the twenty-first century, '*when the great age of us Germans will also lie in the past*'.[33]

Regarding Spengler's view of the Germans as the chosen people of Western *Zivilisation*, it should not be taken as read that Spengler's choice of Germany as the last nation of the *Abendland* flows logically from his theory of world history.[34] To take one example, Spengler's comparison between Germany and Rome in *The Decline of the West* is particularly unconvincing. He argues that both had always been vilified and that Germany can emerge as quickly as a power as Rome once did. But such a flimsy assumption seems very much in the mould of the arbitrary analogies for which Spengler criticises von Ranke and other historians, as we discussed in Chapter 3. Nonetheless, Spengler's ideological commitment to the German nation is, as we have seen, not entirely divorced from his theory of world history either. He does not view Germany as a nation of culture that could 'escape the dilemmas of an increasingly soulless modernity'.[35] The process of *Zivilisation* is of such an all-encompassing nature that Germany cannot free herself from the degenerative effects of this process, as some – particularly *völkisch* thinkers – appear to imply. Rather, he views Germany as 'the last nation of the West' (129), which, although she cannot turn the clock back on the historical process to become a pioneer of culture, can nonetheless produce the statesmen, generals, industrialists and engineers required to lead the world for the first time. As he once put it: 'We Germans will never produce another Goethe, but we may produce a Caesar.'[36]

*Pace* Demandt, therefore, *The Decline of the West* does have much to say on what is to be done in the age of Faustian *Zivilisation*. At the same time, the principles that underpin the book's conception of political leadership are slightly abstract and – as with his conviction that pre-democratic forms can flourish in an era of war and dictatorship – perhaps even contradictory. This immediately raises a number of questions. How does Spengler seek to realise in practice these authoritarian-nationalist perspectives? Which principles does he modify or adapt, and how are these modifications influenced by the events of his time? What does his political career as a whole reveal about the relationship between his politics of decline and his philosophy of world history? These are the questions we will now seek to answer through an analysis of his most important political activities and publications between the founding of the Weimar Republic in 1919 and its overthrow by the National Socialists in 1933.

## Notes

1. Dakin (ed.), *Today and Destiny: Vital Excerpts from the 'Decline of the West' of Oswald Spengler*, 364.
2. Kroll, '"A Biography of the Soul": Oswald Spengler's Biographical Method and the Morphology of History', 69, emphasis added.
3. This particularly applies to Fischer, *History and Prophecy: Oswald Spengler and the Decline of the West* and Fennelly, *Twilight of the Evening Lands: Oswald Spengler – A Half Century Later*.
4. Fischer, *History and Prophecy*, 68.
5. Fennelly, *Twilight of the Evening Lands*, 173.
6. Stutz, *Die philosophische und politische Kritik Oswald Spenglers*, 1.
7. Osmančević, *Oswald Spengler und das Ende der Geschichte*, 108, emphasis added.
8. One notable exception is Freud, who refuses to treat the two phenomena separately. As a fundamentally rationalist thinker, he rejected the normative distinction between a purportedly superior organic, poetic reasoning and the supposedly inferior nature of scientific reasoning. The difficulty in accurately rendering the binary terms *Kultur* and *Zivilisation* in English is highlighted by the title of Samuel Huntington's controversial *The Clash of Civilizations*, which has been translated into German as *Kampf der Kulturen*: Huntington, *The Clash of Civilizations and the Remaking of World Order*; Huntington, *Kampf der Kulturen. Die Neugestaltung der Weltpolitik im 21. Jahrhundert*.
9. For more on the distinction between *Kultur* and *Zivilisation* in German thought more generally, see Agard and Beßlich (eds), *Kulturkritik zwischen Deutschland und Frankreich (1890–1933)*; Beßlich, *Wege in den 'Kulturkrieg'. Zivilisationskritik in Deutschland 1890–1914*; Bollenbeck, *Tradition, Avantgarde, Reaktion. Deutsche Kontroversen um die kulturelle Moderne 1880–1945*; Bolz, *Auszug aus der entzauberten Welt. Philosophischer Extremismus zwischen den Weltkriegen*; Kamphausen, *Die Erfindung Amerikas in der Kulturkritik der Generation von 1890*; Ringer, *The Decline of the German Mandarins: The German Academic Community, 1890–1933*, esp. 87–90 and 259–66.
10. Demandt, *Untergänge des Abendlandes. Studien zu Oswald Spengler*, 185.
11. Spengler, *Der Untergang des Abendlandes. Umrisse einer Morphologie der Weltgeschichte*, 1167. All subsequent references to the text will be placed in parentheses.
12. On Sieyès and the 'Nichtstand', see Spengler, *Der Untergang des Abendlandes*, 1011; and de Berg and Large (eds), *Modern German Thought from Kant to Habermas: An Annotated German-Language Reader*, 142.
13. See the studies mentioned in footnote 9 above.
14. In his critique of the modern press, Spengler uses almost exactly the same terminology as the leading Marxist thinker Karl Kautsky (1854–1938), who in 1905 speaks of the preponderance of a commercially bribable (*käuflich*) press as a necessary condition for the flourishing of bourgeois society. This notwithstanding, Kautsky criticises as one-sided certain left-wing thinkers who, not unlike Spengler, equate the existence of parliamentary democracy with the rule of the bourgeoisie without further ado; Lewis (ed.), *Karl Kautsky on Democracy and Republicanism*, 163. As we will discuss in the following chapter, Spengler appears to be well-versed in the socialist press, as this is not the only instance where he employs some of the rhetoric and metaphors of the German socialist movement of his time.
15. Naeher, *Oswald Spengler*, 11.
16. See Graf, 'Die "Krise" im intellektuellen Zukunftsdiskurs der Weimarer Republik', 77–106.
17. Ibid., 105. In a footnote, Graf wonders whether Spenglerian pessimism actually existed at all. But he does not develop this point further and merely references Spengler's 1921 article 'Pessimismus?', which we discussed in Chapter 1; ibid., 105, fn. 126.
18. Demandt, *Untergänge des Abendlandes*, 47.
19. Tartsch, *Denn der Mensch ist ein Raubtier. Eine Einführung in die politischen Schriften und Theorien Oswald Spenglers*, 192–93.

20. Note, for instance, the similarity between Spengler's ideas and those of the British Tory statesman Georg Canning in his poem: 'The demon of *faction* that over them hung; In accents of horror their epitaph sung; While pride and venality joined in the stave; And canting *democracy* wept at the grave'; Canning, *Memoirs of the Life of the Rt. Hon George Canning*, Vol. 2, 58. For more on this, see Carey, *The Intellectuals and the Masses: Pride and Prejudice among the Literary Intelligentsia, 1880–1939*.
21. Spengler, *'Ich beneide jeden, der lebt'. Die Aufzeichnungen 'Eis heauton' aus dem Nachlaß*, 13.
22. Spengler to Hans Klöres, 18 December 1918, in Spengler, *Briefe 1913–36*, 111–14.
23. Fischer, *History and Prophecy*, 222; Struve, *Elites against Democracy: Leadership Ideals in Bourgeois Political Thought in Germany, 1890–1933*, 247.
24. We will leave a discussion of the dubious terminology of blood and race and their significance in Spengler's politics of decline to the later chapters.
25. Bloch, 'Spenglers Raubtiere und relative Kulturgärten', 319.
26. A partial exception to this is his text *Prussianism and Socialism*. As we will explain in Chapter 5, the concept of Caesarism plays a marginal role in this text.
27. Klemperer, *Germany's New Conservatism: Its History and Dilemma in the Twentieth Century*, 102.
28. Günther, 'Wandlung der sozialen und politischen Weltanschauung des Mittelstandes', 408.
29. Ibid.
30. 'Politik ist, daß man Gottes Schritt durch die Weltgeschichte hört, dann zuspringt und versucht, einen Zipfel seines Mantels zu fassen'; cited in Meyer, *Bismarcks Glaube im Spiegel der Lösungen und Lehrtexte*, 9–10.
31. Shakespeare, *Julius Caesar*, 120 (Act IV, Scene 3).
32. Neurath, 'Anti-Spengler', 168.
33. Spengler to Klöres, 14 July 1915, in Spengler, *Briefe 1913–36*, 45, emphasis added.
34. Martin Falck is most helpful on this point; see Falck (ed.), *Zyklen und Cäsaren. Mosaiksteine einer Philosophie des Schicksals. Reden und Schriften Oswald Spenglers*, 130–31.
35. Herf, *Reactionary Modernism: Technology, Culture and Politics in Weimar and the Third Reich*, 35.
36. Spengler, 'Pessimismus?', 71.

CHAPTER 5

# Spengler's Prussian Socialism

Spengler's first attempt to shape the political events of his time comes in the form of his large pamphlet *Prussianism and Socialism*, originally published in 1919. This year is a momentous one in his life. The continued success of Volume 1 of *The Decline of the West* establishes him as a venerated thinker on the German right. The second volume of his main work is eagerly awaited and he is often invited to address a variety of political associations and clubs. However, against the backdrop of the foundation of the Weimar Republic, Spengler feels compelled to focus on *Prussianism and Socialism*. The essay is a fascinating *précis* of his ideas at the time; it reveals much about the nature of his thought and the radically polarised environment in which it is developed. It instantly becomes another bestseller, and this success further emboldens him in his efforts to influence the development of German nationalism. What is most important about *Prussianism and Socialism* is that it helps us understand how Spengler views political leadership and social change at a key turning point in German history. The pamphlet addresses this issue long before he returns to the matter in Volume 2 of *The Decline of the West*, which we discussed in the previous chapter. *Prussianism and Socialism* is, then, crucial to understanding the evolution of his ideas. A closer reading of the text allows us to determine whether and to what extent Spengler's conception of political leadership changes between 1919 and the publication of Volume 2 of *The Decline of the West* in 1922.

There are only a handful of thorough discussions of *Prussianism and Socialism* in the secondary literature. Moreover, with the exception of the chapter that Farrenkopf devotes to the text in his *Prophet of Decline*, all of these commentaries have been published in German and tend to compare the ideas developed within *Prussianism and Socialism* to those of other right-wing figures at the time, such as Ernst Jünger and Adolf Hitler.[1] Existing research has not only downplayed and thus misrepresented Spengler's intriguing intellectual relationship with the German socialist movement and some of its leading thinkers, but has also led to a number of misleading claims regarding his political priorities at this point in his career. In his pioneering study of the German elite's critique of democracy, for instance, Walter Struve claims: 'Naumann and Weber recognized the existence of a working class, as did Rathenau and Nelson, who sought, if partly by terminological sleights of hand, to abolish it. Spengler refused to acknowledge its existence.'[2] This contention – yet another example of a generalising conclusion drawn solely from *The Decline of the West* – is a seriously misleading assessment of Spengler's thought in 1919 and will be challenged in this chapter.

At first glance, the title of the pamphlet seems somewhat paradoxical. We have already discussed the centrality of the idea of Prussianism (*Preußentum*) in his plans for German world hegemony, but what about *socialism*? It seems highly counterintuitive that a thinker such as Spengler, whose contempt for democratic forms is obvious from even a cursory reading of Volume 1 of *The Decline of the West*, should devote an entire book to a discussion of socialism. After all, this project is generally viewed as encompassing egalitarian social aims pursued by organisations of the working classes, such as parties, trade unions, cooperatives and so forth.[3] But, as we have seen, Spengler appears to have an animus against the notion that any other social class than the aristocracy can successfully preside over the state. Given this, how are we to explain his focus on Prussian socialism? What does Spengler mean by the term? How does it relate to his political alternative of *Preußentum*?

In order to address these questions, this chapter will do the following. After a contextualisation and overview of the work, it will discuss exactly what Spengler understands by a German socialist state, analyse how he engages with a variety of socialist thinkers and, finally, discuss what *Prussianism and Socialism* reveals about the interplay of principles and pragmatism, of method and motivation, in his political thought. In so doing, this chapter will bring out the specificity of the position he occupies as a thinker of the anti-democratic, authoritarian Conservative Revolution in Germany after the First World War by exploring his relation to the socialist movement: does his understanding of socialism follow logically from his culture-centred morphology of history or is he seeking to catch the historical tide by appropriating ideas and concepts at odds with his worldview in the name of short-term political expediency?

## Bavarian Disgust and Common Enemies

The immediate backdrop to *Prussianism and Socialism* is Spengler's disgust at what he deems the 'rabble revolution' of November 1918, when sailors in various ports in the north of Germany mutiny, disarm their officers and seize control of the ships in protest at being ordered to embark upon, in the name of national 'honour', a senseless suicide mission against the British navy, which would cost thousands of lives. Then, on 4 November, the revolutionary sailors in Kiel establish a workers' and soldiers' council inspired by the soviets of the Russian Revolution of 1917. The council demands, among other things, press freedom, the release of political prisoners and the repudiation of officer privileges. It rapidly recruits soldiers, union branches and local members of the main workers' parties of German Social Democracy (the SPD and the USPD), thus gaining a huge following. Kiel becomes the model for other workers' and soldiers' councils throughout the country. In a complicated series of events lasting from November 1918 to the agreement of the Weimar Republic's Constitution in August 1919, these workers' and soldiers' councils clash with forces within and outside the powerful workers' movement that try to stymy the upsurge. It speaks to the impact of Spengler the politician that Gustav Noske, the leading SPD journalist, politician and self-proclaimed 'bloodhound' of the German Revolution, acknowledges that Spengler's 'Prussian socialism' runs in his veins as he mobilises military forces to crush the radical communist-inspired workers' and soldiers' councils, which wish to create a council-led state.[4] For the conservative Ernst Jünger, *Prussianism and Socialism* forges 'the first weapons … following Germany's disarmament'[5] and the revolutionary turmoil.

Spengler is directly affected by the German Revolution. His resident Bavaria is the first German state to become a republic, declared by the USPD activist Kurt Eisner ('the moron Eisner', as Spengler calls him).[6] In January 1919, Bavaria becomes Germany's first socialist republic, but its existence is beset by crisis and conditions of civil war. The skirmishes between the revolutionary movement and the military and paramilitary forces loyal to the government in Berlin land on Spengler's own doorstep in the *Agnesstraße* in Munich and only reach a conclusion on 4 May 1919.[7] On 21 February 1919, just one day after the assassination of Eisner by the nationalist, anti-Semitic baron Anton Graf von Arco auf Valley, Spengler goes for a long walk with his friend August Albers, editor of the newly established publishing house now responsible for publishing Spengler's writings, C.H. Beck.[8] Albers is particularly interested in what Spengler thinks about the question of socialism and its place within his morphology of history. Following the lengthy answer Spengler provides, Albers is convinced that Spengler should publish these thoughts on the revolution and the debates around the future of Germany as a standalone publication. Spengler, after all, has a unique perspective on the events unfolding before him. On the one hand, he is adamant that the mob uprising must be thwarted and thus sympathises with some of the forces – not least the paramilitary groupings such as the anti-Communist *Orgesch* organisation led by his friend Georg Escherich – clamping down on the councils and self-styled socialist governments.⁹ On the other hand, he insists that Germany's transformation into a parliamentary republic is inimical to her successful re-emergence as a power following military defeat and social disintegration. As he puts it in *Prussianism and Socialism*, parliamentarism in Germany is 'nonsense or betrayal'¹⁰ – either an idealistic endeavour to re-enact the past failures, such as the *Paulskirche* experiment during the Revolution of 1848, or a conscious attempt to weaken Germany by subjecting her to the Allied demands for peace with Germany (US President Woodrow Wilson's '14 points'), which include the insistence that postwar Germany be democratised.

When setting out to write *Prussianism and Socialism*, Spengler is able to draw on material he has been working on since 1913. This material not only encompasses some of the aphorisms and notes that form part of his ongoing work on the second volume of *The Decline of the West*, but also an extended manuscript entitled *Romans and Prussians*, which he had initially hoped to publish in September 1918.¹¹ As we saw in this previous chapter, the title of this draft alludes to Spengler's conviction that the Germans can and must become a modern-day Rome (the *Imperium Germanicum*). Spengler's decision to modify the title to *Prussianism and Socialism* can be explained with reference to the spirit of the age, in which socialist rhetoric, ideas and slogans are not only debated in the councils and on demonstrations, but also at the level of government. In January 1919, the SPD is elected as the major governing partner, alongside the liberal German Democratic Party (DDP) and the Catholic Centre Party (Deutsche Zentrumspartei), of the so-called Weimar coalition. The choice of title can, additionally, be understood with reference to Spengler's conception of the potential significance of the unfolding events. While he is disgusted by the radical egalitarian and internationalist aims of the council movement in particular, he nonetheless views the polarised political climate as an unprecedented *opportunity* for the forces of German nationalism: 'I do not view Germany's increasing radicalisation as misfortune. We *have to* get through it.'¹² 'First the socialists, then the Prussian socialists' could have been his motto.

This immediately raises the question of what Spengler exactly understands by socialism. This question is difficult to answer in two respects. For one, his view of socialism is often counterintuitive, in that it has more in common with the ideals of monarchism, nationalism and warfare than with the values of democracy, internationalism and anti-imperialism usually associated with the socialist movement. For another, already in Volume 1 of *The Decline of the West* Spengler draws a distinction – one that is far from clear or consistent in *Prussianism and Socialism* or his work as a whole – between *ethical* socialism and *economic* socialism.

By ethical socialism, Spengler means the inevitable metaphysical outcome of what he sees as Faustian culture's moral dynamism, which attempts to impose its own values on others at all costs. As with the Faustian drive to imperialism, the universal values of socialism – that all should be treated equally without exception – can only be explained with reference to the ethical imperatives of the 'expansive tendency' that he locates in Faustian ethics.[13] This innate drive is unconsciously active within all its subjects. It is an irrepressible energy – 'something demonic and monstrous' – which ensures that the Faustian peoples are not content simply to develop their own views in splendid isolation (Spengler is here thinking of Buddhism as an analogous phenonemon in the late period of Indian culture), but must fight for these values to be taken up at all costs: 'a world-feeling ... that pursues its own opinion in the name of all'.[14] For this reason, he claims that the socialist movement of his time, for all its anti-imperialist and anti-colonialist rhetoric, will one day become a 'most noble pillar' of imperialism and expansion and will carry it 'with the vehemence of fate'.[15] That, at least, is his aim. For what is decisive is how this culturally determined tendency towards socialism manifests itself. Spengler is thus by no means implying that the precise form that socialism will assume in his time is set in stone.

While Spengler speaks positively of ethical socialism and ascribes its purest manifestation to what he sees as Prussian discipline and collectivity, he is scathing about another product of Faustian culture: *economic socialism*.[16] This is the distortion of the Faustian ethical imperative and its reduction to a focus on economics and money, as reflected in the demands of the socialist movement for wage increases, reduced working hours, social provision and so on. It is sympomatic of the urban, soulless *thinking in money* in the age of Faustian *Zivilisation*: bourgeois-materialist values, but turned on their head. It is hardly surprising that *Prussianism and Socialism* sets itself the task of combating this degenerate manifesation of socialism, even if, somewhat confusingly, it does so in the name of socialism. Spengler occasionally refers to what he views as the economic form of socialism as *Marxism*, but this is by no means always the case. Hence, the reader must be wary of how exactly Spengler employs the term *socialism* both in *Prussianism and Socialism* and throughout his work, as it is not immediately apparent whether he is using the term in a pejorative or a laudatory fashion. With this in mind, let us now discuss Spengler's main arguments in *Prussianism and Socialism*.

*Prussianism and Socialism* consists of five chapters, each of which is further divided into numbered sections. The first chapter is entitled 'The Revolution' (sections 1–7); it is followed by 'Socialism as a Way of Life' (sections 8–9); 'Englishmen and Prussians' (sections 10–18); 'Marx' (sections 19–21); and finally 'The International' (sections 22–24). At the outset, Spengler describes the issue of socialism, as reflected in the political discussions of Germany in 1919, as 'not the most profound, but the loudest question of the age' (3). This quote summarises the book's core argument that the noisy debates around socialism and capitalism are but a faint echo of two much more profound antagonisms in the Faustian world: the conflict between moneyed republicanism and traditional authoritarianism over the nature of the form of the state, and, relatedly, the struggle between the Prussians and the English over global leadership. Let us discuss the conflict over the state first.

*Prussianism and Socialism* reflects Spengler's daring venture to propound a socialist politics defined by opposition to what he views as the common enemies of the working class and the aristocracy: liberalism and Marxism. Both ideologies are the necessary and predetermined outgrowth of Faustian *Zivilisation*, as are the baleful phenomena of parliaments, political parties and the press. And while liberal thought's emphasis on individual initiative and the pursuit of happiness may seem at odds with the collective ethos found in movements such as the trade unions and the SPD, Spengler claims that both liberalism and economic socialism can be traced back to the soulless, formless economic thought of the bourgeois *Nichtstand* and its perogatives. In Volume 2 of *The Decline of the West*, Spengler will later describe this outlook as 'materialist nonsense' and Marxist socialism as the logical conclusion of such *thinking in money*: the 'most extreme consequence of rationalism'.[17]

In the previous chapter, we discussed why as a consequence Spengler rejects the bourgeoisie as a political class and finds in the values and traditions of the aristocracy the basis of true national leadership. But why in *Prussianism and Socialism* is he seeking to create a political alternative premised on the aristocracy *and* the working classes, whom in Volume 2 of *The Decline of the West* he will later dismiss as 'the radical nothing'?[18] Does this quote not justify Walter Struve's assertion that Spengler dismisses the existence of the working classes as a socio-political factor?

In the first section of *Prussianism and Socialism*, entitled 'The Revolution', Spengler clarifies his focus on the German working class by emphasising that the real German revolution takes place not in 1918, but with the German war effort in 1914. For him, this was a time when the country came together in a heroic attempt to fight for the national interest, with workers and peasants fighting and dying alongside the Kaiser's generals. The symbolic representation of this unity between the worker's party and the aristocratic estate is the SPD parliamentary fraction's approval of German war credits in August 1914, with the party embracing the policy of 'civil peace' (*Burgfrieden*) earlier summarised by the Kaiser as: 'I no longer know of any parties, but only Germans'.[19] Spengler's focus on the working class, then, stems from his conviction that genuine German socialism could be found not in the increasing opposition to the war on the home front, but on the frontlines of battle: 'Genuine socialism stood in the last struggles at the front or lay in the mass graves across half of Europe. It was the socialism that arose in August 1914 which was betrayed here' (9).

The narrative of betrayal reflects a guiding trope of the nationalist, authoritarian and anti-communist Conservative Revolution in postwar Germany, with Spengler echoing the stab-in-the-back myth (*Dolchstoßlegende*) popularised by the Prussian general Paul von Hindenburg. According to this notion, the German army was on the brink of victory, only to be stabbed in the back by leftists and liberals on the home front. Indeed, for *Prussianism and Socialism*, the so-called German Revolution of 1918 ('the most senseless act in German history') is a sheer betrayal of the true *Burgfrieden* revolution of 1914, which assumed 'legitimate and military forms' (12). This treachery to the German cause comes in two acts: the June 1917 peace resolution agreed in the Reichstag and the abdication of the Kaiser in November 1918. Both represent desertion of military duty and a capitulation to *England* – at this point in time, Spengler sees France as a minor player in global politics and little more than an extension of England's dominance. However, as we will see in Chapter 7, he later realises that France is becoming a major player in its own right.

Spengler is therefore not addressing himself to the German working class as currently constituted, but rather seeking to win over those sections of it – what he calls 'the sensible part'[20] – that can eschew their narrow economic interests and commit themselves to the cause of the German nation. Seen in this light, the Prussian socialism that Spengler envisages is a unification of what he calls the two truly socialist parties in Germany: not, as desired by many, of the SPD and the USPD, but of the German socialist movement and the Conservatives. The aim is to create a German state that *can* win wars again by establishing it on the principles of duty and self-sacrifice, not the imperatives of profit and economic growth: 'The whole is sovereign. The King is only the first servant of the state (Frederick the Great). Everybody is assigned their place. Orders are given and obeyed' (15).

In order for such a state to come into being, several conditions must be met on both sides of the bargain between the aristocrats and the workers. The German aristocracy has to recognise that it must overcome 'all traces' of the feudal-agrarian narrowness that belongs to the past phase of Western *Kultur*.[21] Equally, it has to reject the values of liberalism and its attempts to plant parliamentarism in alien Prussian soil, where it cannot and will not grow. In turn, the German working-class movement needs to break with the alien, anti-German ideology of Marxism and embrace German nationalism.

One of the central aims of *Prussianism and Socialism*, then, is to free 'socialism' from the 'socialists' or – to return to the distinction above – to free the ethical socialist imperative from its vulgar economistic arrangement that Spengler finds in the workers' parties of his time. The foregrounding of economic issues by these parties degrades the real meaning of existence: 'life according to Meister Eckhart becomes life according to political economy' (23). In a similar phrase to that used by his fellow conservative revolutionary, Arthur Moeller van den Bruck ('socialism begins where Marxism ends'),[22] Spengler deems it necessary to 'liberate' German socialism from Marxism (4). In order to do this, he attempts to lay bare what he calls the *English* roots of both Marxism and liberalism and to conduct a struggle against the insidious forces championing them within the new Germany. *Prussianism and Socialism* thus serves as both an invocation and a warning: unless the German nation can come together as it purportedly did in the spirit of civil peace in the war effort of 1914, unless an organic community (*Gemeinschaft*) beyond class and individualism can be created in line with the Prussian socialist spirit, the German people will be brought to its knees by the rule of 'English' banks, profiteering and speculation.

## Knights and Vikings

Here we arrive at the second antagonism that *Prussianism and Socialism* locates as lying at the core of Faustian *Zivilisation* and that forms the longest section of the book, entitled 'Englishmen and Prussians'. Given the importance Spengler attributes to the conflict between these peoples, *Englishmen and Prussians* might have been a better title for the work, insofar as this title more accurately reflects what is at stake politically. For Spengler argues that the First World War is but one manifestation of a historically rooted Anglo-German antagonism, a struggle between the two great Germanic peoples. Such antipathy will invariably lead to more struggles between the modern English people, born in the seventeenth century, and the Prussian people, born in the eighteenth century. The inevitability of such a conflict, as well as the impossibility of mediation or reconciliation between these peoples, is rooted in Spengler's understanding of the Faustian *will to power* and its drive to universality. Referring to the nations of Faustian *Zivilisation*, he writes:

> We know no limits. By means of a new Migration of the Peoples we have made America a part of Western Europe. We have constructed on every continent our special kind of cities, and have subjected the native populations to our own way of life and thought. Such activity is the highest possible expression of our dynamic sense of world-feeling. All are supposed to believe what we do. All are supposed to want what we want. And since life has come to mean for us external, political, social, and economic life, all must submit to our political, social, and economic ideal, or perish. (24)[23]

In a similar fashion to the distinction he draws between the ethical socialism described here – 'that which is common is us all'– and economic socialism, Spengler proceeds to make the case that the expansionist dynamism common to both the English and the Prussians results in two mutually exclusive world outlooks: an individualist one and a collectivist one. While Spengler had already alluded to 'the English intellect' and even spoke of the 'English-Judaic' thought of Marx and Bentham in Volume 1 of *The Decline of the West*,[24] *Prussianism and Socialism* is the first text in which he makes the case for the fundamental difference between the Prussians and the English as two of the leading nations of Faustian culture. Later, it will become an important theme in Volume 2 of his major work. In *Prussianism and Socialism*, he asserts that the respective 'soul' of the two peoples derives from the fact that they have different origins. The Prussians are knightly peoples and the English are Vikings, ensuring that the Faustian outlook they both share assumes a different form:

> But the Viking spirit and the communal spirit of the Teutonic knights gradually gave rise to two antithetical ethical imperatives. One side carried the Germanic idea actively within itself, while the other felt subject to it: personal independence on the one hand, and suprapersonal community spirit on the other. Today we call these concepts individualism and socialism. (31)

Therefore, Faustian moral dyanism can take an individual or a collective form, ensuring that the looming conflict between money and tradition in the era of Faustian civilisation is overlaid by a clash between an English community of economic contentment and a Prussian community of duty – salary versus rank, job versus occupation, free trade versus autarky, 'the Englishman's garb' versus the Prussian 'wearing of uniforms' introduced by the soldier-king Frederick William I of Prussia (37). The watchword of this battle is: 'Every man for himself: that is English; every man for every one else: that is Prussian' (34).

Spengler then proceeds to discuss 'Socialism as a Way of Life'. He describes Prussian socialism as ingrained in the instinct and consciousness of the Prussians, who form a 'race in the spiritual sense' (22) and are metaphysically predisposed to leading an ethical existence defined by self-sacrifice. Here it becomes apparent that Spengler's essentialist view of cultures also applies to his understanding of the various nations and peoples within those cultures. It must be stressed, however, that Spengler is not claiming that *all* Prussians or English people are destined to act in a particular way. Moreover, on several occasions, *Prussianism and Socialism* highlights how there are many *biological* Prussians who nonetheless entertain anti-Prussian, English ideas, such as the text's main bogeyman, 'the German Michel' (8). 'Michel' entertains a host of illusions in democracy and republicanism. Indeed, Spengler himself is no Prussian in terms of his birth and heritage. As with *The Decline of the West*, Spengler's description of the Prussians and the English as *races* is a metaphysical category, not a racial one.

Nonetheless, there is one passage in *Prussianism and Socialism* in which Spengler talks of *race* as expressing itself in certain 'physical qualities' (29). Presumably this relates to the way in which habitual and typical conditions, particularly in the way in which individuals move, eat, talk, dress and comport themselves, express both individual choices and social norms or values. However, given the abundance of the term 'blood' within *Prussianism and Socialism*, it is not entirely clear whether those reading Spengler's book would have been able to grasp the distinction between biology and metaphysics in respect of the traits he sees as marking out certain peoples and 'races' from others. He is possibly even counting on this. That is to say, perhaps the invocation of blood is a rhetorical device within a text that abounds with bombast and calls to political action, a way of infusing his target audience with nationalist fervour and pride. A racialist-inspired conservative reading this text would certainly have no objections to Spengler's emphasis on the historical significance of 'Viking blood' (32) or to his contention that the socialist traits of the Prussians 'are not to be found on paper, they are in the blood' (53). These and similar statements seem to give credence to the idea that the biological basis of a particular people largely determines its socio-political life and the inevitability of its coming into conflict with other peoples. In Chapter 7, we will see how Spengler's problematic rhetoric on race relates to his discussion of the so-called Jewish question in his attempt to outline a theory of race distinct from that of the National Socialists.

In the short section on Marx that follows 'Englishmen and Prussians', Spengler contends that Marx's thought conflates the struggle between these great peoples with the struggle between social classes. Marx's approach is 'purely English' (71) insofar as it is English political economy turned on its head. Although Marx develops a critique of thinkers such as Adam Smith, Spengler claims that this critique proceeds from the same fundamental assumption that human behaviour can be best understood through the prism of concepts such as wealth, labour, commodities and profit. Spengler calls this outlook the 'capitalism of the working class' (75) because, he argues, Marxism foregrounds the proletariat's envy of the propertied classes and their wealth: 'Class egoism is raised to a principle' (ibid.). It is for this reason that Spengler dismisses working-class strike action as the embodiment of a money-driven, Marxist outlook. Such action represents the most *un*socialist act imaginable: 'the most unsocialistic aspect of Marxism. It is the classical feature of its origins in a trader philosophy that Marx adhered to by instinct and habit' (77). True socialism, by contrast, would never seek to organise one section of society against another, but would merely ask how those in various professions, estates and classes can serve the whole.

Spengler claims that Marx 'was merely the stepfather of socialism. There are elements of socialism that are older, deeper and more fundamental than his critique of society. Such elements existed without him and continued to develop without him and actually in opposition to him' (3). Spengler argues, moreover, that true – Prussian – socialism is instinctual and has no need of the elaborate theoretical concepts in Marx's 'sparkly construction' (69). The quantification of labour power is an alien concept to the true Prussian: work can never be understood as a mere commodity to be bought and sold. It is a calling, as expressed in the German word *Beruf*, 'a duty towards the community' (77). It is for this reason that Spengler accuses Marx of being a good materialist but a poor psychologist (69). The elaborate models of political economy are ignorant of the different cultural souls and dispositions of the various peoples within the late Faustian world. They cannot explain why in Prussia social status is defined not by wealth, but by social rank as a reward for best serving the community. Finally, Spengler claims that Marx's ideas will not be able to exert an enduring influence on the late Faustian world because the age of *Zivilisation* will be one of action, not theory and programmes: 'We latecomers of the West have become sceptics. Ideological systems will no longer lead us astray. Programmes belong to the previous century. We do not want any more sentences. We want to be ourselves' (4).

This dismissal of Marx as a superficial socialist whose thought represents the most ideological version of rationalist, urban thought in *Zivilisation* allows Spengler to develop his more fundamental point that Marxism and socialism are not variations on an overarching political theme or shades of opinion within the same movement, but as at odds with each other as are the two souls of the two great Faustian nations.

## Work and Wages

Given the space that Spengler devotes to Marx, it is worth pointing out that this rejection of Marx as a thinker who understands humans as exclusively material beings is problematic for at least two reasons. To begin with, Marx does not, as Spengler implies, treat labour like any other commodity. Marx describes capitalism as generalised commodity production in which labour power itself becomes a universal commodity for exchange, but he is adamant that labour power is a *special* commodity: it is unique in that it is able to produce value above and beyond its own value. This is what Marx calls surplus labour as the basis of surplus value – including in the form of producing and repairing machinery. Indeed, Marx's critique of the capitalist division of labour is not restricted to pointing out that capital incessantly robs the worker of this surplus labour in the quest for surplus value, or what he calls 'dead labour, which, vampire-like, lives only by sucking living labor, and lives the more, the more labour it sucks'.[25] Above and beyond this basic point, Marx's oppositon to alienated labour under capitalism is informed by the idea that humanity has been subsumed by the profit-driven division of labour and the kind of thinking in money of which Spengler is so scathing. Instead of facilitating the full and rounded development of each and every individual in harmony with the general good ('From each according to his abilities, to each according to his needs!'),[26] the capitalist division of labour stultifies individual and social development through work that is degrading and alienating.

Marx's critique of alienated wage labour also informs his understanding of the significance of strike action under capitalism. This is far from as one-sided and 'English' as Spengler seeks to portray it. For Marx, the conflict between workers and their employers – whether in the form of go-slows, laziness, absenteeism or full-blown strikes and sabotage actions – is an inevitable feature of the capitalist mode of production. It will occur whether or not there is an influential Communist Party informed by Marxist principles. For this reason, in his seminal speech to the General Council of the International Workingman's Association in 1865, Marx refers to strikes as the 'unavoidable guerilla fights incessantly springing up from the never ceasing encroachments of capital'.[27] Although such actions can give the workers an impression of their own strength and the importance of their organisation, trade unions and strikes do not inherently pose a challenge to capitalism and the logic of the wages system. Quite the opposite, in fact: the limitation of working-class organisations to trade unions and strikes, particularly in the form of calls for 'fair pay' or a bigger share of the wealth of what Spengler calls the 'community', is fully compatible with the understanding of labour as a commodity. Marx's fundamental point is that it is precisely the lessening of human labour to a thing to be bought and sold on the market that must be overcome. As he points out, trade unions can actually represent an *obstacle* to this endeavour: 'Instead of the *conservative* motto: "*A fair day's wage for a fair day's work!*" they [the trade unions] ought to inscribe on their banner the *revolutionary* watchword: "*Abolition of the wages system!*"[28] Spengler is thus misplaced in trying to portray Marx as a typical representative of 'the truly English proletarian formulation' of the 'unequal distribution of wealth' (45).

Spengler's critical engagement with Marx is nonetheless a captivating one and, as we will see below, Marx is not the only important socialist thinker with whom he engages in his attempt to rally the German workers to the banner of Prussian socialism.

*Prussianism and Socialism* concludes with a section entitled 'The International', which highlights the illusion of a peaceful world order, as heralded by the outbreak of the First World War. Spengler argues that further military conflicts are a given and sketches out a future in which the whole world will be economically coordinated and administered. Yet will this world be run by Spengler's dedicated, self-sacrificing, dutiful Prussian soldiers and civil servants or by ruthless, self-interested, exploitative English bankers and traders? These questions conclude the work, alongside the warning that even though this question is yet to be decided, the all-conquering Faustian soul in its final days makes one thing certain:

> A genuine International is only possible as the victory of the idea of a single race over all the others, and not as the mixture of all separate opinions into one colorless mass. Let us have the courage of our scepticism and throw away the old ideology. In history as it really is, there can be no reconciliation. Whoever believes in reconciliation must suffer from a chronic terror at the absurd ways in which events pan out, and he is only deceiving himself if he thinks that he can control them by means of treaties. There is but one end to all the conflict, and that is death – the death of individuals, of peoples, of cultures. Our own death still lies far ahead of us in the murky darkness of the next thousand years. (84)

Leaving no doubts as to which side he chooses in the epic clash between Prussian socialism and English capitalism before the eventual demise of Faustian culture, Spengler writes, in a flurry of collective pronouns: 'We Germans, situated as we are in this century and bound by our inborn instincts to the destiny of Faustian civilization, have within ourselves rich and untapped potential, but we have immense tasks ahead of us too' (ibid.).

This is a significant point regarding Spengler's political thought. Far from being the determinist he is often portrayed as, he recognises that the possibilities for the advance of the German nation are not simply provided by the forces of history, but depend on the conscious action of historical actors seeking to organise the nation with the values and ideas it needs in order to succeed against others. That he chooses to throw his weight behind the Germans thus reveals more about Spengler as a politician than it does about the logic consistency of his historical morphology. As we will see in the following chapters, depending on the particular context in which Spengler is writing and organising, this commitment to the German nation finds reflection in a variety of political plans and projects.

What is most striking about *Prussianism and Socialism*, however, is that it makes the case for Germany in emotionally charged rhetoric about the inherently *socialist* nature of its inhabitants. Although secondary literature has recognised that Spengler, as a thinker of the Conservative Revolution, is embracing the 'ingenious' idea of reformulating 'a potentially threatening idea, socialism, to suit indigenous German traditions', discussions on what Spengler exactly understands by a German Prussian-socialist state or how he attempts to intervene directly in the politics of the SPD have hardly been forthcoming.[29]

## The Prussian-Socialist State of the Future

Now that we have summarised the main arguments of *Prussianism and Socialism*, let us take a closer look at how Spengler describes a state informed by the principles of Prussian socialism in this text. Perhaps because of his idea that political programmes and ideologies belong to a past age and must be discarded if Germany is to advance, *Prussianism and Socialism*'s description of Spengler's Prussian-socialist state is not particularly detailed. Towards the end of the text, however, there is a long passage that is worth quoting in its entirety:

> The 'state of the future' is a state of civil servants. That is one of the inevitable final conditions toward which our civilization is steadily moving ... The big trusts have already virtually become private states exercising a protectorate over the official state. Prussian socialism, however, means incorporating these economic states of the individual professions into the state in its entirety. The point of contention between conservatives and proletarians is actually by no means about the need for an authoritarian socialist system, which could be avoided by adopting the American system (that is the hope of the German liberals), but about the question of supreme command. It may seem as though two socialist alternatives exist today, one from above and another from below, both in a dictatorial form. Yet in reality both would gradually end up in the same ultimate form. (90)

What becomes apparent from this description of Spengler's ideal state is that the democratic basis of the Weimar Republic established in 1919 must be overturned if Germany is to succeed. Moreover, at this point in his career, Spengler wishes to see the return of a monarch who will preside over the strong state and act according to the principle once expressed by Frederick the Great: 'I am the first servant of the state' (87). The seeming victory of the republican principle in Weimar Germany amounts to nothing other than the state's purchase by moneyed interests: 'If we set aside all illusions, today a republic means the corruptability of the executive wing of the state by private capital' (91). Whereas many of the followers of Marx and Engels believe that a democratic republic can become the form of working-class rule,[30] Spengler claims that 'it is precisely the republican form of government' that has 'nothing to do with socialism' (13).

The only mention of democratisation in *Prussianism and Socialism* comes in relation to the equal esteem in which all forms of work will be held within Spengler's proposed state: 'there is no difference in the ethical value of labour – this is Prussian-style democratization. The judge and the scholar perform "work" just as much as the miner or the lathe operator do' (77). This is no mere rhetorical flourish, for Spengler hopes that the state will exert such an influence over society that it will determine the wages of each and every kind of employment in the country: 'planning the scales carefully according to the overall economic situation of the time, in the interest of all and not of any one profession. That is the principle of salary scales for civil servants, applied to all occupations' (77). The executive organ overseeing this work will not be a democratically elected parliament, but an appointed 'administrative council' (66). Spengler thus posits that history has presented Germany with three paths of development: the dictatorship of capital in the form of republicanism, the dictatorship of the proletariat, and his desired option of a dictatorship of the civil servants in an almost martially organised, top-down state – from each according to his ability, to each according to the needs of the military state.

Spengler's remarkable sketch of German socialism reflects the extent to which he and other thinkers of his time from conservative, liberal and socialist traditions are animated by notions of what we would now call postcapitalist economics. The aim of such thinking is to create a command economy that can rein in the the negative social consequences of market economics. In Germany, this idea – war socialism (*Kriegssozialismus*) – becomes prominent as a result of the experience of the rationalising and planning of economic resources needed to conduct a full-scale war.[31] The concept is personified by the statesman Walter Rathenau in his leadership of the War Department of Raw Materials (*Kriegsrohstoffabteilung*). The notion of the superiority of a state-run economy has significant purchase beyond Germany too. In December 1916, for instance, Lenin looks to the German military state's Weapons and Munitions Procurement Office (WuMBA) as an example of what rationalised state planning could achieve: 'All propaganda for socialism must be refashioned from abstract and general to concrete and directly practical: expropriate the banks and, relying on the masses, carry out in their interests the very same thing the W.U.M.B.A. is carrying out in Germany!'[32]

At first sight, Spengler's emphasis on state planning, mechanistic economic decisions and rationalist wage-setting appears to be at odds with his organicist understanding of state and society that we discussed in Chapter 3. However, just as Spengler claims that the German aristocracy must not hark back to the feudal past, but must assert its values using the means and methods of the modern world, so he argues that a true community can only succeed in Faustian *Zivilisation* if it draws on the the latest developments in communications and industrial technology. Reflecting the ideological spirit of the circles such as those around the economically left-wing but politically right-wing journal *Die Tat*,[33] Spengler hopes that authoritarianism and monarchist tradition can combine with modern working practices and state planning in order to create a third way between the Russian Revolution and the spirit of English Viking capitalism.

## Factional Gambles

How does Spengler make the case for his peculiar brand of socialism and why does he appear to be convinced that this idea might take root in Germany, where Marxist socialism is a far more powerful force in the workers' movement than in England? In order to answer these questions, we must turn to Spengler's intervention into the factional politics of the SPD. In this respect, *Prussianism and Socialism* is engaged in a peculiar balancing act. On the one hand, it seeks to cast certain aspects of the SPD's politics and achievements as a shining example of Spengler's own Prussian socialist outlook. On the other hand, it portrays as English those aspects of the socialist movement with which he disagrees.

Spengler is well aware of the language of German social democracy in his time and of the factional shades within its ranks. One example of this comes in *Prussianism and Socialism*'s citation of *Drei Jahre Weltrevolution* (46), a pamphlet written in 1917 by the German SPD Reichstag deputy Paul Lensch.[34] In 1914, Lensch and his allies in what will become *Die Glocke* group (a publication established in 1915) come to the conclusion that the First World War actually represents a revolutionary process, in which a German victory can break Britain's supremacy in the world and thus open up a space for genuinely Marxist, German SPD-type organisations to develop, as opposed to the Labourite, trade unionist organisations that dominate the British workers' movement. In other words, Germany must be victorious in the name of social progress.[35] What is remarkable about this is that Lensch was once a pupil of Rosa Luxemburg and a household name of the radical, anti-imperialist wing of the SPD.

On occasion, the SPD leadership draws on the arguments of *Die Glocke* in order to make the case for continued SPD support for the politics of civil peace, but the overtly chauvinist tone of those in Lensch's faction ensures that it is generally viewed with suspicion by the SPD as whole. Hence, the group has to chart a course between its erstwhile allies from the left, who are now opponents, and the pro-war majority of the party. In the ideologically charged atmosphere of the November Revolution, however, there is a cross-fertilisation of nationalism and socialist-inspired ideology – spawning such projects as Hitler's National Socialism, Spengler's Prussian socialism and Ernst Niekisch's National Bolshevism[36] – and the ideas of Lensch and his co-thinkers play a significant role in this process. Spengler himself is clearly interested in the group and even has some connections with it: he corresponds both with Lensch and another of the leading figures around *Die Glocke*, the trade unionist and SPD parliamentarian August Winnig, who laters becomes a prominent *völkisch* opponent of both the Weimar Republic and the SPD itself. Lensch writes to Spengler 'on the occasion of Goethe's 170th birthday' in August 1919 to thank him for his 'wonderful book' (Volume 1 of *Der Untergang des Abendlandes*), of which Lensch writes a glowing review in the *Deutsche Allgemeine Zeitung*.[37] Spengler arranges for his publisher to send Winnig a copy of *Prussianism and Socialism*, for which Winnig is most grateful.[38]

These personal and intellectual connections, which have been largely overlooked by secondary literature,[39] are crucial to an understanding of *Prussianism and Socialism* in two respects. First, it is clear that Spengler believes that his arguments will be received with enthusiasm by certain nationalist circles in and around the SPD: his gamble on winning over the 'sensible' sections of the German workers to his project is thus informed by the conviction that his ideas will fall on fertile ground. Second, although Lensch and his co-thinkers, such as Heinrich Cunow and Konrad Haenisch, remain – in contrast to Spengler – committed to developing the politics of Marxism, there is a striking overlap between Spengler's and Lensch's analysis of the role of England and the English workers' movement, which are seen as embodying a variety of thinking-in-money in its uninspired syndicalism. By contrast, both Lensch and Spengler see the German SPD as a truly nationalist organisation that fights for political power, not economic improvement.

Spengler portrays the SPD as a once great institution that has recently fallen from grace through its role in ending the war and overthrowing the Kaiser's state. He views these actions not as the culmination of the party's anti-war and republican-Marxist propaganda over four decades, but as betraying its true essence, which was once expressed during the stewardship of its most iconic leader, August Bebel (1840–1913). Bebel's extraordinary career sees him rise from extreme poverty to international prominence as a Social Democratic leader and gifted SPD parliamentarian through his activity in both the Leipzig Workers' Education League and several women's campaigning groups.[40] For Spengler, the SPD under Bebel is less a Marxist-inspired proponent of economic socialism than a genuinely *Prussian* product of an almost dictatorial leadership. Bebel comes in for much praise by Spengler, who, as we saw in Chapter 1, liked to listen in on the SPD leader's famed Reichstag speeches as a student. Had Bebel not died in 1913, then – Spengler feels – he would have had no hesitation, in 1918, in reaffirming the party's true Prussian spirit of 4 August 1914 by ushering in a dictatorship that would violently impose its will on society: 'this is the way to give back the standing that the monarchy, the authority of the state and the military appear to have hopelessly lost'; only this can lead Germany out of disgraceful situation she finds herself in..[41]

In a fashion not dissimilar to the German communists' accusations of SPD betrayal – 'Who betrayed us? The Social Democrats!' (*Wer hat uns verraten? Sozialdemokraten!*') – Spengler makes the audacious claim that if Bebel had not died before the revolution, the party would have embarked on the Prussian-socialist course championed by Spengler. So not only does the Spengler of *Prussianism and Socialism*, pace Struve's claims about Spengler's overlooking the workers,[42] recognise the existence of the working class as a political factor, he actually attempts to gain the ear of those sections of the SPD who feel disgruntled by the role of the party in the revolution. In seeking to do so, Spengler's critique of the SPD's behaviour during the November Revolution occasionally borders on the voluntaristic. He is convinced that, under the 'Prussian' Bebel, heads would have rolled under the rule of his 'iron hand' (8) and the SPD would have renounced democratic forms and alliances with bourgeois parties in the Weimar Coalition. After all, he asks, was the SPD not organised rather like a military machine under Bebel that could be expanded to the German state as a whole? It is Bismarck, whose worker protection laws had created Prussian socialism, that the SPD should be looking to emulate, not his liberal or Catholic opponents. Arguing that the English and Prussian workers' movements are irreconcilably different, Spengler claims:

> The wages paid to Prussian officers and civil servants since the days of Frederick William I were ridiculously small in comparison with the sums required to belong even to the middle classes in England. But the Prussians had worked harder, more selflessly, and more honestly. The real compensation for this work is rank. It was the same in the SPD under Bebel. This workers' state-within-a-state did not want to get rich, it wanted to rule. During their enforced strikes these workers more than often went hungry, but they did so in the interest of gaining power, not of higher wages. They struck in support of a philosophy that was purportedly or actually opposed to that of their employers. They struck for a moral principle, and a defeat in their battle could ultimately mean a moral victory. English workers are completely unable to understand this. (46)

This 'Prussian' reading of the SPD's history and its leader Bebel, who until his death is popularly known as the 'Shadow Kaiser',[43] is sentenced to over two years in jail for treason and *lèse-majesté* and is seen as the figurehead in the struggle for Marxist socialism against Bismarckian state socialism, is of course deeply problematic. Nonetheless, Spengler is able to recognise and exploit what he views as an ambiguity within German social democracy over its attitude to the war and the question of Germany defending herself against foreign belligerence and aggression – not least in the face of the charge that the party was little more than an organisation of *scoundrels without a fatherland*. While Bebel was certainly no advocate of war with England and generally favoured rapprochement between the European powers,[44] in a famous speech at the SPD's Essen Congress in 1907, he claimed that if Germany were to be invaded from the East by Russia, then he would be the first to defend the fatherland, 'to put my rifle on my shoulder and to go off to war against Russia'.[45] Indeed, he argued, the defence of Germany without the support of the SPD would be inconceivable.[46] Spengler appears to be tapping into this controversy over the role that socialists should play in the event of war, a controversy that continued even after the First World War.

As with his critique of Marx, the question of whether Spengler's argument is accurate or reasonable is secondary: what is most noteworthy is the fact that he deems it politically expedient to engage polemically with the SPD in this fashion. His narrative about the purportedly authoritarian SPD and Bebel also allows him to spin the political behaviour of the SPD during the November Revolution as a stab in the back by the invisible English forces within the country, as a case of 'insubordination in the army and in the workers' party at the same time' (46). As such, he claims, the SPD's Prussian will to power under Bebel has become anglicised, degenerating from a philosophy of power into an obsession with penny-pinching, trade-union struggles.

Spengler's critique aims to show how things could have been, and still could be, different. However, this is not the end of his discussion of German social democracy. Spengler cites Ferdinand Lassalle's *Was nun?* (1863)[47] as an inspiration for his proposed alliance between the German aristocracy and the genuinely Prussian working class, thereby creating further distance between his socialism and that of Marx, who is highly critical of the contradictory Lassalle.[48] (Spengler omits to mention Bebel's contribution to the 'Eisenacher' wing of the SPD in its ideological struggle against Lassallean ideas).

Through his strict, dictatorial leadership of the General German Workers' Association (ADAV), Lassalle contributes to breaking the German working class from liberalism and to establishing an independent working-class party, as outlined in his famous *Offenes Antwortschreiben* (1863),[49] which makes the case for the working class forming its own social institutions. Widely read and discussed, this open letter created the basis of the ADAV and thus the SPD, whose rallies and demonstrations are often fronted by pictures of Lassalle alongside Marx. Simultaneously, however, Lassalle holds a number of opinions that are inimical to the idea of the German working class pursuing its own political project. These include his view that the Prussian state should provide funding for worker cooperatives and his flirtation with a possible alliance with Bismarck and the German *Junker* class against the bourgeoisie. In this limited sense, Lassalle might be considered an intellectual forefather of Spengler. At this point in his career at least, Spengler appears to share Lassalle's view that the rise of the bourgeoisie can only have incapacitating effects on the state. Both, interestingly enough, write their doctoral dissertation on Heraclitus. Spengler doubtless finds something of aristocratic virtue in Lassalle too, who died in a duel for the love of Countess Sophie von Hartzfeld.

It is striking just how conversant the conservative Spengler is with the various socialist discourses of his time. Hence, Horst Möller is incorrect to argue that Spengler's specific interpretation of socialism 'had nothing to do with Bernstein's revisionism or the socialism of social democracy'.[50] We have demonstrated just how acquainted Spengler is with the various competing understandings of socialism within the SPD throughout its existence.

There are two overriding reasons why Spengler is not successful in his attempts to win over the working classes to nationalism at this time. First, as recent historiographical scholarship has shown, the model state outlined in *Prussianism and Socialism* – that is, the supposed coming together of the German nation on 4 August 1914 – is more myth than reality.[51] For all of Spengler's criticisms of ideological systems and schemes, his desired Prussian state and the reality of *Burgfrieden* in Germany is an idealised one. Worried by what the conflict will mean for their existence, German peasants and workers do not flood into the town squares in order to express their joy at the outbreak of war; such sentiment was largely restricted to students and the middle classes. Second, Spengler clearly feels that those such as Lensch and Winnig represent important sections of the nationalist-influenced German working class that can be won over to his project. But these figures and their followers in the workers' movement gradually sink into insignificance during the early years of the Weimar Republic. Lensch leaves the SPD altogether in 1922. Winnig is expelled from both the SPD and the trade-union movement following his support for the aborted putsch against the Weimar state in March 1920 led by the generals Wolfgang Kapp and Walter von Lüttwitz. However, as we will see in the following chapters, Spengler's attempts to overthrow the Weimar Republic extend well beyond that year.

## Method and Motivation

Having discussed how Spengler seeks to intervene in the socialist movement of his time, we should now consider a further contextual factor in the development of his Prussian socialism – the dominance of notions of Germanness (*Deutschtum*) during and after the First World War. There are two influences in particular that should be taken into consideration when analysing the emergence of his Prussian socialism. They highlight how both the *Prussian* and *socialist* aspects of his Prussian socialism are perhaps not the invention of Spengler, but a sign of the times in which he is seeking to apply his philosophical ideas to the world around him.

First, it is evident that the creation of an antagonism between English and German culture is no invention of Spengler's, but is in the mould of the ideological mobilisation of the German people during the war, and the attempts on the part of philosophers such as Rudolf Eucken and Paul Natorp to create what Hermann Lübbe calls a 'metaphysics of Germanness' ('Deutschtumsmetaphysik').[52] This attempt to formulate philosophically a unique German identity distinct from the other warring nations is a guiding principle of the Conservative Revolution. Ernst Troeltsch, Johann Plenge and Werner Sombart are pioneering in this regard, with the latter publishing a 1915 treatise under the revealing title *Traders and Heroes* (*Händler und Helden* – the latter, of course, being the Germans). Troeltsch distinguishes, as does Spengler, between the individualism of the English gentleman's trader philosophy and German ideas of self-denying community. Spengler also shares with his allies in the German conservative movement a focus on the youth – students in and around the fraternities and conservative clubs in particular – as an agent of reasserting Germanness. He refers to this 'young generation' not in terms of their age, but rather their 'power of judgement' and their 'sense of responsibility'; those who have neither will always be far too young for politics, he adds.[53]

Second, several terms and concepts within Spengler's historical morphology – not least the emphasis on *Faustian* culture and the philosophical distinction between *Kultur* and *Zivilisation* discussed in the previous chapters – are important tropes in the competing political discourse on both sides of the trenches in the First World War. Whereas French and British pro-war intellectuals claim to be fighting for 'civilisation', those in Germany inscribed on their banners the slogan of 'culture'.[54] As Georg Lukács puts it, *Kultur* is a leitmotif in 'reactionary German philosophy', with the ideological struggle against the democratisation of Germany taking place behind the banner of this antagonism, with *Zivilisation* representing everything bad about capitalism, particularly Western democracy, and with truly German, organic *Kultur* standing opposed to it.[55]

Notwithstanding Spengler's position within this broader current of German-nationalist intellectuals, John Farrenkopf speciously claims that Spengler cannot be accused of jumping on the ideological bandwagon of metaphysical Germanness in the way that those such as Plenge and Troeltsch do.[56] The reason Farrenkopf offers is that, for Spengler, it is the overarching, cyclical conception of history that is ultimately decisive, not an idealisation of Germanness. However, this contention overlooks the significance of Spengler's understanding of the modern Germans as metaphysically unique and predisposed to stamping their authority on the great struggles of the twentieth century. As such, it is another example of scholarship underestimating the subjective, German-nationalist factor in the development of Spengler's political and historical thought. Farrenkopf's assertion nonetheless raises a key question regarding the relationship between Spengler's morphology of history and his concrete proposals to influence the remaining days of Faustian *Zivilisation*. Let us conclude our discussion of *Prussianism and Socialism* by looking at this matter in more detail.

Clemens Vollnhals argues that Spengler's Prussian socialism merely amounts to 'playing games with the concept of socialism … a flirtatious pose occasioned by the time'.[57] The implication here is that Spengler's socialism is little more than unprincipled short-termist political posturing through which he seeks to popularise his authoritarian-nationalist project at a time when socialist discourse dominates parties and movements from the far left to the far right. In a similar vein, Stefan Vogt contends that 'authors such as Spengler or [Edgar Julius] Jung had no intention of changing the capitalist economic system' and, unlike thinkers such as Hans Freyer, Hans Zehrer and Otto Strasser of the *Tatkreis*, do not envision 'forms of planned economy and the socialization of certain means of production'.[58]

Nonetheless, against Vogt's claim, we have already established how the Spengler of *Prussianism and Socialism* actually does sketch out a form of military 'planned economy' for postwar Germany. Moreover, we have seen how, contrary to Vollnhals, already in Volume 1 of *The Decline of the West*, Spengler claims that *socialism* – at least in his particular appropriation of the idea – represents the epochal destiny of the Faustian people in the age of *Zivilisation*. To dismiss out of hand the substance of Spengler's commitment – however fleeting – to a German nationalist form of socialism at this point in his life is to overlook two important aspects of his political thought: for one, it underestimates the utopian nature of his writing in the context of the Conservative Revolution after the First World War; and, for another, it is oblivious to something more fundamental about the originality and inventiveness Spengler shows in the constantly evolving nature of his political thought. While his approach is always informed by fundamental principles that flow from his morphology of history (in this case, the rejection of democracy and the embrace of *ethical* socialism), he is invariably pragmatic when seeking to apply these principles to his political activities and assessing the implications that the events around him should have for his plans for the future of Germany.

Moreover, it should be noted that *Prussianism and Socialism* is not the first time that Spengler attempts to modify some of his principles in order to make them appeal to a working-class audience. Before the fall of the Hohenzollern monarchy, Spengler was an 'opportunistic advocate of the quasi-democratization of the Second Reich' who was willing to abolish the three-tier suffrage system in Prussia.[59] This system effectively excluded the working class from the ballot box by linking the weight of the popular vote to the amount of tax that each voter paid to the state. Spengler felt that putting an end to this injustice might help to dampen the strong opposition of the working class in Prussia and integrate it into the Wilhelmine Empire. Once again, this is a matter of efficacy, of 'instinct', over political principle – a concession even to Spengler's hated democracy in an attempt to strengthen the nation.[60] To understand Spengler's political thought, therefore, it is necessary to consider *both* his methodological claims to objectivity *and* his subjective motivations and instincts at any given point, and not to draw all-encompassing conclusions from just one of his texts.

However, as we will establish in the following chapters, the abundance of socialist rhetoric in *Prussianism and Socialism* proves rather short-lived in Spengler's career; his commitment to socialism is certainly not an enduring feature of his thought. By the publication of Volume 2 of *The Decline of the West* in 1922, Spengler appears to have abandoned altogether the notion that the working class can meaningfully contribute to the bold political leadership demanded by Faustian *Zivilisation*. There his focus is squarely on the virtues of aristocratic leadership. Moreover, as we have seen, Spengler's particular emphasis on *ethical* socialism actually entails the inversion of *socialism* in any meaningful sense of the word: democracy becomes the authoritarian state, internationalism becomes imperialism, and the eradication of inequality gives way to an embrace of rank and hierarchy. In contrast to other thinkers who attempt to win over the working classes to a project of national unity, such as Max Weber, Friedrich Naumann or even Lensch, the Spengler of *Prussianism and Socialism* has next to nothing by way of proposals to address the social question (*die soziale Frage*) in German society. Seen in this light, the concluding passage of *Prussianism and Socialism* – 'We are socialists. We do not wish to have been so in vain' (99) – reads almost ironically. This must have also been the the case for the tens of thousands who read the pamphlet, for such bombastic statements only blur the already vague distinction between economic and ethical socialism, which is far from readily apparent or understandable from an informal reading of the pamphlet. (As we will see in Chapter 7, Spengler is later compelled to respond to this very criticism on the part of some of his detractors on the German right.)

The socialist rhetoric and the 'utopian traits'[61] that characterise *Prussianism and Socialism* must therefore be explained with reference to the context within which they are written. The idealistic and future-orientated prose of *Prussianism and Socialism* reflects, and feeds into, the heady ideological atmosphere of the time and belies the dominant reading of his thought as pessimistic or fatalistic. Even H. Stuart Hughes's more nuanced distinction between short-term optimism and long-term pessimism in Spengler's ideas does not actually apply to *Prussianism and Socialism* – the work abounds with optimistic references to the future and little by way of the gloomier, longer-term predictions for the fate of the *Abendland*.[62] What is particularly noteworthy with regard to the evolution of Spengler's thought is that the concept of *Caesarism* – alluded to in Volume 1 of *The Decline of the West*, but not explained in detail until Volume 2 in 1922 – appears just once in *Prussianism and Socialism* to describe the destiny of party politics in all the nations of Faustian *Zivilisation*: 'The relationship between party leaders and the party, between the party and the masses, will become more raw, more transparent, and more brazen. That is the beginning of Caesarism' (67). In 1919, then, this concept is by no means as central to his thought as it will later become in both Volume 2 of *The Decline of the West* and his subsequent publications.

The only critic who has grasped something of Spengler's tendency to restyle himself politically as and when he feels the situation demands is Ernst Bloch. He writes: 'He [Spengler] first bet on a German victory, then he airily turned himself into a "socialist" and there he salvaged some of the Prussian rhetoric that he had kept at the ready.'[63] Accordingly, Bloch talks of several Spenglers: the historical morphologist, the journalist prophet completely detached from this historical morphology, and then a third, isolated and overly trenchant Spengler whose life is characterised by the pretence of prophecy, but who no longer possesses the intellectual abilities he once did.[64]

Bloch never fully develops this noteworthy point of departure through a focused study of the developments and changes within Spengler's political thought across his career. But now that we have outlined Spengler's alternative of Prussian socialism and what the book reveals about him as a historical actor in revolutionary Germany, we are in a position to trace further the development of his ideas through an analysis of how he works with others in the anti-republican German conservative movement to overthrow the Weimar Republic. Moreover, we can establish whether and to what extent the ideal future state of *Prussianism and Socialism* and the concomitant rhetoric of the Conservative Revolution find reflection in his subsequent political writings.

## Notes

1. Farrenkopf, *Prophet of Decline: Spengler on World History and Politics*, 145–65; Boterman, *Oswald Spengler und sein 'Untergang des Abendlandes'*, 218–59; Falck (ed.), *Zyklen und Cäsaren. Mosaiksteine einer Philosophie des Schicksals. Reden und Schriften Oswald Spenglers*, 73–88; Felken, *Oswald Spengler. Konservativer Denker zwischen Kaiserreich und Diktatur*, 95–114; Henkel, *Nationalkonservative Politik und mediale Repräsentation. Oswald Spenglers politische Philosophie und Programmatik im Netzwerk der Oligarchen (1910–1925)*, 223–49; Maaß, *Oswald Spengler. Eine politische Biographie*, 31–53; and Lübbe, 'Oswald Spenglers "Preußentum und Sozialismus" und Ernst Jüngers "Arbeiter"'. On the similarities and differences between *Prussianism and Socialism* and the ideas of Hitler, see Koktanek, *Oswald Spengler in seiner Zeit*, 215–36.
2. Struve, *Elites against Democracy: Leadership Ideals in Bourgeois Political Thought in Germany, 1890–1933*, 248–49.
3. I have published extensively on the German socialist movement between 1875 and 1933. For an introduction to the organisations and aims of that movement, see, for example, Lewis, 'The Four-Hour Speech and the Significance of Halle'.
4. Noske, *Von Kiel bis Kapp. Zur Geschichte der deutschen Revolution*, 68; Felken, *Oswald Spengler*, 94.
5. Cf. ibid., 114.
6. Cited in Henkel, *Nationalkonservative Politik*, 245. For an introduction to Kurt Eisner's life and work, see Eisner, 'Kurt Eisners Ort in der sozialistischen Bewegung'.
7. Spengler to Hans Klöres, 27 December 1918, in Spengler, *Briefe 1913–36*, 114–15.
8. Naeher, *Oswald Spengler*, 84.
9. Given Spengler's association with these and other paramilitary organisations, it is slightly bizarre for Naeher to claim that Spengler was 'not a militant anti-Bolshevik'; ibid., 82.
10. Spengler, *Preußentum und Sozialismus*, 54. Subsequent references to *Preußentum und Sozialismus* in this chapter will be placed in parentheses in the main text.
11. Felken, *Oswald Spengler*, 95.
12. Spengler to Hans Klöres, 6 March 1919, in Spengler, *Briefe 1913–36*, 123.
13. Spengler, *Der Untergang des Abendlandes. Umrisse einer Morphologie der Weltgeschichte. Erster Band: Gestalt und Wirklichkeit* (1920 [1919]), 52. This edition has been cited here because we wish to discuss Spengler's arguments in the earlier editions of *Der Untergang des Abendlandes*, not the revised edition of 1923.
14. Ibid.
15. Ibid.
16. Somewhat confusingly, Spengler also refers to this form of socialism as *political socialism*. However, since he claims in *Prussianism and Socialism* that true ethical socialism is fundamentally concerned with political power – 'socialism means power, power and once again power' – *economic* socialism is a much more helpful way of framing the distinction between two forms of socialism; Spengler, *Preußentum und Sozialismus*, 98.
17. Spengler, *Der Untergang des Abendlandes. Umrisse einer Morphologie der Weltgeschichte*, 2 vols (1997 [1923]), 1129.
18. Ibid., 1004.
19. Cf. Nübel, *Die Mobilisierung der Kriegsgesellschaft*, 32.
20. Spengler to Hans Klöres, 6 March 1919, in Spengler, *Briefe 1913–36*, 123.
21. Spengler to Hans Klöres, 27 December 1918, in ibid., 115.
22. Cited in Sontheimer, *Antidemokratisches Denken in der Weimarer Republik. Die politischen Ideen des Nationalismus zwischen 1918 und 1933*, 351.
23. Both in terms of the idea it discusses and the language used, this statement is similar to one of the *Communist Manifesto*'s most notable descriptions of the bourgeois epoch: '[The bourgeoisie] *compels* all nations, on pain of extinction, to adopt the bourgeois mode of production; it compels them to introduce what it calls civilisation into their midst, i.e.,

to become bourgeois themselves. In one word, it creates a world after its own image. The bourgeoisie has *subjected* the country to the rule of the towns'; Marx and Engels, *Manifesto of the Communist Party*, 113, emphasis added.

24. Spengler, *Der Untergang des Abendlandes* (1920 [1919]), 206; 190. We will leave to one side the question of 'Jewish' thought in Spengler's work for now and will return to this important matter in Chapter 7.
25. Marx, *Capital Volume I*, 342.
26. Marx, 'Critique of the Gotha Programme', 21.
27. Marx, *Value, Price and Profit*, 29.
28. Ibid.
29. Herf, *Reactionary Modernism: Technology, Culture and Politics in Weimar and the Third Reich*, 37.
30. Engels, 'Zur Kritik des sozialdemokratischen Programmentwurfes', 227–40.
31. The seminal account of this idea and its implications from a liberal perspective is Heuss, *Kriegssozialismus*.
32. Lenin, 'Theses for an Appeal to the International Socialist Committee and All Socialist Parties'.
33. The best overview of the history and impact of the *Die Tat* magazine remains Sontheimer, 'Der Tatkreis'.
34. Lensch, *Drei Jahre Weltrevolution*.
35. On Lensch, see Lewis, 'The SPD Left's Dirty Secret', 10–11.
36. On Niekisch and National Bolshevism, see Rühle, 'Haßliebe zu den niederen Dämonen: Ernst Niekisch und der Nationalbolschewismus', 192–206. For Niekisch, Spengler's state of the future in *Prussianism and Socialism* represents 'the old authoritarian state once again, which the worker must blindly obey'; Niekisch, *Gewagtes Leben. Begnegungen und Begebnisse*, 135.
37. Paul Lensch to Spengler, 28 August 1919, in Spengler, *Briefe 1913–36*, 139–40.
38. August Winning to Spengler, 27 August 1920, in ibid., 169.
39. One exception is Henkel, who points to the links between Spengler and those such as Lensch and Winning, and even provides an unattributed quote to Spengler, according to which the most important thing that the nationalist right needs is a group of capable 'worker leaders'; Henkel, *Nationalkonservative Politik und mediale Repräsentation*, 252.
40. For an overview of Bebel's life and work, see Schmidt, *August Bebel. Kaiser der Arbeiter*. I have written briefly on Bebel's contribution to Marxism and women's liberation; see Lewis, 'Bebel's Forgotten Legacy'.
41. Spengler to Hans Klöres, 27 December 1918, in Spengler, *Briefe 1913–36*, 114–15.
42. Struve, *Elites against Democracy*, 248–49.
43. Cf. Maehl, *Shadow Emperor of the German Workers*.
44. Schmidt, *August Bebel*, 136.
45. Sozialdemokratische Partei Deutschlands (ed.), *Protokoll über die Verhandlungen des Parteitages der Sozialdemokratischen Partei Deutschlands. Abgehalten zu Essen vom 15. bis 21. September 1907*, 255.
46. Ibid.
47. Lassalle, *Was nun? Zweiter Vortrag über Verfassungswesen*.
48. For an overview of Lassalle's life, see Bernstein, *Ferdinand Lassalle und seine Bedeutung für die Arbeiterklasse. Zu seinem vierzigsten Todestage*.
49. Lassalle, 'Offenes Antwortschreiben an das Zentralkomitee zur Berufung eines Allgemeinen Deutschen Arbeiterkongresses'.
50. Möller, 'Geschichte im Dienste der Zeitkritik', 54.
51. On what he describes as the myth of 'an all-embracing enthusiasm for war in August 1914', see Ziemann, *War Experiences in Rural Germany 1914–1923*, at 16–27 in particular.
52. Lübbe, *Politische Philosophie in Deutschland*, 185.
53. Spengler, 'Vorwort', in *Politische Schriften 1919–1926*, 11.

54. In philosophical terms, Lübbe traces the *Kultur/Zivilisation* dichotomy back to Immanuel Kant, but argues that this distinction only becomes politicised in the early twentieth century, as part of what he describes as a 'Fichte Renaissance'; Lübbe, *Politische Philosophie*, 191 and 199.
55. Lukács, *Die Zerstörung der Vernunft*, 375.
56. Farrenkopf, *Prophet of Decline*, 128.
57. Vollnhals, 'Praeceptor Germaniae. Oswald Spenglers politische Publizistik', 178.
58. Vogt, 'Strange Encounters: Social Democracy and Radical Nationalism in Weimar Germany', 271.
59. Farrenkopf, *Prophet of Decline*, 113.
60. For this reason, Farrenkopf's claim that it is simplistic to maintain that Spengler was 'a virulent antidemocratic thinker' downplays Spengler's consistent opposition to democracy as a hindrance to the efficacy of the state; ibid., 2.
61. Falck (ed.), *Zyklen und Cäsaren*, 97.
62. Hughes, *Oswald Spengler: A Critical Estimate*, 87.
63. Bloch, 'Spengler als Optimist', 195.
64. Ibid., 195–96.

CHAPTER 6

# Rebuilding the German Reich
## *Illusion and Failure*

The focus of this chapter is Spengler's political work, launched by the enormous impact of his *Prussianism and Socialism*, in the 'years of crisis'[1] faced by the young Weimar Republic. Particularly in the period between 1919 and 1924, Spengler is an influential publicist, networker and organiser in the broad nationalist movement that devotes its energies to dislodging the Weimar Republic in the course of the latter's troubled existence. This represents a particular challenge for him because he must draw on his detailed understanding of the epoch to develop solutions to rapidly changing problems.

This chapter will shed light on Spengler's political practice in this period in two main respects. First, it will provide an outline of the role played by Spengler in the consolidation of the German right and its plots to replace the Berlin government with a National Directorate (*Direktorium*). Spengler contributes to these plans through his close connections with politicians, captains of industry and press barons. Second, this chapter will provide an overview and critical assessment of his *Rebuilding the German Reich* (1924). This 100-page book is worthy of a detailed discussion because, although less commercially successful than *Prussianism and Socialism* and *The Hour of Decision*, it is the closest thing to a political programme that Spengler ever publishes. As we saw in the previous chapter, he is generally dismissive of political programmes and objectives as ideological and divorced from the reality of Faustian *Zivilisation*. For this reason alone, *Rebuilding the German Reich* represents a milestone in the development of Spengler's political thought.

In spite of this important fact, however, secondary literature has almost without exception failed to discuss the text in any detail. The outcome is that Spengler research has not been able to account for the true significance of *Rebuilding the German Reich* and how it is reflective of Spengler's shifting political priorities and objectives. The only chapter-length analyses of the text can be found in the studies by Sebastian Maaß and Thomas Tartsch. Maaß's book, as we discussed in Chapter 2, was pulped by the publisher. Tartsch's study remains utterly marginal even in Spengler studies.[2] Other commentators on *Rebuilding the German Reich* view it as reflective of a thinker whose political outlook is more tempered, moderate and less radical than in the immediate aftermath of the November Revolution of 1918. Domenico Conte, for instance, is of the view that *Rebuilding the German Reich* and other texts from this period, unlike *Prussianism and Socialism*, display a classically conservative character.[3] Similarly, Markus Henkel claims that, notwithstanding Spengler's 'conservative-revolutionary frame of reference', his politics should be placed within 'the context of a German "Tory Conservatism"'.[4] The aim of this conservatism, Henkel adds, is 'to help Germany to its old greatness and to a *modern political system*, that should be *up to the tasks* of the current democratic age as well as the politics of the future that will be shaped by Caesarism'.[5]

This chapter will challenge these readings of *Rebuilding the German Reich*. It will do so by reconstructing the context in which the text is written and published, as well as through a discussion of how its demands to rebuild Germany relate to the exhaustion of democracy and Caesarism that Spengler finds in the late days of Faustian culture. In contrast to Conte and Henkel, this chapter will demonstrate how *Rebuilding the German Reich* reflects Spengler's continued commitment to overthrowing the democratic basis of the Weimar Republic and establishing the constitutional framework for the emergence of a Caesar on German soil.

Finally, this chapter will offer a brief assessment of the other continuities and discontinuities within Spengler's political thought in the tumultuous period between the publication of *Prussianism and Socialism* in 1919 and *Rebuilding the German Reich* in 1924. In so doing, we will further develop our understanding of Spengler's pragmatism – or opportunism, depending on one's interpretation – when seeking to apply his philosophy of world history to the day-to-day contingencies of politics and power.

## A Philosopher Lost in the Maze of Politics?

Spengler's political activities following his newly found fame as a conservative thinker can be broken down into three main categories. First, he corresponds extensively with a range of leading German nationalists from various areas of public life. Second, he expands his profile by giving a range of speeches on the pressing issues of his time to various right-wing associations. Third, by means of telegrams, letters and face-to-face meetings that take place across the whole of Germany, Spengler uses his ties to industry in particular to set the political agenda by all means at his disposal.[6]

Spengler's correspondence during the early period of the Weimar Republic forms something of a 'Who's Who' of the German conservative elite. It makes it clear that he must count amongst the best-connected thinkers of his age. Besides links with the Crown Prince of Bavaria, he is close to influential representatives from the core of the German economy. These include industrial champion Paul Reusch, the mining millionaire Hugo Stinnes, the media tycoon and leading German National People's Party (DNVP) member Alfred Hugenberg, whose 'Hugenberg press' provides a platform for an array of nationalist causes, and Gustav Krupp, the steel magnate. In this period Spengler considers himself to be a tireless campaigner and – although he might have disliked the term – lobbyist for German industrial interests. On one occasion, for instance, he attempts to organise a committee of industrial and agricultural representatives in order to prepare a bill on taxation policy.[7] As we will see below, this shift in political focus from the nationalist sections of the working classes to German commercial interests finds reflection in the nature of his writings and proposals, even if he often becomes frustrated at the leading industrialists' not always following his advice to the letter.

Spengler gives speeches to the GÄA-Gesellschaft, a society that provides a 'forum for the exchange of ideas and the coordination of policy' among the German elite and counts among its exclusive membership 'politicians, writers, businessmen and officers';[8] the Juni-Klub, a grouping of conservative-revolutionary intellectuals established in Berlin by Arthur Moeller van den Bruck and others, named after the month in which Germany signed the Treaty of Versailles they hold in such contempt; and elite clubs of German industry in the Ruhr and Hamburg, such as the Hamburger Überseeclub, which is founded in 1922 by the banker Max Warburg in order to promote closer ties between industry and scholarship. These appearances make Spengler something of a celebrity in the conservative movement and facilitate his role as a networker within those circles. His links, moreover, transcend party-political affiliation and extend to all those he deems loyal to the German nation. Thus he rubs shoulders with Franz von Papen and Martin Spahn, both of whom belong to the Catholic Centre Party (Deutsche Zentrumspartei); Alfred von Tirpitz and Paul von Lettow-Vorbeck of the DNVP; and Gustav von Kahr, a 'most traditional monarchist'[9] and member of the Bavarian People's Party, the Bavarian wing of the Centre Party. In addition, von Kahr is an important figure in the crisis of 1923, which we will discuss below.[10]

Spengler's connections do not stop at officially recognised organisations. In Bavaria, he enjoys close contact with the extraparliamentary right. He corresponds with various figures from paramilitary groupings, many of which are established in defiance of the restrictions on Germany's military forces imposed by the Treaty of Versailles. Such figures include

Carl Wäninger (founder of the Bavarian Stahlhelm); Georg Escherich of the so-called Orgesch; and Captain Hermann Erhardt of the *Freikorps*, who headed the Consul organisation, one of Germany's various patriotic associations (*vaterländische Verbände*). All these semi-legal groupings are viciously anti-communist and committed to the overthrow of the Weimar Republic. Spengler contributes to raising funds to strengthen and expand these paramilitary defence associations, especially those based in Bavaria.[11]

At the same time, Spengler seeks to gain the ear of the parliamentarians and even the presidents of the republic he is seeking to overthrow. He often does so by offering information and access to influential contacts in Germany and abroad.[12] A case in point comes in his letter to Gustav Stresemann on 23 September 1923. Spengler claims to be in contact with the European representative of the right-wing South African General Jan Smuts, who will shortly be visiting England. He feels that Stresemann may be able to use Smuts's influence in order to achieve the best possible outcome from German negotiations with the Entente powers over reparations.

The immediate aim of this activity is twofold. On the one hand, Spengler is attempting to unite in a single coordinating body, beyond the party-political affiliations he despises, the very best and brightest representatives of anti-Weimar German nationalism from the fields of politics, economics, the military and the media. This is no straightforward task, for the forces of the right in Weimar Germany are as disparate as they are determined. On the other hand, Spengler expends much of his time and energy on establishing a clandestine press headquarters (*Pressezentrale*) to steer the output of the press with an invisible hand and thereby improve the standing of right-wing and nationalist ideas in society.

Taken together, these projects are integral to Spengler's overriding ambition of German national renewal by ridding her of all republican ideas and traditions. He is not particularly unique in his plans to overthrow the Weimar Republic from the right. Several such plots are being formulated at this time and, from the early 1920s, Spengler's resident Bavaria is increasingly the focal point of extreme right-wing organisations and activities. In order to explore further Spengler's attempts to intervene in, and thus influence, Germany's future in the era of Faustian *Zivilisation*, let us now take a brief look at his attempt to establish a *Pressezentrale* to further the cause of conservatism.

In Chapter 4, we noted how *The Decline of the West* makes the case that the 'free press' is a mere illusion and that the print media as a whole are subordinate to the interests of a small number of individuals who seek to tailor the political and intellectual agenda to their own interests.[13] Somewhat paradoxically, therefore, those calling for the press to be free are, in fact, facilitating the continued concentration of the media in a few hands. The 'free press' is thus grist to the mill of the emerging phenomenon of Caesarism. Spengler maintains that this is doubly true when local and national publications are beset with financial difficulties, as they are in the early 1920s. In the face of such hardship, he is convinced that money becomes even more significant to the evolution of the German print media. In return for financial incentives, press outlets can be open to editorial influence, with cash-strapped editors being coerced into running prominently placed nationalist articles or opinion pieces. As he puts it: 'Granting credit and providing financial support through advertisements allows us to demand that certain articles and news pieces be published'.[14] Obviously, the financial backing of his allies in German industry would be indispensable to his plans to shape the headlines, as these forces preside over the necessary credit and funds.

In a memoir written in July 1922 and circulated amongst close contacts, Spengler outlines the rationale for his work in seeking to influence the press agenda:

> We are concerned with taking the first steps to a non-public organisation of the right-wing press.
> The two most important reasons for such a body as are as follows:
> 1. The economic collapse of the newspapers, which has already affected a third of them and, following the figures provided by the newspaper publishers at their last conference, will affect another third by October (confidential) ...
> 2. The urgent necessity of arriving at uniform tactics in response to unfolding political and economic events ... Until now, the individual editorial offices were left to their own devices and their attitude was accordingly a mere expression of personal ambition, academic unfamiliarity with the world and complete helplessness when faced with the actual tasks of political journalism.[15]

In order to pave the way for such nationalistic reportage – the 'actual tasks of political journalism' – his proposed *Pressezentrale* has four main objectives: to promote right-wing articles in various publications through financial pressure; to unify the political line of newspapers owned by figures sympathetic to the cause of the anti-Weimar right; to provide 'material support for those press outlets ... who are capable of higher political tasks and outlooks'; and, finally, to discredit the left-wing and liberal press, and harangue it with constant threats of expensive libel cases.[16]

Plans are even made for the central office of his *Pressezentrale*. Spengler foresees its leadership as consisting of three men – Martin Spahn, Paul Nikolaus Cosmann, editor of the *Süddeutsche Monatshefte*, and Spengler himself, who is to run the office. Since Spengler is certain that Germany's future depends in no small measure on developments abroad, he plans to establish an Intelligence Bureau for Foreign Affairs.[17] This is to be run by Ernst Graf zu Reventlow, a naval captain who toys with ideas of National Bolshevism and eventually becomes a National Socialist. These plans provide further evidence of how Spengler's networks cut across the various shadings of the German right and, indeed, across the political spectrum. It should be noted that in 1923 zu Reventlow joins with Moeller van den Bruck in contributing articles to the German Communist Party's publication *Die Rote Fahne*. These articles constitute a polemic with leading German communists over the role and significance of German nationalism in the highly charged atmosphere of 1923.[18]

As evinced by his extensive correspondence from this period, Spengler is optimistic regarding the prospects of his initiative. Through Reusch in particular, he arranges for the transfer of rather large amounts of money for political allies.[19] Ultimately, however, his plans come to nothing and this is a source of desperate frustration. According to Paul Hoser, Spengler's failure can be traced back to the role played by Hugenberg, who seeks to gain from Spengler's notoriety, but is unwilling to countenance a longer-term alliance with Spengler in a prominent role:

> Spengler is only of value to Hugenberg because of his extensive contacts and in his reputation as a philosopher of history who propagates a world view that is both acceptable and useful to industry. Hugenberg does not dare to think of helping such an outsider to establish such a central position of power in the German press that could become even been more influential than his own.[20]

Hoser's account of Spengler's inability to bring into existence his desired press bureau is a familiar one in Spengler studies. For Hoser, Spengler's real talent and drive is for questions of philosophy, not politics. So when literary success launches Spengler into public prominence, he becomes lost in the maze of *Realpolitik*.[21] When Spengler's 'simplistic understanding of steering and influencing the press' meets with the concrete realities of politics in Weimar Germany, only failure can result. Spengler's 'fantastic petty-bourgeois dream'[22] for the press is ultimately out of step with the complex reality of the modern media. His dream is based on the past, when Spengler's heroes – Machiavelli, Talleyrand and others – were supposedly able to change the course of history with a subtle whisper here or a cunning manoeuvre there. Now, Spengler is certainly frustrated with the outcome of his work on a *Pressezentrale*, as is evident in a lecture he gives to the GÄÄ-Gesellschaft: 'No other country in the world has such a politically unusable press', he fumes.[23] However, Hoser's accusation is slightly simplistic. Spengler clearly draws inspiration from his heroes of a past age. Yet his attempts to mobilise right-wing thought, unite the various anti-Weimar political strands and create an agenda-setting press office are all weapons of the modern party-political arsenal. They prefigure the role played by psephologists, spokespersons and spin-doctors in modern-day parties, lobbies and think tanks. Moreover, Spengler's wide-ranging activities in the field of the media discussed above underscore how his conception of the modern press is not a determinist one: Spengler does not view the media as merely a rigidly determined structure that aids and abets the end of democracy without further ado. What matters is the particular direction in which it can be guided by those who recognise its true nature.

Simply because Spengler does not realise his plans for a right-wing media organisation should not obscure the fact that, as a *political philosopher*, he is intensely involved in applying his views on Faustian *Zivilisation* to the contingencies of unfolding events. It is thus misleading to suggest, as Hoser does, that Spengler the *philosopher* becomes lost in the world of *politics*. The two facets of his thought are integrated, albeit – as we will establish at several points in this volume – in constant flux. An instance of this tension comes in his endeavour to cohere a nationalist 'invisible lodge'[24] – a political party in all but name – while being opposed to the political party as a manifestation of modern Western decadence. His attempt to establish a *Pressezentrale* is not the only occasion during the period under consideration when Spengler experiences the difficulties involved in applying a detailed worldview to fluid political situations.

## 1923: The Lost Year of Decision

Notwithstanding his continued exasperation at the failure of his press plans, at the beginning of 1923, Spengler has not given up on his plan to rejuvenate the German right; quite the opposite, in fact. When a series of crises – international, economic, regional and military – intersect later that year, he has good reason to feel closer to power than ever before. The Weimar Republic is shaken to its foundations by the continued burden of reparations, crippling inflation, and the occupation of the Ruhr by French and Belgian troops. Beginning in January 1923, the occupation ensures that the seething social discontent brought about by soaring prices often assumes a nationalist form. It is this backdrop which ensures that leading German communists write eulogies for openly fascist militants.[25] For the German right, the intertwining of nationalist and oppositional sentiments inspires hope in the possibility of another 'civil peace' (*Burgfrieden*), the true German revolution to which Spengler first aspires in *Prussianism and Socialism*.

The unfolding catastrophe – which contributes to a vote of no confidence in the non-aligned pro-business Chancellor Wilhelm Cuno's government and his replacement by Gustav Stresemann of the German People's Party (DVP) – exposes several weaknesses of the young Weimar state. Spengler has long been critical of the DVP for being the 'Judas' of German conservatism due to its involvement in several coalition governments in the early Weimar years.[26] In a letter to Reusch of 17 August

1923, Spengler claims that the switch from Cuno to Stresemann represents 'a defeat for industry'.[27] At the same time, he is confident that Stresemann's administration will achieve little more than to 'plaster over the existing crisis'.[28] Further, with reference to his political work, Spengler notes that the increasingly precarious situation demands 'that industry finally take its political safeguards resolutely in its hands'.[29] He warns that 'a bloody incident' is potentially on the cards.[30]

Spengler's call for the political representatives of industry to cohere their forces points to a significant shift in perspective since the publication of *Prussianism and Socialism*. Whereas his focus in that text was on the German nationalist working classes and the aristocracy, he now appears to recognise that the success of his political project is contingent on the flourishing of his contacts with German industry. In September 1923, for example, he feels that the unfolding events are forcing Hugenberg to devote more energy to the secretive press project than had previously been the case.[31] Spengler's letter to Reusch cited above additionally conveys the impression that the time is ripe for putting an end to the Weimar experiment. When, in September 1923, Gustav Stresemann's government makes the controversial decision to call off the policy of passive resistance to the occupation of the Ruhr, this is the last straw for Spengler.[32] He is convinced that Stresemann and his finance minister, the SPD economist Rudolf Hilferding, are disingenuously invoking the needs of German *industry* in order to justify this decision. By contrast, Spengler places the blame squarely on the role played by *finance* and the burden of reparations. He is livid and even castigates close allies such as Hugo Stinnes, who in the face of such a propaganda offensive on the part of the government remain unwilling to heed Spengler's advice and coordinate a campaign of 'newspaper defamations' that could undermine their opponents in press outlets friendly to Stresemann and Hilferding.[33] So Stresemann has to go. But who, and what, is to replace him?

Spengler sees in General Hans von Seeckt a potential figurehead for an elite Directorate to replace the Berlin government. Von Seeckt becomes Commander in Chief of the German army in the wake of the failed Kapp Putsch in March 1920, which attempts to overthrow the government and install a conservative administration in its place. But Spengler is well aware that von Seeckt is no defender of the republic from the right and that von Seeckt's appointment had been made 'despite his refusal to allow the army to defeat the putsch'.[34] One of the few areas where the putsch attempt of 1920 was successful, after all, was in Spengler's resident Bavaria, a stronghold of right-wing extremism. The Bavarian administration of the time comes into existence in 1920, after having ousted Adolf Hoffmann's SPD government. Instrumental in these developments is Spengler's ally von Kahr, who had first been appointed as head of the Bavarian government in

1921, only to resign following the national government's decree against 'the enemy on the right'.³⁵ By the end of 1923, in a situation of unrest and martial law in Bavaria, von Kahr is appointed State Commissioner of Bavaria. He oversees an administration that becomes something of a model for right-wing authoritarians opposed to the rule of Berlin. Some want the Bavarian bulwark of reaction to set out on its own path and split away from the German state altogether. Others, Spengler included, are opposed to these small-state perspectives (*Kleinstaaterei*), maintaining that Bavaria must pioneer a struggle against Berlin rather than isolate itself through secession.

There are also plans to overthrow the Weimar Republic from the left. In early October 1923, the German communists join local state governments in Saxony and Thuringia in order to pave the way for a seizure of power across Germany on 9 November.³⁶ This move becomes one of the catalysts for the German right's subsequent efforts to seize power. While troops are suppressing the revolutionary movement in the German East, von Kahr formally breaks off relations between Bavaria and Berlin. Thus, von Kahr, as de facto head of Bavaria, and von Seeckt, as head of the army, both become key players in the ensuing crisis. In a tense exchange between Friedrich Ebert, the SPD President of Germany, and von Seeckt, the former asks which forces the soldiers stand behind, to which von Seeckt famously replies: 'Behind me!'³⁷

Sensing that the historical horizons are opening up, Spengler meets with von Seeckt on 20 October 1923. He attempts to convince von Seeckt that power lies in his hands and that decisive action is required. Spengler even offers his services in any alternative administration that von Seeckt might lead.³⁸ But his efforts are to no avail and he henceforth speaks of von Seeckt as a 'downright opportunist'.³⁹ Indeed, by early November it becomes clear that, for all his ambitions, von Seeckt cannot countenance using his position to turn his forces against the republic. He upholds his loyalty to the Weimar Constitution when it needed him most.

Despite this disappointment, Spengler remains committed to the general position 'that if we are to prevent everything falling apart, it is necessary to replace the dictatorship of Stresemann and Seeckt with a non-parliamentary dictatorship'.⁴⁰ In this quote, we once again find evidence of Spengler's conception of crisis as opportunity. He is convinced that a dictatorship (of parliament and finance) already exists, so why not replace it with a genuine (non-parliamentary and thus German) dictatorship that has the nation's best interests at heart? His contacts are even informing him that such a prospect might be on the cards. Many officers in the German army are becoming estranged from their leader von Seeckt. Writing at the end of October, just nine days before the event that has gone down in history as the Munich Beer Hall Putsch, Spengler is convinced that:

> The German army is falling apart. The people and the young officers are against him [von Seeckt]. From here things can go anywhere. An opportunist at the head is the worst thing possible. Stresemann would have been finished a long time ago if it wasn't for von Seeckt … in 14 days the army can disintegrate, just as the old army did in November 1918.[41]

We need only recall the world-historical significance Spengler ascribes to the dissolution of the German army in November 1918 to grasp how pronounced is his impression that a fundamental overhaul of the structures of the Weimar Republic is now a distinct possibility. In fact, Spengler's prediction would come to be tested not within 14 days, but in just over a week, during the showdown between Berlin and Bavaria in the wake of the Beer Hall Putsch of 7–8 November 1923.

## Failure and Anger

Spengler's correspondence dries up somewhat during the period in and around the putsch. The final letter he sends before the attempted coup is from 4 November, but the next one is from 18 November.[42] This letter, sent to the banking director Hermann Münzing, expresses Spengler's expectation that the German Mark is about to plummet, and that Stresemann is seeking to hold on to power at all costs. The letter ends with a plea to destroy the correspondence: 'Please destroy this letter.'[43]

This expectation comes just ten days after the Beer Hall Putsch, to which Spengler is an eyewitness. The putsch sees Hitler and his supporters interrupt a speech given by von Kahr and proclaim the national revolution against the 'Marxist government' in Berlin. In a dramatic chain of events, Hitler holds von Kahr and his close allies – General Otto von Lossow and Colonel Hans von Seißer – captive and attempts to win them over to his plans. Von Kahr, von Lossow and von Seißer are committed to a national revolution, but feel that the Berlin administration has now 'weathered the worst of the crisis' and that the prospect of such a revolution is now over.[44] Hitler negotiates with the three hostages while holding them at gunpoint. When even this fails, General Ludendorff intervenes and wins them over. Convinced that all is well, Ludendorff then releases the men, whereupon they immediately arrange for the following day's uprising to be suppressed. Both Hitler and Ludendorff recognise that the success of their 'March on Berlin' requires not merely the unity of far-right groupings, but also 'the wholehearted support of the civilian and military authorities'.[45] The latter is now lost. And the outcome of the putsch, despite its later National Socialist instrumentalisation as embodying a key turning point in German history, is a farcical stand-off in the streets of Munich. The uprising is easily suppressed.

It is difficult to overstate Spengler's outrage at the events in Munich. On the one hand, he is furious at Hitler and Ludendorff. This is not because they are mistaken in attempting to seize the historical moment by marching on Berlin, but because their movement is too plebeian and inspired by a racist *völkisch* ideology, towards which Spengler is consistently sceptical. Moreover, the Hitler-Ludendorff putsch is timed to undermine the authority of the very men whom Spengler views as the statesmen required for a genuine Prussian alternative to the state structures created by the November Revolution. To Spengler's dismay, the lamentable upshot of the actions of the Hitler movement is the reconciliation of Berlin and Bavaria. As such, the Nazis play into the hands of Stresemann, who from the outset had been working towards such a rapprochement.

This assessment of the role played by the Hitlerites is shared by Elisabeth Förster-Nietzsche, who later becomes a committed National Socialist and chastises Spengler for not having gone down the same path. However, a foreshadowing of her subsequent veneration of Hitler is already apparent at this stage. In a letter dated 13 March 1924, she expresses her disappointment with the Hitler trial and hopes that nobody is punished, 'since, after all, they all acted passionately and patriotically to try and do the right thing for the fatherland'.[46] On the other hand, Spengler's frustration is aimed at figures such as von Kahr and von Seeckt for not grasping the opportunity that history has presented them. Yet it is unclear which alternative tactics Spengler could have proposed in order to accelerate the overthrow of the Berlin government. Although he welcomes the news that Ludendorff hopes to succeed the hesitant von Seeckt as head of the army, and meets with the former regularly for tea and political discussions,[47] it is uncertain whether Spengler's distrust of Hitler and the Battle League (Kampfbund) would have precluded some kind of short-term tactical alliance with those behind the 'March on Berlin'. When pressed by correspondents, Spengler often speciously refers to the egotism and inadequacy of the leaders as the root of the failure, but avoids further details. In a letter to Elisabeth Förster-Nietzsche written on New Year's Eve 1923, for example, he is rather nondescript in his assessment: 'I prefer to remain silent on everything that has been wasted in terms of political possibilities and ideals. It is a shame for the youth that they have fallen into the hands of such inferior leaders.'[48] He fails to draw a balance sheet of what had happened. When his allies press him for further information, he omits to mention what could have been done differently. This highlights both Spengler's ambivalent position in, and his assessment of, the crisis of 1923.

On another occasion, however, Spengler argues that the right-wing press should face some responsibility for the failure of the national revolution. In a letter to Nikolaus Cosmann, one of his hopes for a seat on the proposed *Pressezentrale*, Spengler chides the conservative media for failing to achieve clarity on the Hitler-Ludendorff movement. The *Münchner Neueste Nachrichten* (a 'rag')[49] comes under fire for failing to produce a coherent editorial line on Hitler and the young NSDAP. Instead of constructively criticising this movement from a conservative perspective – and thereby helping to rein in its radicalism and expose its illusions before an audience that would naturally be sympathetic to at least some of its aims – the *Münchner Neueste Nachrichten*, he claims, mainly pursued 'a tactic of silence … tantamount to support'.[50] It even printed statements by those such as Hitler and Ludendorff in prominent places.[51]

Spengler notes how he had constantly pushed the *MNN*'s editor, Fritz Gerlich,[52] to enter into polemics with the Hitler movement, but that such writings were hardly forthcoming. Things were so bad that the *MNN* was not even able to give extra prominence to pieces advertising meetings of the right-wing associations and groupings that desired a national overhaul, but also opposed Hitler.[53] These mistakes ensure that, when the *MNN* eventually takes a more explicit stand against Hitler in the aftermath of the events of 8–9 November, Spengler feels that these articles are characterised by embarrassing or embarrassed undertones. Even worse, in the wake of the putsch attempt, the *Münchner Neueste Nachrichten* carries articles promoting Bavarian-secessionist, small-state politics.[54]

Similarly, Spengler – convinced, as we have seen, that the press is crucial in making or breaking political movements – feels that the *Münchner Neueste Nachrichten* and other right-wing newspapers had contributed to von Kahr's inability to seize the moment. There was no constructive criticism of him or any coordinated attempt to push him along a distinct, alternative path. In Spengler's eyes, von Kahr's vacillation and hesitancy, which left a vacuum all too easily filled by Hitler and his supporters, could have perhaps been prevented: 'All this could have been avoided if Kahr had a press behind him that drove him on, instead of just registering what he had to say'.[55] Regardless of whether this objection flows from an inflated sense of self-importance, this is the closest thing Spengler offers to a critical reflection on the events of November 1923.

It should be noted, however, that Spengler is not yet of the view that the historical opening represented by the crisis of 1923 has passed. The letter to Elisabeth Förster-Nietzsche cited above expresses his conviction 'that we still need a terrible crisis in order for everything that we have inherited from 1918 to be swept away, and in the coming months there is every prospect of this'.[56] His belief that another national emergency – and thus an opening – lies in the near future, as well as his continued hope that the German nationalists will soon address their failings regarding a coordinated political and media assault, form the backdrop to his *Rebuilding the German Reich*.

## Demands for Rebuilding

The first reference to *Rebuilding the German Reich* within Spengler's correspondence can be found at the end of 1923. He informs Elisabeth Förster-Nietzsche that he has just completed another 'political book' that will be published in January 1924.[57] It eventually appears in May 1924, following several months of intense political engagements. These include Spengler giving five speeches in ten days on a trip to Switzerland, as well as an address he gives to a conservative student circle in Würzburg on 26 February 1924.[58] This speech is published as a standalone pamphlet entitled *The Political Duties of the German Youth*. In this address, held on the same day as the opening of the prosecution against Hitler and Ludendorff, Spengler seeks to deter the right-wing students from involvement in the ostentatious, short-termist radicalism of the Battle League and to devote themselves to a project of informed, self-sacrificing and statesman-like nationalism.

Spengler is convinced that the German youth are central to fulfilling the nation's 'mission' of emerging from its current plight and playing 'a historical role'.[59] However, in order for the next generation to contribute to this re-emergence of Germany, they must become conscious of how long and difficult the path is to Germany's revival as a country with a great future: 'It is your holy duty, gentlemen, not only to encourage others to achieve this goal, but to educate them to do so. Volition alone achieves nothing. Politics is an art that is most difficult to learn'.[60]

At this time – this point bears repeating – Spengler still believes that the opportunities for the advance of the German right have not yet passed. However, by the time *Rebuilding the German Reich* is published in May, however, the radically polarised environment of 1923 appears to be over. The Weimar elections of May 1924 confirm support for Wilhelm Marx, who had formed a minority administration on 30 November 1923 following the collapse of the Stresemann government. This marks the dawn of what Eberhard Kolb deems 'the phase of relative stabilization' in the history of the Weimar Republic.[61]

For this reason, Koktanek claims that *Rebuilding the German Reich* is a *post festum* publication. It does not exert the impact it might have done if it had appeared at the time when Spengler feels that Germany is undergoing a crisis comparable to that of November 1918. *Rebuilding the German Reich* thus does not experience the fortuitous timing of publication enjoyed by his magnum opus back in 1919; far from it. The changing nature of Spengler's correspondence makes it clear that by the autumn of 1924, he is far less occupied with campaigning work[62] and much more with intellectual endeavours. These include his appearance at the annual Orientalist Conference in Munich on 2 October and his keynote speech at the Nietzsche Archive, entitled 'Nietzsche and His Century' on 15 October.[63] This is the beginning of what is justifiably viewed as Spengler's 'return to research',[64] his temporary withdrawal from the political stage. If we are to understand the aims and outcomes of Spengler's political activities during his heightened political activities in 1923–24, it is essential to bear in mind the context in which *Rebuilding the German Reich* is conceived and published. Let us now turn to its arguments and demands.

*Rebuilding the German Reich* breaks down into eight chapters. The first and longest is entitled 'The Swamp'. It is a biting critique of the Weimar Republic, which Spengler lampoons as a sick, bitterly divided society – a formless swamp of base, competing material interests and divisions. It has ensured that political life has degenerated from a noble 'art of governance' (20) into – in a twist on von Clausewitz's definition of war – 'the continuation of private transactions by other means' (11).

Spengler claims that, after fighting and enduring hardship for four years 'like perhaps no other people before', Germany is now characterised by 'a pitifulness that is without precedent in world history' (3). Post-1918 Germany has entered the equivalent of the 'Directory period' (16) of the French Revolution. This period is the last governmental form of the Revolution, which sees executive power reside in a Directorate consisting of five Consulates. This body is then overthrown by Napoleon, who is elected First Consul a day later. Spengler maintains that the early years of republican Germany have been far inferior to the dramatic events of the decade after 1789, because the German Revolution 'possessed no belief in ideas or institutions. It had no personalities, no deeds – it was not even confident that its own rule would last' (16). He expands this historical analogy by referring to the *völkisch* movement in Germany as the contemporary manifestation of the gilded youth, the *jeunesse dorée*, during the French Revolution. These were gangs of wealthy, stylish young men who organised counter-revolutionary street actions. Both movements, he says, are excitable and committed, but they lack the necessary cool consideration and informed statesmanship to provide a viable alternative to the states established by the revolutions.

Spengler contends that only 'when tremendous adversity befalls a man does he show what is strong and good in him' (3). The duty of those disgusted by the tragedy of Germany's current situation is 'ruthlessly to locate the ulcer on the German body in order to heal a longstanding, insidious illness' (ibid.). For, in spite of Germany's enormous problems, historically she has been a pioneer in the fields of industry, religion, the officer corps and the state bureaucracy.

'The Swamp' further includes a historical overview of the perceived shortcomings of political leadership in Germany since Bismarck. Naturally, Spengler praises Bismarck, but adds that, for all his achievements, Bismarck was unable to train a new generation to carry on the baton of bold statesmanship. Spengler argues that this weakness flowed from a key strength. So skilled and far-sighted was the leading Prussian elite around Bismarck and so naturally did it deal with internal and external political challenges that it did not consider it necessary to delegate tasks to others, to educate the population in the conduct of state affairs that this grouping fulfilled almost without thinking. Had talented members of the German parties been awarded leadership of ministries or important diplomatic tasks, then they would have been able to broaden and entrench the ethos of statesmanship that characterised the Prussian elite.

The goal of *Rebuilding the German Reich* is to restore this form of political leadership and to break with the dominance of German parliamentarism; the Reichstag is described as a 'whiners' den' that is 'desolate, narrow-minded, philistine and conceited' (7). For when the men of the first generation of the German elite died off or left politics, a complete absence of 'political education' was the result, with 'schools, parties and the press' equally failing in this key task (7). Thus, the 'personalities' had been replaced by 'petty strivers, whingers, wirepullers and know-it-alls – all the kinds of untalented people that gather in the proximity of German beer' (6).

The various political demands advanced in *Rebuilding the German Reich* flow from Spengler's overriding aim of redressing this problem and creating the conditions in which strong leaders can emerge. His point of reference lies in the past, but his focus is on the future. As he puts it, '*a leading figure is necessary*, one who combines the creative characteristics of a people in relation to its historical situation and then develops them' (28).

'The Swamp' is followed by the chapter 'Public Service and Personality', in which Spengler expands on this discussion of genuine leadership and outlines his demands for a transformed civil service. This estate of officials must be built on the concept of selfless service, which must form the core of any successful state. To this end, Spengler makes the case for a number of changes to the state bureaucracy. It must be based not on the older, more entrenched members of the bureaucracy with their routine-ism and old habits, but rather the 'bright lads' of 1914, who can inject fresh dynamism into running the country (38). The programmatic aspects of the text come to the fore in this chapter, with Spengler liberally deploying a range of modal verbs alongside objectives and aims: 'The breeding of talent for the civil service *must* be fundamentally different for those in leading positions and those who carry out the orders of those leaders'; 'public service *should* ... have an educational impact beyond the individual offices' (37, emphasis added).

This programmatic approach also applies to the next chapter of *Rebuilding the German Reich*, which outlines Spengler's proposals to overhaul the education system, the smooth functioning of which is a precondition of a reinvigorated civil service. He attaches great importance to this aim of making the German youth 'different, more insightful, cleverer' (40). Indeed, he rather modestly notes that *Rebuilding the German Reich* does not deal with this matter in sufficient detail and promises to return to it in greater detail in a future text (ibid.).

Spengler contends that while humanist education conceived by Wilhelm von Humboldt can boast some impressive achievements, in the age of militarism and expansion, it is much better to focus on technical achievements, the practical use of language and hands-on work. Indeed, Spengler claims that Enlightenment-focused education is in part responsible for the emergence of the outlook of 'the German Michel' targeted in *Prussianism and Socialism*. This education has led to cleverly constructed liberal constitutional models and recitals of past poetry, but an aloofness from the unforgiving power politics of Faustian *Zivilisation*. Knowledge of the German economy, for instance, is far preferable to the natural fields of 'the German Michel', such as law and philosophy (34). This is quite a statement from somebody who, as we observed in Chapter 2, is predominantly remembered by subsequent scholarship as a philosopher of history.

Spengler's proposals for the education system reflect a polytechnic approach to learning. His proposals exhibit yet further modern characteristics insofar as they attempt to cater for those who are unable to excel in the school environment. He proposes that a 'school-leaving examination' or 'national examination' – 'a lesser doctor title' (50) – should be introduced for all adults, regardless of whether they have completed formal secondary education. If there is one area of life where Germany needs democracy, Spengler adds, it is here. Yet his relative egalitarianism, his rather relaxed attitude towards education – he proposes that the school day should last no longer than three or four hours (45) – and his sympathy for those who do not succeed in the school environment are offset by his call for a German Eton and 'to use the English phrase, *debating clubs*' (48). These are hothouses for the cultivation of the next generation of leaders.[65] Ultimately, Spengler's educational reforms are aimed at the breeding (*Zucht*) of the next generation of the elite and not at a rounded education (*Bildung*). There has, he claims, been far too little of the former and far too much of the latter; too much learning of Shakespeare and too little familiarity with *The Times* (42–43).

While some of Spengler's educational proposals may seem forward-thinking from the standpoint of the 1920s, then, his reforms are solely geared towards the elite: 'The separation of the upper classes and the lower classes should not be, like today, blurred by grammar school education or by students being moved up automatically. At the top the aims, traits and tasks are all quite different' (37). The institutions that provide the inspiration for his remodelling of education are the 'General Staff of the former German army and the Roman Senate', for 'the art of governance is not the first problem of high politics, but the only one' (20).

The overall structure of *Rebuilding the German Reich* begins to suffer somewhat with the introduction of the next chapter, 'Law as the Result of Duties'. Here, Spengler launches an attack on the concept of universal law propounded by liberal theory and contends, by contrast, that jurisprudence 'is not only the result of historical development, but above all the inner form of this existence, that is to say, the character of a nation' (49). Such a claim echoes assertions made by the German Historical School of Jurisprudence around thinkers such as Friedrich Karl von Savigny.[66]

Spengler contends that Germany is lacking precisely in a legal system corresponding to its national character, for the continued preoccupation with Roman law and its specific conception of jurisprudence is completely at odds with core Germanic concepts such as honour, property and the family. Germany's ideal legal system is not to be found in codified Roman law, but in the ruthless practice of the Roman praetor. This mix-up is yet another manifestation of history taking bitter revenge on the German people. The praetor did not bother to study Egyptian law, but 'saw himself as a civil servant, military leader and financier in all affairs of the Roman world surrounding him' (50). Rights can only flow from duties, not the other way around. For Germans, duty to the state must be the standard by which legal infringements are punished. Hence, if any individual commits an infringement against the honour of another, whether this be 'personal honour' or 'commercial honour', then this should entail 'a curtailment of rights ... and the rights of honour, freedom and property at that' (55). The primary considerations of Spengler's ideal legal system therefore revolve around determent through severe penalties. He is scornful of the idea that prison should primarily reform criminals, which he views as ensuring that felons live out an existence that is often above and beyond 'the living standards of the middle classes' (60). Finally, in an echo of the violent and often paranoid atmosphere of the times, *Rebuilding the German Reich* demands that it should be permissible for individuals to act, in the name of the state, against criminals when the state itself is absent, including when it comes to dealing with those suspected to be spies (58).

## Property and Socialism

In the next three chapters, 'The German Currency', 'Against Fiscal Bolshevism' and 'Labour and Property', Spengler shifts the focus to a theoretical-historical critique of Marxism that is similar to the arguments we outlined with regard to his *Prussianism and Socialism* in Chapter 5. One noteworthy alteration, however, comes in his discussion of the SPD. In contrast to *Prussianism and Socialism,* there is now only positive mention of August Bebel's achievements. Moreover, the praise for the 'Prussian' qualities of the SPD once expressed in *Prussianism and Socialism* is entirely absent, indicating how Spengler's critique of socialism – Prussian or otherwise – appears to be hardening. Indeed, the sole mention of socialism within *Rebuilding the German Reich* comes not in relation to labour or the innately socialist qualities of the Germans, but in relation to property. In contrast to *Prussianism and Socialism*, where the terms are often conflated, Spengler is referring not to *economic* socialism, but to *ethical* socialism as one *type* of socialism: 'Property, if we understand this word with all the moral seriousness of Germanic life, contains within it a kind of socialism too – a Prussian imperative, not an English one: Treat your property as if it had been *entrusted* to you by the people' (93). Spengler argues that the precondition of a strong German nation is that the propertied classes in that country – the industrial *and* the aristocratic elite – act in accordance with the maxim of 'property obliges'. Such an adage – a subtle dig at the aristocracy in its modification of the term *noblesse oblige* – is purportedly a reflection of the true Germanic conception of property. Unlike in *Prussianism and Socialism*, here Spengler does not dwell on the differences between 'English' and 'German' property as competing expressions of the Germanic outlook. The absence of such a discussion suggests either that this theme is not an enduring feature of his political thought or that he now views England as more of a marginal power on the world stage. As he puts it in *Rebuilding the German Reich*, England's diplomatic shortcomings have placed it 'in the service of French aims' for the first time in centuries (96).

Whereas in *Prussianism and Socialism* Spengler favoured a strong interventionist state and the central fixing of wages, in *Rebuilding the German Reich* these ideas have given way to a pronounced opposition to the taxation policies of the Weimar Republic. Spengler rather hyperbolically views these as a manifestation of Russian Bolshevism within Germany. Yet, it must be stressed that the implicit anti-capitalism of *Prussianism and Socialism* has not disappeared from *Rebuilding the German Reich*; however, it has been reduced to an opposition to *finance* capital. Spengler places great emphasis on the rapidly increasing detachment of possession as being characterised by actually owning something tangible – a process that has been accelerated by the interposition of loans, securities, shares and stakes, with ownership having now become 'moveable, invisible and intangible' (79). The outcome is that nobody really knows who owns a particular enterprise, fleet or factory, nor how much of an individual country's wealth lies beyond its borders. Spengler's opposition to this form of capital as nonproductive and elusive flows from his understanding that it undermines the integrity of the German nation:

> If we want to use the buzzword of the previous century, then there are two types of capitalists: the entrepreneur and the speculator. The latter has *capital*, the former has a factory. The former produces, whereas the latter exploits what has been produced. Money serves the one as an operating resource and the other as the object of a game. (93)

In *Rebuilding the German Reich*, we thus find a toning down of the purported significance of socialism to the German soul when compared to *Prussianism and Socialism*. Where does this significant change in perspective come from? In addition to Spengler's disgust at the role played by the SPD in the early Weimar Republic, it is possible to trace this reduced emphasis on socialism back to three factors.

First, Spengler's proximity to political power and his conviction that an anti-Weimar Directorate, on which he himself may sit, is now a distinct possibility. Many of his allies pursuing this project are highly suspicious of socialism of any stripe. In this respect, the fact that *Rebuilding the German Reich*'s only reference to socialism comes by way of a defence of property is highly revealing.

Second, Spengler's intimate links with German industry and its anti-trade union, low-taxation agenda can account for the shift in emphasis on the importance of socialism. This agenda becomes apparent in Spengler's distinction between entrepreneurship and speculation, as well as in his conviction that Weimar taxation represents 'the social revolution without the bloodshed' (84). He views this silent social revolution as a conscious effort to tax disproportionately those entrepreneurs who are selflessly advancing their capital in order to build up the German nation. The spectral nature of finance capital, by contrast, makes it largely impervious to taxation and thus parasitic on the productivity of Germany's economy. He thus sees a paradoxical sense in which the international workers' movement and international finance often unwittingly pull in the same direction in their demands for taxing the rich.[67] His distinction between what the National Socialist thinker Gottfried Feder later calls 'schaffendes' and 'raffendes' capital (capital that creates and capital that reaps profit) has wide purchase across the German right of the time.[68] However, there is no discernible anti-Semitic dimension to Spengler's opposition to finance and the workers' movement. The main motivation flows from his position as a lobbyist for industrial interests, not from biological or metaphysical considerations of Germanness and *race*. His position on this is much less clear in his last political publication, however, as we will discuss in the following chapter.

Third, the shift away from socialism can be seen to be reflective of his overwhelmingly negative experience of the fledgling National Socialist movement and the Battle League during the turmoil of 1923. Downplaying the prominence of socialist ideas within his thought therefore enables him to distance his project from organisations on the left *and* on the right.

There is nonetheless a certain continuity within Spengler's arguments on socialism between 1919 and 1924. As we have seen, the overriding concern of his Prussian socialism is that Germany's contending classes should rally behind a guiding idea of sacrifice, service and duty. This project presupposes eliminating the baleful influence of Marxism. The fact that Spengler reprints the opening section of *Prussianism and Socialism* ('The Revolution') as a standalone publication entitled *The Revolution Is Not Over* in 1924 also testifies to the fact that he views the arguments he outlined in 1919 as a roadmap to the events of 1924.

In total, Spengler produces four political publications in 1924. In addition to *Rebuilding the German Reich*, he publishes three editions of some of his earlier writings: *The Revolution Is Not Over* and standalone reprints of two chapters from Volume 2 of *The Decline of the West* ('The State' and 'The Economy'). *The Revolution Is Not Over* was published as part of the of 'Texts to the Nation' Series.[69] Hence, we find pragmatic modifications and adaptations of his ideas and a shifting target audience during these five years, but there is a clear underlying continuity. The shifts in his thought appear to stem from the spirit of the times in which the texts are written and the nature of the plans he is pursuing. The core theme of *Preußentum* is present in both, but the grand narrative of Prussian socialism has been overshadowed by the focus on *Realpolitik* and programmatic objectives in *Rebuilding the German Reich*.

The final chapter of the book, 'On the World Situation', explores how developments in Germany interrelate with, and are influenced by, the global situation. Spengler's attention is aimed at the enemy on both fronts. Looking to France, he is scathing. Instead of pursuing the kind of civilising imperialism he envisages as part of Faustian culture's tendency to impose its own ideals universally, France represents 'the bloodiest, and the same time the most successful coloniser that there is' (98). French *revanchism* strives to transform Germany into a 'reparations colony', a 'European India' (14). To the East, Spengler is keeping a close eye on developments within Soviet Russia, following the death of Lenin in

January 1924. He describes this event as marking the shift of Bolshevism from a largely European phenomenon to an Asiatic one.

In our overview of *Rebuilding the German Reich*, we have outlined how Spengler advances a range of demands in relation to Germany's state bureaucracy, the law, the education system and the economy as part of his programme to revitalise the sick German political body. In so doing, we have demonstrated how *Rebuilding the German Reich* evinces Spengler's consistent opposition to democracy as a manifestation of decadence, his elitist conception of politics and education, and his polemics against Marxism. We have further shown how the context in which *Rebuilding the German Reich* is written finds reflection in the text's arguments and demands.

More generally, we have made the case that, given its focus on *Realpolitik* and immediate demands for an alternative conservative government, *Rebuilding the German Reich* is Spengler's most explicitly programmatic text. At the same time, we have seen how its length, lack of internal coherence and the dispersion of its demands among typically Spenglerian historical excurses ensure that it can only be viewed as programmatic with reservations. Hence, the book amounts to an uneasy balance between the determined aspects of Spengler's diagnosis of Western decline and his programmatic or interventionist prognosis. The outcome of this tension is Spengler's pragmatism in modifying or updating certain ideas in his scheme (socialism being a case in point), but also his retention of others (such as his opposition to parties, even at a time when he is actively trying to coordinate a German-nationalist *lodge*).

Compared to *Prussianism and Socialism*, in which sweeping rhetoric overshadows detailed plans for an alternative state, the constitutional proposals in *Rebuilding the German Reich* are more concrete. As a result, the text exhibits a disjuncture between his lofty attempts to ready the German state for the global power struggles ahead and his rather prosaic, or banal, proposals. These proposals include the idea that civil servants should remain sharp-minded by participating in sport in their spare time (as in England, apparently), that uniforms and titles should be upheld and respected, that relations between colleagues should be characterised by 'example, criticism and instruction' (36) and that any local official should be offered possibilities for promotion (ibid.). On occasion, his programme for the state is more akin to a modern-day management restructuring programme geared towards the minutiae of the state bureaucracy than to a *longue durée* exposition on the end of democracy. For all his continued emphasis on the significance of politics on the grand scale (*Großpolitik*) to Germany's future, this section reveals a man who feels compelled to concern himself with the machinations of petty politics (*Kleinpolitik*) in remarkable detail.

## Two Stages towards the Caesar

How does Spengler envisage the realisation of the aims scattered across *Rebuilding the German Reich*? What kind of governmental form can achieve the changes he wishes to bring about? Is the text's comprehensive discussion of *Kleinpolitik* indicative of a more moderate thinker who largely dispenses with the 'heroic realism'[70] of *Prussianism and Socialism* to embrace a more 'classically conservative'[71] or even German Tory[72] approach? Answering these questions will shed further light on Spengler's political theory by demonstrating his ideal state form at this point in his career and by revealing how it relates to his concept of Caesarism.

Our discussion of *Rebuilding the German Reich* has not yet had occasion to discuss the concept of Caesarism in any detail. In fact, the idea is nowhere near as central to the text as it is in Volume 2 of *The Decline of the West*. Nonetheless, *Rebuilding the German Reich* concludes with a striking statement on the emergence of strong personalities and dictatorial political forms:

> and with this, an awareness of no longer being tied to the existing forms emerges on the other side too – the side of tradition, of national power, of honour and inherited property. Today, coups and dictatorships are integral components in the style of political action – and all the more so, since they are more than compatible with the preservation of parliamentary forms, even of English ones.
>
> But the decision thereby moves from problems of form to the existence and will of strong personalities. Soviet Russia *was* Lenin, South Africa *was* Rhodes, Mussolini *is* Italy. Today, no parliament, no party, no army has the decisions in its hands. Everywhere, these are exclusively in the presence or absence of individual men – their *personal* decisions, ideas and aims ... These are the prospects for even the smallest country. The preparedness is all. (104)

It should come as little surprise that Spengler explicitly affirms the need to break with 'the existing forms' of political representation, or that he calls for putsches to overthrow government power and establish a strong political dictatorship. We have already discussed his conviction that Caesarism will eclipse the era of parliamentary democracy and have seen how, in practical terms, Spengler conspires with co-thinkers for a coup that, he felt, could avert the ruin of the German nation. However, what is more surprising is that the alternative state outlined in *Rebuilding the German Reich* allows for the formal existence of a Reichstag legislative body chosen by universal election. For this reason, the text is sometimes viewed as indicative of a less radical stage in Spengler's career following the failure of the radical putschism in 1923. Koktanek, for instance, argues that Spengler's attitude towards parliament is 'not consistent, even if it is generally dismissive' and notes that the constitutional arguments in *Rebuilding the German*

*Reich* testify to a point in Spengler's career when his disdain for the parliamentary form is less pronounced. Koktanek's assertion that in *Rebuilding the German Reich* 'parliament is not to be abolished, but in keeping with the demands of the new period, is to be turned into an expert assembly' is formally correct.[73] Yet, as we will see below, this statement overlooks how Spengler's proposals to weaken the German parliament are tantamount to that body's negation as a democratically representative institution.

Markus Henkel's study, *Nationalkonservative Politik und mediale Repräsentation. Oswald Spenglers politische Philosophie und Programmatik im Netzwerk der Oligarchen (1910–1925)*, is the most impressive discussion of Spengler in the 1920s and is successful in demonstrating 'the significance of Spengler as a "disruptive factor" in politics'.[74] Nonetheless, when it comes to Spengler's ideas in the 1920s, Henkel claims that – despite Spengler's 'cultural-philosophical' recognition that, in the longer term, democracy is doomed and Caesarism looms large on the historical agenda – Spengler's political-programmatic project is that of a reluctant democrat. Henkel claims that even though Spengler despises parliamentary democracy in Germany as an alien and artificial phenomenon, Spengler nonetheless feels that parliament should be exploited in a pragmatic-conservative fashion to *stall* or *offset* the emergence of Caesarism. Henkel describes this as Spengler's 'openly declared belief in an (unbeloved) pluralistic democracy'.[75] Henkel thus claims that Spengler pragmatically sees the necessity of embracing parliamentary democracy in order to 'be able to *counteract* the Caesarism that was heralded abroad in the wake of the seizure of power by leader figures such as Rhodes, Lenin and Mussolini'.[76]

However, Henkel's argument fails to address Spengler's praise for *certain types* of Caesar figures, not least Rhodes and Mussolini. Spengler by no means views these men as the products scraped from the bottom of a barrel of an increasingly decadent political leadership, but rather as the incarnations of the true ruler (*Herrscher*) demanded by their countries in Faustian *Zivilisation*. In this instance, Henkel's study is unable to show how Spengler's politics develop not merely *in opposition* to his metahistorical considerations, but also in *harmony* with them.

Sebastian Maaß goes further than Henkel and Koktanek. He claims that *Rebuilding the German Reich* not only reflects a change from the radicalism of the Spengler of the Conservative Revolution to a more pragmatic conservatism, but also that Spengler strives to integrate 'a democratic element' into his political philosophy.[77] In Chapter 2, we described how the secondary literature on Spengler is unduly indifferent to changes and developments within Spengler's ideas and how it tends to view his political thought as an unchanging whole. In this instance, however, we will make the opposite case: to wit, that Maaß's and Koktanek's noting of a change in Spengler's conception of democracy is erroneous.

In order to see why this is the case, we need only highlight Spengler's consistent admiration for what he sees as the sham of parliamentarism in England. Here, the ruling aristocracy still sits comfortably in the saddle of power, not *despite* but *because* of the existence of parliament. As he puts it:

> Since George I, the focus of authority is to be found in the cabinet, which does not even exist in the constitution, as the committee of the faction of the aristocracy that is ruling at the time. Absolutism is present, but it is that of a representation of the estates. The concept of *lèse-majesté* is transferred to parliament, just as the inviolability of the Roman kings was to the Tribunes.[78]

This apparent state of affairs is clearly what Spengler has in mind when claiming that his proposed dictatorship is compatible with the 'preservation of parliamentary forms, even of English ones' (104). His proposals can thus be viewed as allowing for the continued de jure existence of the German Reichstag, but its de facto abolition.

A closer look at Spengler's constitutional proposals in *Rebuilding the German Reich* will illustrate how he foresees this process. He wishes to see 'an extraordinary strengthening of the government's power with great responsibilities' (24) relative to parliament. This amounts to giving the Reichstag the status of something along the lines of the 'fig-leaf of Absolutism'[79] it once enjoyed in the days of the North German Confederation and in the German Kaiserreich. And perhaps it would be even more toothless an institution than in the days of the Kaiser. For instance, Spengler proposes that this body, while elected by universal suffrage, should meet but twice a year, 'for short meetings' (25). These sittings will not be a forum to debate policy or to criticise the executive branch of government. They will merely vote on matters such as legislation and the budget. In addition, they will reject or approve the government's annual report. As Spengler puts it: 'It is not aims, but results that should be subject to criticism [expressed by the Reichstag]' (24).

All the while, in Spengler's plan the government retains the right to dissolve the parliament whenever it sees fit – a power also enjoyed by Wilhelm II, for instance – and to convene new elections. In these elections, only four parties are permitted to stand candidates (Spengler does not elaborate which parties he has in mind). If a party fails to achieve 10% of the popular vote, then it will be denied representation altogether. The Reichstag will be limited to a body of 150 seats and will contain as few party officials as possible. Ideally, it should be composed of experts. This technocratic conception of politics, in which the smooth functioning of the state machine trumps any considerations of democratic legitimacy and accountability, even leads Spengler to entertain the possibility 'of demanding a kind of qualifying certificate from parliamentary representatives', thereby excluding 'the bawlers, the drummers and the pipers' from various party organisations (26).⁸⁰ Even this is slightly more democratic than a proposal he entertains at another point, namely to kick out all of the Reichstag deputies and replace them with 400 economic experts: 'In my view, the best "election to the Reichstag" would be if the four hundred most significant representatives of our economy were brought into the building and the rest were thrown out.'⁸¹

The Chancellor presides over enormous power relative to parliament: 'the ministers are responsible to him alone and he alone is responsible for the ministers' (24). He should possess the authority to create his own general staff and have complete freedom to choose the number, composition and organisation of the ministries and the entire government apparatus. Although this presidential power could perhaps be slightly offset by the existence of a second chamber, a Staatsrat, which is a feature of a number of modern constitutions, this body cannot make any decisions. It can only discuss proposals and make suggestions: Spengler argues that it should focus on discussing proposals and thereby become a higher school for young talent (ibid.) – a salon for future success to accompany Spengler's German Eton and the 'debating clubs'.

Contrary to what Koktanek and Maaß claim, then, Spengler does not moderate or modify his stance towards parliamentarism in any meaningful sense. Nor, as Henkel puts it, can his proposals be viewed as embodying a modern state in keeping with the demands of the democratic age.⁸² At best, Spengler's incorporation of a parliament with highly attenuated powers into his plans to overthrow Weimar Germany is not dissimilar to his engagement with *socialism* in *Prussianism and Socialism*. He incorporates a concept into his political proposals in order to rid it of its real content at the same time. His disgust at the existence of parliamentary democracy in his theory of history remains a fundamental tenet of his political thought.

Spengler is explicit that his proposals for Germany have more in common with monarchism than with modern parliamentarism. Whereas he once made the claim that the Germans are inherently socialist in nature, he now maintains that a monarchism lies dormant in their soul: 'The Germans are a monarchical people due to their ancient Germanic traits of adherence and submission to the leader that they inwardly recognise.'⁸³ He adds that 'one day, when some sunshine falls on us again, the sleeping desire for this symbolic crowning of the state will be fulfilled' (27).

But how do Spengler's thoughts on a German monarchy relate to his understanding of Caesarism? For Thomas Tartsch, the head of Spengler's proposed state will not necessarily be a Caesar figure, as a monarch could fulfil the same function.⁸⁴ However, this is misleading, for *Rebuilding the German Reich* views the power of the monarchy as consisting in its political symbolism. It is no substitute for an emerging Caesar to preside over the state. In order to make this point, Spengler once against looks across the Channel, arguing that English parliamentarism's 'greatness is based on the fact that *formally speaking*, it is the King that chooses the Prime Minister' (ibid., emphasis added). While this is a mere formality, with the monarch invariably assenting to the proposal from the party with the most seats,[85] Spengler feels that this act of appointment is historically momentous. It provides the nation with a figure who stands 'above all parties and commercial interests' and thus provides moral foundations for the country (ibid.). This cohesion reflects the country's historical and dynastical traditions, and such emblematic national unity is utterly absent when parties wrangle over who is to be the head of state. In their entirety, therefore, the proposed reforms in *Rebuilding the German Reich* – even in the absence of a restored German monarchy – do not amount to Spengler's rapprochement with democracy, but rather to its effective dissolution. As in 1919, Spengler is convinced that the Weimar Constitution and its structures must be overhauled.

There is a more fundamental sense in which statements regarding Spengler's purported moderation in *Rebuilding the German Reich* are misguided. They overlook the way in which his conception of the state relates chronologically to the emergence of the German Caesar of Faustian *Zivilisation*. In other words, they fail to grasp how Spengler's constitutional proposals in 1924 are tantamount to his earlier plans for a Directorate, befitting of Germany's own Directory Period. In Spengler's proposed state, the executive wing of government, particularly the Chancellor, would be so dominant, so decoupled from popular sovereignty and so overwhelmingly composed of the German elite that it would form something akin to the French Directorate at the end of the eighteenth century before its overthrow by Napoleon.

The fact that Spengler outlines his constitutional alternative at some length underlines the point we made in Chapter 5: his use of the term *Zufall* to describe the emergence of a Caesar to banish the exhausted forms of democracy should be understood not in terms of 'chance' or 'accident', but rather 'contingency'. This significant point is entirely absent in the secondary literature on Spengler's politics.

In a similar fashion to Maaß and Henkel, for example, Walter Struve asserts that 'Spengler's rhapsodic discourses on Caesarism obscured his basic goal – the establishment of a single, stable elite upon much the same social basis as the *Junker*-bourgeois coalition in Wilhelminian Germany except that big businessmen would play an even more important role'.[86] However, the alternative state proposed in *Rebuilding the German Reich*, as its concluding passage underlines, is neither a *Junker*-bourgeois state form that is an end in itself nor a mere holding measure to await the arrival of a German strongman, but a very *precondition* of that figure's arrival. It is not, as Spengler's contemporary Theodor Heuss has it, the 'business project of a dictator' per se,[87] but rather a transitional framework to create the conditions within which a future dictator can appear from the elite layer of experts and officials. As we have seen, Spengler envisages his political strongman emerging not from the streets, but from the salon, not from rabble-rousing processions and rallies (here we need only recall his comments on the *jeunesse dorée* during the French directorate period), but in close consultation with the very business and political forces with which he is allied at this time. It is for this reason that Mussolini's close consultation with the business world receives particular acclaim from Spengler: 'But fascism at least understood how to consult with the most significant forces in the economy at the right time, for it was concerned with success and not with programmes and parades.'[88] Taken together with his other proposals and demands for a revitalised and effective state bureaucracy, *Rebuilding the German Reich* endeavours not to bring into being the final Caesarist state form, but to create the conditions within which world-historical figures of Caesarian magnitude can be cultivated.

*Rebuilding the German Reich* sheds important light on the precise nature of Spengler's proposed course of political action for Germany. Our discussion of the text has facilitated an understanding of how his thought has developed since the publication of *Prussianism and Socialism* against the backdrop of the revolutionary crisis of 1919. By outlining the context in which both texts are composed, we can account for the shifts in emphasis and modifications in Spengler's outlook on socialism, the monarchy and the changing nature of his ideal German state, but also locate the continuities in his ideas. By 1924, the realism of what Maaß calls Spengler's 'heroic realism' appears to have become more dominant.[89] As we have seen, however, the fact that Spengler seems to be more pragmatic and detailed in his political plans should not lead us to the conclusion that he has become more moderate in his outlook and aims.

Spengler's commitment to the development of a German Caesar, as opposed to another Goethe, is as unswerving in 1924 as it was in Volume 2 of *The Decline of the West*. But what will Spengler's Caesarist figure look like? We have already observed that the final lines of *Rebuilding the German Reich* offer praise for Mussolini. What is more, in the speech Spengler gives to the conservative student group in Würzburg in February 1924, he states explicitly that those present are witnessing:

> the end of democracy. Not its collapse, but its irrevocable inner decay: the less that democratic forms mean in future, the less we will have to worry about allowing its forms to continue to exist. This process would not have been understood before the war; today it is impossible to overlook: wherever you look in Europe and in America, where the farmers' movement essentially wants the same thing as Italian fascism. The best Germans, and not only the Germans, are waiting for a man to

appear, in whose hands we can place the destiny of the country, with the authority to repulse all those who, in the interests of individual groups, seek to curtail this authority.[90]

Particularly in view of the rise of Hitler less than a decade later, this implicit equation of Caesarism with fascism is quite a remarkable statement, as it suggests that the coming Caesar might just resemble a German Mussolini. It is to this highly controversial matter of Spengler's intellectual relationship with fascism – and National Socialism in particular – that we will turn in the next chapter of this book.

## Notes

1. Kolb, *The Weimar Republic*, 34.
2. Maaß, *Oswald Spengler. Eine politische Biographie*, 55–62; Tartsch, *Denn der Mensch ist ein Raubtier*, 135–47.
3. Conte, *Oswald Spengler. Eine Einführung*, 63.
4. Henkel, *Nationalkonservative Politik und mediale Repräsentation. Oswald Spenglers politische Philosophie und Programmatik im Netzwerk der Oligarchen (1910–1925)*, 414.
5. Ibid., 412, emphasis added.
6. This aspect of his career was first highlighted by Anton Mirko Koktanek's biography of Spengler in 1968: Koktanek, *Oswald Spengler in seiner Zeit*. Henkel is nonetheless the only thinker to appreciate the significance of this period in Spengler's political thought.
7. Spengler to Paul Reusch, 30 December 1924, in Spengler, *Briefe 1913–36*, 373.
8. Struve, *Elites against Democracy: Leadership Ideals in Bourgeois Political Thought in Germany, 1890–1933*, 240. Struve claims that the name of the grouping is 'probably not an abbreviation', but 'may have referred to the Greek earth goddess Gaea'; ibid., fn. 33.
9. Koktanek, *Spengler in seiner Zeit*, 290. Von Kahr is associated with Crown Prince Rupprecht and helps the latter in his attempts to return to the throne.
10. Ibid., 276.
11. Ibid., 46.
12. Spengler to Gustav Stresemann, 26 September 1923, in Spengler *Briefe 1913–36*, 271–72.
13. Spengler, *Der Untergang des Abendlandes. Umrisse einer Morphologie der Weltgeschichte*, 2 vols (1997 [1923]), 1119.
14. Cf. Hoser, 'Ein Philosoph im Irrgarten der Politik. Oswald Spenglers Pläne für eine geheime Lenkung der nationalen Presse', 440.
15. Ibid., 438.
16. Ibid., 436, 438, 441.
17. Ibid., 440.
18. The entire discussion is available as a pamphlet published by the KPD: Frölich, Reventlow and Moeller van den Bruck, *Schlageter. Eine Auseinandersetzung*.
19. One instance of this is Spengler gaining Reusch's agreement to transfer 150,000 German marks to a certain Major von Wäninger in January 1923. Reusch is concerned about transferring such a princely sum directly to von Wäninger and so arranges for it to be sent via Spengler instead; Spengler to Reusch, 3 January 1923, in Spengler, *Briefe 1913–36*, 234–35.
20. Hoser, 'Ein Philosoph im Irrgarten der Politik', 448.
21. Cf. Koktanek, *Spengler in seiner Zeit*, 284.
22. Hoser, 'Ein Philosoph im Irrgarten der Politik', 456.

23. Cf. Henkel, *Nationalkonservative Politik*, 303.
24. Koktanek, *Spengler in seiner Zeit*, 269. In all likelihood, Koktanek's use of the term 'invisible lodge' is a reference to Jean Paul's *Die unsichtbare Loge*.
25. See, for example, Karl Radek's obituary of the murdered far-right activist Leo Schlageter; Radek, 'Leo Schageter, der Wanderer ins Nichts'.
26. Spengler, *Neubau des deutschen Reiches*, 13. Subsequent references to this publication in this chapter will be placed in parentheses in the main text.
27. Spengler to Reusch, 17 August 1923, in Spengler, *Briefe 1913–36*, 260.
28. Ibid.
29. Ibid.
30. Ibid.
31. Spengler to Gerhard von Janson, 9 September 1923, in ibid., 266–67.
32. Henkel correctly claims that the Ruhr crisis, alongside the First World War and the November Revolution, has the biggest impact on the development of Spengler's politics: Henkel, *Nationalkonservative Politik*, 306.
33. Spengler to Paul Reusch, 9 September 1923, in Spengler, *Briefe 1913–36*, 268.
34. Kolb, *The Weimar Republic*, 37.
35. The words of SPD Chancellor Joseph Wirth in a Reichstag speech held one day after the assassination of Walther Rathenau in June 1922. According to Wirth's biographer, Ulrike Hörste-Phillips, Wirth was not seeking to make a sweeping condemnation of the Weimar right as a whole, but rather to single out those forces that had created the atmosphere in which such an assassination could occur; see Hörste-Phillips, *Joseph Wirth 1879–1956. Eine politische Biographie*, 464. However, as Spengler's activities demonstrate, the organisational and ideological boundaries between the traditional German right and the paramilitary organisations are most porous.
36. An excellent summary of these developments can be found in Broué, *The German Revolution 1917–1923*, 791–816.
37. Cf. Schäfer, *Die Militärstrategie Seeckts*, 167.
38. Koktanek, *Spengler in seiner Zeit*, 289.
39. Spengler to Paul Reusch, 31 October 1923, in Spengler, *Briefe 1913–36*, 284.
40. Spengler to Gerhard von Janson, 30 October 1923, in ibid., 281.
41. Spengler to Reinhold Quaatz, 30 October 1923, in ibid., 283.
42. The absence of some of Spengler's responses to questions from correspondents has prompted J. Vogt to call into question Koktanek's editorship of Spengler's published correspondence; Vogt, 'Rezension zu Oswald Spengler, "Briefe 1913–36"', 462. However, for Henkel, there are 'clear gaps' in the Spengler archive when it comes to his correspondence from the 1920s; Henkel, *Nationalkonservative Politik*, 26, fn. 55. This seems to suggest that Spengler – and the people to whom he wrote – destroyed some of their seditious exchanges (as in the case of Spengler's letter to Hermann Münzing cited in footnote 43 below). As we will see in Chapter 7, Spengler's fear of his more sensitive correspondence falling into the hands of the Nazi regime leads to him to destroy several of his letters.
43. Spengler to Hermann Münzing, 18 November 1923, in Spengler, *Briefe 1913–36*, 287.
44. Carr, *Hitler: A Study in Personality and Politics*, 18.
45. Ibid., 17.
46. Elisabeth Förster-Nietzsche to Spengler, 13 March 1924, in Spengler, *Briefe 1913–36*, 306.
47. Erich Ludendorff to Spengler, 21 October 1923, in ibid., 279.
48. Spengler to Förster-Nietzsche, 31 December 1923, in ibid., 296. Henkel views this letter as an expression of Spengler's disillusionment, but it can equally be viewed as an indication of Spengler's unwillingness to discuss the event in any detail; Henkel, *Nationalkonservative Politik*, 324.
49. Cf. Hoser, 'Ein Philosoph im Irrgarten der Politik', 454.
50. Spengler to Nikolaus Cossmann, 1 December 1923, in Spengler, *Briefe 1913–36*, 291.
51. Ibid., 290.

52. According to Koktanek: 'However, Spengler's hopes of working with Professor Nikolaus Cossmann to give this newspaper a profile that corresponded to his own ideas did not materialise, particularly because the editor Dr. Fritz Gerlich went his own way'; Koktanek, *Oswald Spengler in seiner Zeit*, 282. Gerlich's later journalism was extremely critical of Hitler; he eventually died in a Nazi concentration camp.
53. Spengler to Cossman, 1 December 1923, in Spengler, *Briefe 1913–36*, 290.
54. Spengler to Reusch, 2 December 1923, in ibid., 293.
55. Spengler to Cossman, 1 December 1923, in ibid., 291.
56. Spengler to Förster-Nietzsche, 31 December 1923, in ibid., 296.
57. Ibid.
58. Spengler to Hilde Kornhardt, 18 February 1924, in ibid., 300.
59. Spengler, 'Politische Pflichten der deutschen Jugend', 129.
60. Ibid.
61. For a discussion of this period, see Kolb, *The Weimar Republic*, 51–95.
62. Nonetheless, there are scattered references to his continued plans for the German right, as expressed in his letter to Reusch; Spengler to Reusch, 30 December 1924, in Spengler, *Briefe 1913–36*, 372.
63. Spengler, 'Plan eines neuen Atlas Antiquus', 85–92; Spengler 'Nietzsche und sein Jahrhundert', 98–110.
64. Koktanek, *Spengler in seiner Zeit*, 309.
65. Accordingly, Markus Henkel's description of these demands as a form of 'social education policy' seems a little far-fetched; Henkel, *Nationalkonservative Politik*, 374.
66. A school of thought criticised by Marx as reactionary: see de Berg and Large (eds), *Modern German Thought from Kant to Habermas*, 129, fn. 21.
67. It should be noted that he also makes this point in Volume 2 of *The Decline of the West*; Spengler, *Der Untergang des Abendlandes*, 1073.
68. On this, see Herf, *Reactionary Modernism: Technology, Culture and Politics in Weimar and the Third Reich*, 190.
69. Spengler, *Die Revolution ist nicht zu Ende*, Schriften an die Nation, 35.
70. Maaß, *Oswald Spengler*, 23.
71. Conte, *Oswald Spengler*, 63.
72. Henkel, *Nationalkonservative Politik*, 414.
73. Koktanek, 'Spenglers Verhältnis zum Nationalsozialismus in geschichtlicher Entwicklung', 36.
74. Henkel, *Nationalkonservative Politik*, 358.
75. Ibid., 416.
76. Ibid., 376.
77. Maaß, *Oswald Spengler*, 57.
78. Spengler, *Der Untergang des Abendlandes. Umrisse einer Morphologie der Weltgeschichte*, 1049.
79. The words of Wilhelm Liebknecht in 1867 during a parliamentary session of the Reichstag des norddeutschen Bundes, cited in Eisner, *Wilhelm Liebknecht. Sein Leben und Wirken*, 40.
80. This is probably a dig at Hitler, who was sometimes called the 'drummer' of National Socialism. See Tyrell, *Vom 'Trommler' zum 'Führer'. Der Wandel von Hitlers Selbstverständnis zwischen 1919 und 1924 und die Entwicklung der NSDAP*.
81. Cf. Koktanek, 'Spenglers Verhältnis', 36.
82. Henkel, *Nationalkonservative Politik*, 412.
83. In retrospect, this is a badly chosen term. However, given the discussion above, it is evident that Spengler is not thinking of Adolf Hitler.
84. Tartsch, *Denn der Mensch ist ein Raubtier*, 147.
85. However, Spengler overlooks how the monarch must not necessarily choose the leader of the majority party as the Prime Minister. In 1894, Queen Victoria passed over the claims of Sir William Harcourt and appointed Lord Rosebery to become Prime Minister instead; in 1923,

George V appointed Stanley Baldwin, not Lord Curzon, who was previously the Deputy Prime Minister.
86. Struve, *Elites against Democracy*, 269. Struve qualifies this statement by claiming that the great leader needed to achieve this aim will be if not 'a true Caesar', then his 'precursor'. But there is no discussion of the connections between Spengler's reforms and the establishment of Caesarism in Germany.
87. Heuss, 'Das Geschäftsprojekt des Diktators'.
88. Spengler, 'Politische Pflichten der deutschen Jugend', 152.
89. Maaß, *Oswald Spengler*, 23.
90. Spengler, 'Politische Pflichten der deutschen Jugend', 144.

CHAPTER 7

# Decisive Years
## *Spengler and National Socialism*

Almost without exception, the scholarly studies of Spengler discussed in Chapter 2 devote entire sections to an analysis of his understanding of National Socialism.[1] It is, after all, one of the first questions that spring to mind when his name is mentioned.

Secondary literature tends to oscillate between two extremes when it comes to Spengler and National Socialism. On the one hand, there are outright condemnations of him: either as a proto-Nazi or as a forerunner of National Socialism whose ideas garner profoundly anti-democratic and authoritarian sentiments in Weimar Germany. Clemens Vollnhals, for instance, suggests that Spengler's denunciation of the Weimar Republic as a historical aberration manufactured by the Allies 'pre-empted ... the slogan of "National Socialism" that was propagated by Hitler soon afterwards'.[2] In a similarly teleological fashion, GDR historiography sought to portray Spengler as a precursor of fascism insofar as his 'ultra-reactionary bourgeois outlook corresponded to the ruling interests of the German monopoly bourgeoisie' – the class that, so it was claimed, was the driving force behind the ultimate success of the Hitler movement.[3]

On the other hand, far more apologetic accounts exist, which portray Spengler and his conception of late Faustian, Caesarist nationalism as a bona fide, viable *alternative* to the rise of Nazism. According to Sebastian Maaß, for example, Spengler is best understood as a 'dissenter' from the Nazi cause.[4] Maaß is suggesting here that there could have been a Spenglerian alternative for Germany that was free of the pitfalls of both National Socialism and Bolshevik-inspired communism.

There are also more nuanced accounts. Thus, Detlef Felken claims that Spengler should be seen neither as a principled opponent of National Socialism nor as a supporter of the NSDAP who publicly endorses that movement. To make this case, Felken provides a comprehensive overview of Spengler's engagement with Hitler and National Socialism. He concludes that Spengler cannot be accused of *opportunism* in his response to the Nazi regime:

> If he was really an opportunist, then he would have taken the opportunity on Potsdam Day [21 March 1933 – see below] to throw himself into the arms of National Socialism with an unctuous speech. He certainly could have secured for himself a laureate role in the Third Reich. But Spengler thought too much in dimensions of his own greatness to content himself with the part of an ideological window-dresser. His *conditio sine qua non* for cooperating with the regime was a concrete influence on political development in order to push through his own understanding of the revolution. He wanted nothing less than to provide thought-provoking impulses, which he felt Hitler so urgently needed.[5]

Although this is true, Felken's discussion of Spengler and fascism is weakened by the conviction that Spengler's politics, including vis-à-vis National Socialism, are invariably the logical manifestation of his philosophy of history. This approach cannot account for Spengler's complex, shifting and multifaceted intellectual interaction with the phenomenon of fascism. If there is one instance in Spengler's career when the tension between his diagnosis of the rise of Caesarism and his response to unfolding events becomes most apparent, then it is in the 1930s.

For this reason, Walter Struve's distinction between two phases in Spengler's attitude towards the German National Socialists is more useful. In the first phase, lasting until 1933 or 'perhaps as late as the middle of 1934', Struve says, Spengler 'welcomed them [the Nazis], but he wished to see them used and held in check by those on the Right to whom he felt closer'.[6] In the second phase, by contrast, Spengler is convinced that the Nazis might be interfering with the emergence of genuine Caesarism. Struve notes: 'His basic position during the two phases was similar; what changed was his assessment of the consequences of Nazi tactics.'[7] However, Struve's account of Spengler and National Socialism is rather pinched and does not involve a detailed discussion of Spengler's *The Hour of Decision* (*Jahre der Entscheidung*), first published in 1933. In this chapter we will build on Struve's point of departure, but will make the case that Spengler's relationship with National Socialism is best viewed as the culmination of his own metahistorical views *and* the specific outcome of a variety of contingent day-to-day events that could have turned out differently: not merely Spengler's response to 'Nazi tactics'. We will demonstrate how at various junctures Spengler makes an assortment of seemingly contradictory statements on National Socialism. Taken in isolation, these have facilitated his paradoxical reception as both a proto-Nazi and as one of that regime's rare public critics. Finally, we will be able to reframe Felken's discussion of *opportunism* not in terms of *careerism* (as we will see, Spengler never seeks personal gain from the Nazi regime), but in terms of the question of whether Spengler's political thought is more reactive than proactive, more pragmatic than prophetic, in this fateful period of European history.

In order to explore these questions, this chapter will contextualise Spengler's engagement with the National Socialist movement in the early 1930s and will explore his ideas on the rise of Hitler as Chancellor. First, we will provide a concise historical overview of the most significant events leading up to the Nazi seizure of power and discuss Spengler's relationship with Hitler and the Nazi intellectual Gregor Strasser. Second, it will examine Spengler's *The Hour of Decision* (1933) and will discuss some of the National Socialist response to it. In our discussion of *The Hour of Decision*, close attention will be paid to what his ideas on race, the Jews and Prussian socialism reveal about the changing priorities of his political ideas and aspirations.

## Strasser, Spengler and Hitler

The years of crisis following the 1929 Wall Street Crash not only breathe life into extremist right-wing organisations such as the National Socialists, but also generate a renewed interest in politics for Spengler. So intense is the crisis resulting from the economic crash that by 1932, the National Socialist Party is in a strong position to contest the German elections – five of which are held in 1932. We know from his sister's diaries, which are preserved in his papers, that Spengler not only votes for the NSDAP, but that he is willing to hang swastika flags from the window of their shared house in order to greet a Nazi procession.[8] In private, however, Spengler repeatedly stresses that Hitler should urgently gather some intelligent advisers around him if he wishes to take advantage of the convulsions to come. As we saw in the previous chapter, Spengler's experience of the Beer Hall Putsch in 1923 did not exactly convince him of Hitler's political acumen. Other, more insightful strategists would be needed to harness the energy and devotion of Hitler's movement, and channel it into a feasible alternative focused on the corridors of business and power, not on street actions. In this, Spengler is reflective of the German establishment's understanding of Hitler at this point, as expressed in the common denunciation of him as 'the private from Bohemia'.[9]

Spengler's explanation of this attitude to the Nazis, provided in a letter to André Fauconnet in 1927,[10] typifies his criticisms of the NSDAP as a populist (and thus inherently flawed) political phenomenon at the time:

> Not only have I kept away from the National Socialist movement, which led to the Munich Putsch, but I have even tried – in vain, unfortunately – to prevent the

worst ... I am of the view that politics must not be based on a sentimental romanticism, but on sober facts and deliberations.[11]

However, just two months later, Spengler strikes up a close intellectual relationship with Gregor Strasser, the Munich-based leader of the 'left' wing within the NSDAP. Strasser writes to Spengler to inform him that *Rebuilding the German Reich* is 'virtually a treasure trove of highly constructive and realist-practical politics'.[12] Unlike several leading Nazis, whom Spengler sees as 'hopelessly stupid',[13] he obviously holds Strasser in high regard. He describes him as 'the smartest chap, alongside Hugo Stinnes, that I ever met'.[14] Spengler's correspondence with Strasser (much of which was unfortunately destroyed by Spengler following Strasser's murder in 1934) is indicative of two thinkers engaged in a genuine exchange of ideas. It is largely devoid of the uncritical flattery that characterises the attempts of other leading Nazis, such as Joseph Goebbels,[15] to engage with Spengler and to win him over. Before we look at the intellectual relationship between Spengler and Strasser, let us briefly recall the latter's life and career.[16]

Strasser was an army volunteer in the First World War and was awarded the Iron Cross. He studied pharmacy in Munich and joined a *Freikorps* paramilitary grouping during the November Revolution. He then led a comfortable existence as a chemist in Landshut. He joined the NSDAP in 1921 and participated in the Beer Hall Putsch of November 1923. He was arrested for his involvement in the coup, but from prison was elected to the Bavarian parliament as a representative of the Völkischer Block, which succeeded the outlawed NSDAP. His politics were strongly shaped by his experience as a soldier and the idea that social inequality and class differences were a hindrance to the strength of the German nation. For Strasser, the emphasis on anti-capitalism and German socialism was more prominent than *völkisch* and anti-Semitic ideas. He advocated a German socialism that was not too far removed from some of Spengler's radical proposals in *Prussianism and Socialism*. Among its key elements were the subjection of the economy to the state and the integration of the working class into an organic national community. At the Hannover Conference of the NSDAP in 1926, Strasser proposed that the party adopt this course of German socialism. However, Hitler and his allies were able to outmanoeuvre him. They did so in an attempt to appeal to the interests of German industry. They defeated Strasser's call for a social revolution within the party programme and also ensured that a party conference would no longer have the right to change that programme.

Strasser thanks Spengler for the 'extensive response'[17] to his letter (sadly, Spengler's response seems to have been destroyed) and appears to concur with some of his criticisms of National Socialism. Yet he disagrees with Spengler's dismissal of the National Socialist movement as utopian. Strasser stresses that his project by no means entails a utopian world revolution akin to that dreamed up by the communists, but rather a social transformation: 'a German revolution by a national socialism'.[18] Strasser feels that such a perspective can be found in Spengler's thought and earnestly seeks to cooperate with him. Given the existence of common ideological points of departure between the two men, Koktanek even suggests that Spengler is actually seeking to gain Hitler's ear through Strasser.[19] Felken makes the same point by noting Spengler's intellectual proximity to *Die Tat*, a magazine that likewise seeks influence over Hitler. Indeed, Spengler and Strasser are rumoured to meet on several occasions shortly before Strasser is liquidated by the Nazi leadership.[20] However, given that their correspondence was destroyed, it cannot be deduced what they are discussing or planning at this time. In retrospect, it can only be concluded that their close relationship never entails either man completely shifting his political priorities. Despite Strasser's repeated insistence that, for all their differences, Spengler is the real prophet of the German socialist movement, Strasser never leaves the NSDAP until that same organisation puts an end to his life. Spengler never joins. Moreover, as we will see, the development of their friendship is replete with historical irony, for the one piece of advice which Spengler offers Hitler – that a true Caesar must deal ruthlessly with opponents in his own party – is precisely the action that costs Strasser his life and contributes to Spengler's estrangement from the NSDAP.

Yet, in spite of his private criticisms, during the Nazi rise to power Spengler is generally enthusiastic about the prospects of a national rebirth and an end to Weimar democracy. By February 1933, however, he seems to entertain the view – privately again – that the fate of the national movement might quickly be run into the ground by the 'grotesque inability of its leadership clique'.[21] At this point, he seems to believe that the National Socialist experiment will be short-lived and catastrophic. Nonetheless, just two weeks later, following the Reichstag fire and the elections of 5 March 1933, which see the NSDAP and Franz von Papen's German National People's Party (DNVP) narrowly maintain the joint majority they had first secured in the elections of January 1933. Spengler's enthusiasm in his correspondence is evident: 'Hopefully Ash Wednesday will not come now! Now we can see whether Hitler is just a trumpet.'[22] What is striking about this statement is that Spengler does not seem at all troubled by the nature of the elections, which take place against the backdrop of a smear campaign against left-wing and liberal organisations, as well as intimidation, violence and arrests at the ballot box. Indeed, he even refers to the overthrow of the Bavarian government by the Nazis as a 'great delight'.[23]

Throughout 1933, however, Spengler continues to bide his time when it comes to *public* pronouncements on, or associations with, the Nazi regime. In June he refuses an offer of an academic post at Leipzig and in July he turns down an offer from the University of Freiburg, where Heidegger had held the post of Rektor since April. Moreover, Spengler appears to be concerned that some of his allies on the German right are falling in behind the Nazi project in a rather unprincipled and uncritical fashion. He singles out Roderich Schlubach, chair of the Patriotische Gesellschaft in Hamburg, the conservative publisher Albert Knittel and the industrialist Paul Reusch as examples of this political opportunism.[24]

Spengler, then, is confronted with the dilemma of how to respond to overtures from the Nazi regime. He is torn on the matter, reflecting how he continues to view the so-called national resurgence of 1933 positively, while maintaining his reservations about Hitler and his movement. Spengler's sister recalls the atmosphere in the Spengler household during the March 1933 elections: 'We voted Hitler. Signor [the name given to Spengler by his sister and her daughter] said about it: "Hitler is an idiot, but you have to support the movement."'[25]

Goebbels pushes for Spengler to provide a radio address on the occasion of Potsdam Day. This marks the opening of the new Reichstag on 21 March 1933 in the Garnisonkirche. The Nazis hope that the festivities will emblematically reconcile the old Prussian conservative outlook with the new Nazi order. At this ceremony, Hitler is received by Reichspräsident Paul von Hindenburg in front of the cameras, in a similar fashion to how previous Chancellors were once greeted by the Kaiser. Having Spengler provide an address amidst the pomp and circumstance would thus entail an important symbolic victory for the new administration – the seal of *Preußentum*, as it were. Spengler's initial reaction is to decline, but then he is convinced by others close to him that the address would provide an unrivalled opportunity to speak to potentially millions of people. After further consideration however, Spengler eventually turns down the invitation. His sister nonetheless feels that Spengler will take up such an opportunity at a later stage: 'I think he will actually speak on the radio one day.'[26] That his voice is never heard via what in popular vernacular is known as 'Goebbels's snout' (*die Goebbels-Schnauze*) suggests that at a certain point, something fundamentally changes in Spengler's attitude towards the National Socialists.

Could the 90-minute meeting between Hitler and Spengler at the Bayreuth Festival at the end of July 1933 perhaps account for Spengler's estrangement from the NSDAP, as Demandt implies?[27] The rendezvous is organised for Spengler by Else Knittel, the wife of his friend Albert. Else is a close friend of Winnifried Wagner (née Williams). Winnifried is an orphaned British woman who is adopted at a young age by a German couple and eventually marries Siegfried Wagner, one of the composer's sons. In Bayreuth, she lives next door to another Briton by the name of Houston Stewart Chamberlain. Chamberlain has a reputation as an outspoken anti-Semite on account of his popular *Die Grundlagen des Neunzehnten Jahrhunderts* (*The Foundations of the Nineteenth Century*, 1899). Winnifried and Houston, who always converse in German, become 'two of Hitler's earliest and most ardent acolytes'.[28] Moreover, Winnifried plays an instrumental role in promoting Hitler in general and his associations with the Bayreuth Festival in particular.

Spengler later seeks to portray the meeting as a vindication of his view that Hitler is a poisonous influence on the German nationalist movement. In a letter referring to a Nazi propaganda campaign to present the four major brains of German history as Frederick the Great, Goethe, Bismarck and Hitler, for example, Spengler notes: 'Yes, three great minds and a numskull.'[29] Nonetheless, the meeting with Hitler is not as disappointing or discordant as Spengler or some subsequent scholarship would have it.[30] Contrary to the claim made by the erstwhile Nazi-turned-German-American businessman Ernst Hanfstaengl in his memoirs, published almost forty years after the event, Hitler and Spengler part from each other with the intention of meeting up for another discussion in the near future.[31] Spengler feels that although Hitler does not create the impression of being a significant historical figure, he is nonetheless a 'very decent man': he 'wants something, is doing something, and you can speak to him'.[32] The most extensive account of what the two men actually discuss once again comes from the diaries of Spengler's sister Hilde. She notes how her brother returns from the festival in good spirits:

> A 1.5-hour discussion with Hitler (on France and on the Protestant church controversy). On France, Spengler said, Hitler was exactly right (that is to say, he had the same view as Signor); Hitler regretted that the Protestant church does not have a single outstanding thinker ... when it came to the Reichstag fire trial, Hitler claimed that there was interesting material that would prove how close we were to a Bolshevik revolution, with systematic arson and attacks and murder. Hitler said that the trial would begin in around five weeks.[33]

This account of the meeting is taken from Hilde's unpublished diaries, which are located in Spengler's papers. While it cannot be treated as an objective account of what happened, it does provide an alternative summary of the meeting and of the overlap between Spengler and Hitler on some of the pressing issues of the day. What is particularly striking is that Spengler reports uncritically Hitler's explanation that the Reichstag fire is an example of how imminent a communist uprising was. By November, however, Spengler sees through this pretext. In a letter to Alfons Sack, a lawyer involved in defending Ernst Torgler, the accused leader of the Communist Party of Germany's parliamentary group, in the Reichstag fire trial, Spengler sarcastically notes: 'By the way, the adage that "those who want to prove more than they can, prove nothing", clearly applies to this trial.'[34]

Following their meeting in July, Spengler appears to believe in the possibility of speaking to Hitler and of influencing his decisions. But whether he thinks that he can now achieve his longstanding goal of becoming a 'favourite of a capable ruler', a modern incarnation of what Talleyrand once was to Napoleon, is another matter.[35] Shortly before the meeting with Hitler, he completes his *Jahre der Entscheidung. Deutschland und die weltgeschichtliche Entwicklung. Erster Teil* (*The Hour of Decision. Part I: Germany and World-Historical Evolution*) and – in line with his usual practice of sending free copies of his publications to those he is seeking to influence – arranges for Hitler to receive a personal copy, with the following greeting:

> Esteemed Reichskanzler!
> I have taken the liberty of arranging for a copy of my new book to be sent to you, which I kindly ask you to accept. I would welcome the opportunity to hear your judgement of these issues at some point.
> With loyal greetings,
> Oswald Spengler[36]

As far as it is possible to ascertain, Hitler never responds to this request for another meeting. Is Spengler labouring under the illusion that he can play the advisory political role he always desired? Or is this a passive-aggressive provocation on his part, written safe in the knowledge that Hitler would never respond, given the book's contents?[37] Hitler may never have replied to Spengler's short letter, but the greater issue of how to respond politically to *The Hour of Decision* continues to exercise the Hitler regime for some time. At a meeting of Nazi leaders, Hitler is said to have personally intervened to prevent a ban on the book.[38] Perhaps he does so in the expectation that Spengler's best days are now behind him and that the public's attention is focused on other matters. But another explanation, as we will see, might be that Hitler does not feel unduly threatened or even targeted by the publication itself. Nevertheless, by the end of September 1933, *The Hour of Decision* had sold a staggering 100,000 copies and it becomes evident that the Nazi regime will have to convey its view of the publication and the ideas it contains. Let us now take a closer look at the structure and arguments in *The Hour of Decision* in order to shed further light on Spengler's understanding of fascism in general and National Socialism in particular.

## The Last Bestseller

*The Hour of Decision. Part I: Germany and World-Historical Evolution* is Spengler's last published political treatise. It is an updated and expanded version of a lecture delivered to the Patriotische Gesellschaft in Hamburg on 3 February 1930. It therefore provides a useful summary of the views Spengler forms on fascism in Italy and Germany between 1930 and 1933. Spengler's title for his last bestseller is revealing. First, the foregrounding of *Germany* and its place in world-historical development reflects his career-long hopes for the German nation's self-assertion in a troubled climate. Second, this publication is conceived as one of two volumes dedicated to an analysis of the global political climate. However, for reasons we will discuss below, the follow-up volume is never completed.

*The Hour of Decision* breaks down into four main chapters: 'The Political Horizon', 'World Wars and World Powers', 'The White World Revolution' and, finally, 'The Coloured World Revolution'. The content of the first two chapters will be largely familiar to those who have read Spengler's other works, but the final chapters contain fresh philosophical-historical material and concepts, which we will discuss in more detail below.

Perhaps the most significant section of the book from the point of view of Spengler and National Socialism is the Introduction, in which he refers to the Nazi seizure of power positively as 'the national revolution' and asserts that nobody could have desired such an upheaval as much as he. Conscious of the fact that the book is based on a lecture from 1930 entitled 'Germany in Danger', Spengler updates the title of the published book. He is clearly seeking to avoid creating the impression that the Nazi seizure of power has now placed Germany *in jeopardy*. He is at pains to stress that the Nazi uprising is not what he sees as the danger facing his country, but rather that Germany's problems can be traced back to 1918 and, beyond this, its late development as a nation that has only recently overcome political localism. He calls this 'seven hundred years of miserable provincial small-state-ism without even a whiff of greatness, ideas or aims' (10). By contrast, National Socialism's rise to power is viewed as nothing less than a 'Prussian' phenomenon comparable to 1914:

> The national revolution of 1933 was something tremendous and will remain so in the eyes of the future due to the elemental, super-personal force with which it came about and the discipline of the soul *when it was carried out*. That was something Prussian through and through, just like the awakening of 1914, which transformed the souls [of the nation] at one stroke. (5)

Nonetheless, Spengler argues that even an event of such historical significance is unable to eradicate the dangers on the road ahead. The emphasis on decision (*Entscheidung*) highlights the open-endedness of the historical process he sees unfolding: 'the great spectacle of global politics is not over' (4). He points to a looming global conflict and contends that Germany is 'the world's most decisive country' (7). He makes this claim not merely due to its location 'at the border of Asia', but also because the Germans – unlike the French or the English, who had their own national movements led by Mirabeau and Cromwell – have these events in front of them: the Germans are 'still young enough' (7) to have a real future.

Spengler explains the background to the publication by pointing out that, as of 30 January 1933, the book was printed up to page 106. He then adds that he has changed nothing of the original text before its publication since he is a 'historical connoisseur' (4) who is able to understand the facts of his time and to sketch out future development. This ensures that he thinks not in months, but in years. Spengler's pretensions aside, the book does indeed read as if it were finished before Hitler's rise to the position of Chancellor. The Introduction is the only section of the book that directly refers to the Nazi seizure of power and it feels incongruously appended to a publication that is already out of date by the time it appears.

Spengler avoids taking a position on National Socialism in the text. This is understandable in that it is only just beginning to consolidate its power and thus has novel characteristics, claims and aspirations. As we have seen, some of these appeal to him, some do not. The subtitle of the book makes clear that Spengler is not attempting to theorise a particular event or scene within this spectacle, but rather the plot as a whole: Germany's place within the longer-term development of world history. At times, he speaks of decades (4)[39] and hypothesises about where the world might be at the end of the twentieth century. The English translation of the text as *The Hour of Decision*[40] is therefore misleading. It implies that the decision faced by Germany is an immediate one against the backdrop of the Nazi rise to power. But this is not the case. Surveying what he views as the hollowness of the political process, Spengler bemoans the fact that politicians seem capable of thinking merely in hours and days, not years or decades: 'our age is a tremendous one, but the people are all the smaller for it' (16–17). The choice of *The Hour of Decision* for the title of the English translation, as well as the dominant interpretation of the text, retroactively view the text through the lens of the Nazi seizure of power and the possibility of it being censored. Sebastian Maaß, for instance, calls the text 'in essence an anti-National Socialist one ... which was not however censored due to the fact that it was published at a relatively early stage'.[41] Thomas Tartsch speaks of Spengler as an 'opponent of the National Socialist state' because of his supposed 'unveiled criticism of National Socialism' in *The Hour of Decision*.[42] H. Stuart Hughes writes of the 'dilemma' faced by Spengler when publishing *The Hour of Decision*, which 'was sure to displease the new rulers of Germany, who might even go so far as to suppress the book entirely'.[43] Nonetheless, Hughes argues – fully in line with the view that Spengler's political thought forms an unchanging and coherent whole – that 'it was not in Spengler's nature to withdraw or alter anything that he said'.[44] Contrary to these claims, it must be emphasised that *The Hour of Decision* is no critique of the Hitler regime. It is a text that outlines Spengler's view of the epoch in general. There are, as we will discuss below, only a smattering of references to the phenomenon of fascism as an international movement and even fewer to the exact place of National Socialism within this movement.

*The Hour of Decision* can be more accurately described as a critique of the structures and guiding ideological concepts of modernity than as a polemic against Hitlerism. The publication possesses a typically Spenglerian breadth that is both fascinating and difficult to summarise. It deals with Germany's position within the world order, the emergence of global powers and conflicts, the domination of politics and decision-making by money and finance, the distinction between the class antagonisms of the modern world and the rank-based hierarchies of the past epoch, the emergence of working-class politics in Western Europe and the rise of what Spengler deems the coloured peoples – a most unhelpful term, particularly because Spengler claims that these non-*Abendland* peoples include those from nations as diverse as Morocco and Russia – and their potentially destructive influence on the exhausted *Abendland*. Spengler warns that the *Abendland* must get its act together if it is not to perish. We will return to this novel idea in his thought further below.

The decision presented by Spengler, then, is not one to be made within hours or even years, nor is it a cut-and-dried choice between embracing National Socialism and opting for the politics of Bolshevism or liberalism. The decision on which the future of the 'white peoples' (97) hinges is far more fundamental. It cuts across all the above ideologies and movements. As Spengler puts it, there is a choice between two paths: one that goes to the 'left' and one that goes to the 'right'. This distinction is ably outlined by Michael Thöndl, who argues that the 'left-right' political axis should be turned anti-clockwise by 90 degrees so that 'left' becomes the masses at the bottom and 'right' the elite at the top. Thus: 'It becomes evident that, for Spengler, those parties that represent right-wing values also contain left-wing elements, and that they do so precisely because they are organised as parties.'[45]

The left is represented by what Spengler calls the 'white world revolution' (76). This movement can be traced back to the emergence of rationalism and liberalism in the late eighteenth century. It provides the main impetus for phenomena as varied as liberalism, Bolshevism and fascism insofar as they all focus on mobilising the masses in party formations. For Spengler, the outcome of this trend is an undermining of the socio-political virtues of the aristocracy: tradition, discipline and elite rule give way to the stock market, parties and elections. He summarises this position as follows:

> 'Left' is whatever is a party or whatever believes in parties, because that is a liberal form of the struggle against higher society, of the class struggle since 1770, of the desire for majorities ... for quantity over quality, for the herd over the gentleman. (102)

By contrast, the path to the right creates the conditions for Caesarism and counters this ongoing 'offensive from below' with a 'defensive from above' (100). It does so in order to uphold rank and tradition in the face of the class struggle that has been raging since the rise of the modern world in ca. 1770 and the rise of finance capital in ca. 1840. The proletariat's dominance has ensured that no politician dares to criticise or upset the worker. All parties must appeal to the worker's base and capricious interests in order to chase votes and remain in power. Not only is this situation leading to the collapse of morality, coherence, taste and style, but, most importantly, it is undermining the ability of the Western states to defend themselves militarily. As in *Rebuilding the German Reich*, he claims that finance and the workers' movement surreptitiously work hand in hand to undermine national cohesion:

> By contrast, as I have already shown, *all forms* of worker socialism are thoroughly English in origin. They arose around 1840, at the same time as the victory of the joint-stock company and the rootless 'financial' form of capital. Both were the expression of Free Trade Manchesterism: this 'white' Bolshevism is capitalism from below, wage-capitalism, just as the method of speculative finance-capital is socialism from above, from the stock exchange. (105)[46]

The vertical struggle in society between the masses and the forces of tradition within states takes place in parallel to the horizontal conflicts between states. Any positive resolution of these battles is conceivable only when the forces of Caesarism begin to assert themselves and make the nations 'in form' (106) – ready to wage conflict successfully once more – by restoring the values of *custom*, *duty* and *honour*. This distinction between the masses as 'the radical nothing' and the nobility as the embodiment of a strong state can first be found in Volume 2 of *The Decline of the West*.[47] What is new is his explanation of the baleful influence of the masses and money with reference to the 'white world revolution'. He feels that the economic crisis of 1929 may represent the apogee of this process, although not its conclusion: 'Today the world revolution ... has reached what is perhaps its zenith, but it is far from over' (81).

Another key development in Spengler's thought is his use of the terms 'white peoples' and 'masses of coloured peoples' in relation to imperialism and the colonies (97). He believes that the political and moral decadence of the white revolution has dangerous implications not just for the individual countries of the West, but also for the culture as a whole. He fears that the 'masses of coloured peoples' will be able to seize on the internal weakness of the white world and undermine it (ibid.). Specifically, he worries that those in the colonies of the Western world will deploy the knowledge and technology acquired from their colonial masters not as a means of pursuing the *Abendland*'s quest for infinity, but of destroying it for good. For the first time in his career, he posits the idea that in a globally interdependent world, the struggle between races and the struggle between classes (*Rassenkampf* and *Klassenkampf*) could combine (111) to obliterate the foundations of the *Abendland*. Here he has in mind the anti-colonial uprisings in China, India and Mexico: 'deep down, there is one and the same thing that underpins the Taiping Rebellion in China, the Sepoy uprising in India, the revolt of the Mexicans against Kaiser Maximilian: a hatred of *the white race* and the absolute will to destroy it' (118).

Michael Thöndl seeks to defend Spengler from charges of straightforward racism on this matter. He claims that this position is consistent with Spengler's views on the necessity of defending and upholding the cultural period of the Faustian world in the face of those who – whether because they represent the mass (*Masse*) of Faustian *Zivilisation* or because they have never belonged to such a culture in the first place – threaten to undermine it.[48] Nonetheless, there is an unmistakable sense in which Spengler's use of the term 'race' here is both essentialising and, in contrast to previous uses of the term, appears to be informed more by biology (that is, skin colour) than by a culture's prime symbol (*Ursymbol*). We will return to this point in more detail in our discussion of Spengler's understanding of Jewishness and the Jews below.

How do these world-historical trends located by Spengler relate to the phenomena of fascism generally and National Socialism specifically? As we have seen, Spengler does not mention Hitler by name. This alone irks the Nazi philosopher Alfred Baeumler. He complains that 'neither Hitler's name nor the term National Socialism appear in this work'.[49] However, the term *fascism* appears on a number of occasions in *The Hour of Decision*. When it comes to fascism, Spengler is predominantly thinking of Mussolini's Italian movement, but he also uses *fascism* as an umbrella term to describe the numerous international movements – including in Germany – that have been inspired by the experience of Italy (101). As we will see below, his praise for Mussolini's political strategy allows him – between the lines – to intervene in the German debates on fascism by highlighting its limits as a party-political phenomenon. He does so by contrasting the dead-end of this plebeian fascism with the model example of Mussolini's elitist fascism. As Spengler puts it: 'What pre-empts the future is not the existence of *fascism as a party*, but solely and exclusively the *figure of its creator*' (103, emphasis added). In keeping with his understanding of the terms 'left' and 'right', then, Spengler considers fascism in its mass form to be another manifestation of the 'left', 'partyist' 'white revolution from below':

> Fascism is also a transition. It developed from the urban masses, as a mass party with rowdy agitation and speeches among the masses – tendencies of worker socialism are not alien to it. But as long as a dictatorship has 'social' ambitions and claims to be there for the sake of the 'worker', is active in the backstreets and is popular, it remains a mere *intermediate form*. The Caesarism of the future fights only for power, for a Reich and against all kinds of political parties. (103)

Spengler's fundamental point is that, for all the mutual hostility between movements such as fascism and communism, in the last instance they are peculiar brothers-in-arms: they share the same emphasis on mass participation and veneration of the worker's sectional interests. The Caesarist alternative he has in mind – this point bears repeating – will only be able to lead the late Faustian world if it dispenses with such an approach and repairs the damage caused by parties and parliaments: 'You need to know whether you are on the "left" or the "right", otherwise the course of history itself will decide this for you – and the course of history is more powerful than any theory or ideological dreaming' (101). Rulers, not demagogues, are required to show the way:

> It is here that the path splits to the left and to the right: the demagogue lives with the masses always as one of them; the born ruler can use them, but he despises them. He conducts his most arduous battles not against the enemy, but against the swarm of his all-too-devoted friends. (111)

Hence, Mussolini's variant of fascism comes in for much praise because Spengler feels that Mussolini is the true ruler (*Herrscher*) of Italy. He has shown himself willing to purge the influence of the masses on politics – even, or especially, those within his own organisation (103). Spengler implicitly refers to the 'decision' faced by fascism in Germany with reference to Mussolini's Italy:

> The most difficult victories of a ruler, and the most *essential* ones, are not those won over enemies, but those won over his own supporters, the praetorians, the 'Ras', as they are known in Italy. This is how the best ruler proves himself. He who does not know this and has neither the power nor the courage to do so swims like a cork on the waves, at the top and yet powerless. (103)

Spengler's admiration for Mussolini does not stop there:

> Mussolini, although he was once a workers' leader, is no party leader, but the ruler of his country. Had Lenin lived longer, then he would have probably been Mussolini's role model here. He possessed a superior ruthlessness towards his party and the courage to withdraw from all ideology. Above all, Mussolini is a statesman, ice cold and sceptical, a realist and a diplomat. He really does rule by himself. (103)

This praise is reciprocated. In a book review of *The Hour of Decision*, Mussolini commends Spengler's insights into the nature of the political period and also arranges for a translation of the text into Italian.[50] Contrary to Markus Henkel's claim that Spengler's practical-political proposals are designed to *offset* the emergence of figures such as Mussolini,[51] Spengler leaves no doubts as to the dictatorial nature of the coming Caesarism for which he is striving: 'Caesarism in its finished form is a dictatorship, but not the dictatorship of a party, but rather of a man against all parties – *particularly his own one*' (103). If genuine Caesarism is to be achieved, then the 'Praetorian Guard' within fascist organisations must be eliminated in a 'ruthless' fashion (103). Until this is the case, any political phenomena – plebeian fascism included – will at best amount to 'interim solutions and transitions' (102). In an epoch where 'the age itself is radical', any compromises with, or concessions to, the 'revolution from below' (103) will prove to be short-lived and harmful. Spengler mocks those who fail to realise this fundamental point. In his eyes, they lack the *will to power* demanded of the times and languish in the centrist mentality of what he acidly deems the 'will to the middle' (101) of the political spectrum. He is adamant that only uncompromising Caesarist political forms can do away with the corrupting influence of the masses on democracy and politics:

> The Caesarism of the future will not persuade, but will emerge victorious with weapon in hand. Only when this goes without saying, when the majority is perceived as something to be objected to, when somebody looks down on the masses, on the party in every sense of the word and on all programmes and ideologies, will the revolution have been overcome. (102)

Spengler's call for fascist movements to emulate the example of Mussolini and to deal ruthlessly with their own praetorian guard leads to a turning point in his relationship with German National Socialism. Whether or not Hitler is influenced by Spengler's arguments on fascism and Caesarism, or whether – as Klaus P. Fischer claims[52] – Spengler actually informs Hitler of these ideas in their meeting in Bayreuth, it is most ironic that Hitler's purging of the SA during the so-called Night of the Long Knives in the summer of 1934 provides the occasion for Spengler's disillusionment with National Socialism. As we have already shown in Chapter 1, the Nazi purge brings the death of several of Spengler's companions and contacts. Alongside his friend Willi Schmid – killed as a result of an administrative error in the purges – these include two other figures who are at the heart of political developments on the German right: Strasser and Gustav von Kahr. Strasser is eliminated precisely in a move against a section of the Nazi movement that is more closely associated with German socialism and anti-capitalist, plebeian elements. Indeed, as Koktanek points out, Hitler's move against the SA occasions more support from the captains of heavy industry – the very forces Spengler devotes most of his political career to organising – and ensures that Hitler comes to be viewed as more of a reliable, pro-establishment figure.[53] Spengler views the death of von Kahr as a loss of the kind of traditional, conservative figure who, with the correct political guidance to address some of his past errors, could have contributed to bringing Germany into form once again.

What could, using the language of *The Hour of Decision*, be called Hitler's *decision to the right* therefore seals Spengler's estrangement from the Nazis and from politics as a whole. The kind of decision Spengler had been calling for had been made, but he is horrified by the consequences. Since 1919 at least he is consistent in calling for Caesarist dictatorship and an end to party-political life, but when faced with the reality of this move outlined in his philosophy of history, he is distraught. He later writes with a palpable sense of regret: 'we wanted to get rid of parties – the worst one was left over'.[54] He shelves the planned second volume of *The Hour of Decision*: 'so it is that I have not written a single line of it and it would make no sense to do so now, because I do not write books for them to be confiscated'.[55] As a result, he withdraws into private life and resorts to *aperçus* and jibes against the Nazis in his correspondence. Struve, then, does not tell the whole story when describing Spengler's shifting attitude towards National Socialism as flowing from his assessment of Nazi 'tactics'. His account overlooks the tragic significance of Spengler calling for the measures that cause him to turn his back on National Socialism.

Here the disjuncture between the claims, or predictions, of Spengler's historical philosophy and his political decisions in reaction to unfolding events becomes apparent in the most tragic fashion. Moreover, following his alienation from the Nazi regime, in his last years Spengler seeks to project this estrangement back onto the past: there is no discussion of how his musings on the necessity of authoritarian Caesarian rule may have fed into, overlapped with, or provided fuel to the fire of the Nazi seizure and consolidation of power. Instead, in an attempt to paint himself once more as a prophet of historical development, Spengler merely notes that there is 'much that is correct' in Nazi ideology insofar as it was not created by 'loudmouths', but rather by him and others, such as Bismarck and Frederick William I of Prussia.[56] The Nazis, he concludes, had 'sponged off my ideas'.[57]

It is therefore wrong to claim that *The Hour of Decision* is 'in essence an anti-National Socialist' text.[58] Nor can its author be viewed as one of Nazi regime's 'most prominent critics'.[59] Nor, *pace* Farrenkopf, can the text be seen as a 'politically courageous criticism of the Nazi leadership' that was supposedly 'belatedly banned by Nazi censors ... one of few and the most sensational of the regime-critical works to appear during the Third Reich'.[60] Nor, finally, can it be seen as marking the break between Spengler and National Socialism, as Koktanek suggests.[61]

True, implicit criticism of the Nazis is present between the lines: Prussian statesmanship and elite traditions are called for, not mass mobilisations and rallies. In keeping with long-held ideas on politics as a serious business of statesmanship and devotion, as opposed to mass enthusiasm and intoxication, Spengler feels that the involvement of the masses will obscure a proper, leadership-informed conception of politics: 'The danger with enthusiasts is that they see things far too simplistically' (5).

However, explicit criticism is hardly forthcoming. When it comes to one of the rare instances of such criticism in *The Hour of Decision*, irony yet again plays an important role.[62] In the Introduction, Spengler does mention the Nazis by name and points out that they are seeking to build their 'castles in the sky' without soberly assessing the fact that 'Germany is not an island' (10). His point is a familiar one in his work: Germany can only assert her interests by pursuing *Weltpolitik* and by settling scores with the world around her. Here Spengler has clearly been duped by the peace rhetoric of the early Nazi regime and its claims of setting out on an independent path of nonaggression. This professed foreign policy is summarised by the Nazi writer Johann von Leers as calling for 'the working peoples' to collaborate 'on the basis of these peoples' respect for each other'.[63] In reality, such talk was a smokescreen to conceal the regime's real plans for a new war in Europe. Spengler is thus criticising the National Socialists for not carrying out a policy they are in fact pursuing. Another instance of Spengler's agreeing with the foreign policy of the National Socialists can be seen in his support for the Nazi regime's subsequent decision to withdraw from the League of Nations, which in *The Hour of Decision* is pilloried as a 'swarm of parasites holidaying at Lake Geneva' (34).

Once again, it is possible to detect a dynamic tension between Spengler's philosophy and his politics. While the former to some extent predicts and accounts for the emergence of a movement akin to German National Socialism, the latter is ultimately shaped by unfolding developments that could have turned out differently. Spengler's relationship to National Socialism is thus not that of an all-seeing prophetic historical connoisseur, as he would have it, but of a thinker who is responding to novel developments and rapidly unfolding events beyond his control. Had the Nazis killed the correct man – Willi Schmidt instead of Willi Schmid – and had

Strasser been spared, would Spengler have been won round to the project of a more serious National Socialism that was now breaking with some of its old habits and becoming more state-focused and statesmanlike? Had Hitler not – against Spengler's best advice – taken a turn 'to the right' in 1934, would Spengler have remained open-minded about his involvement with the Nazi regime? These questions can never be adequately answered. The fact that they can be posed at all reveals much about the ambivalence and inconsistency of Spengler's response to National Socialism.

## The Propaganda Campaign

How do the Nazis respond to *The Hour of Decision*? We have seen that they decide not to censor the popular book, so how does the regime deal with its arguments? Before we discuss what *The Hour of Decision* reveals about Spengler's changing attitudes on race and Prussian socialism, let us first discuss what several Nazi writers thought about the book.

Günther Gründel's *Jahre der Überwindung* (*Years of Overcoming*) is an example of a spontaneous response to *The Hour of Decision*.[64] Gründel, a fan of Spengler's, implores him to draw the logical conclusions of his arguments in *The Hour of Decision*: if the world does indeed look rather like Spengler's depiction within the book, then he must surely recognise that the only force that can put an end to this situation is Hitler's NSDAP. When Spengler fails to respond to Gründel's letter, Gründel publishes his own text.[65]

At the same time, there is a coordinated response to *The Hour of Decision*, in which the Nazi Minister for Propaganda Joseph Goebbels plays a key role. Goebbels is becoming increasingly annoyed with the failure of his overtures towards Spengler.[66] In late October 1933, for instance, Spengler accepts in principle Goebbels's offer to provide a public radio address to mark the occasion of the fifteenth anniversary of the Treaty of Versailles, albeit on the condition that the press campaign against him be suspended. This does not happen, so the address does not take place. In December 1933, a Nazi press directive is issued that calls for an end to the discussion of Spengler's work in the media altogether.

Between 1933 and 1934, a range of book-length publications appear on Spengler.[67] Here we will focus on two such works that are reflective of the attitude of leading Nazis to Spengler in the 1930s: Arthur Zweiniger's *Spengler im Dritten Reich. Eine Antwort auf Oswald Spenglers 'Jahre der Entscheidung'* (*Spengler in the Third Reich: A Response to Spengler's 'The Hour of Decision'*, 1933) and *Spenglers weltpolitisches System und der Nationalsozialismus* (*Spengler's World Political System and National Socialism*, 1934), written by Johann von Leers.[68]

The former book reflects aspects of the early Nazi government's radical, worker-orientated and even utopian rhetoric[69] by taking Spengler to task on what Zweiniger considers to be the looming issues of the day. Convinced that Spengler has a 'thoroughly conflicting'[70] relation to fascism, Zweiniger accuses Spengler of failing to understand the real forces of historical change, as well as of an incomprehension of the true significance of Hitler's rise to power. This historic event has ushered in a 'wave of fervent love for the fatherland'[71] so desired by Spengler. For Zweiniger, Spengler's *The Hour of Decision* reveals a thinker who has next to no positive proposals for Germany's future. To the extent that Spengler has any positive demands or desires in this text, they have all been realised in practice by the Hitler regime. And whereas Spengler could once claim to have highlighted the great values and ideals of *Preußentum*, at a point when these very ideals are taking shape, Spengler can only carp from the comfort of his armchair.[72] Zweiniger charges Spengler with 'cold pessimism' and a scepticism of collective action inspired by proud nationalist aims, as well as with an inability to distinguish between 'the masses' (*die Masse*) of the atomised and alienated people and 'the people' (*das Volk*).[73] The former has been overcome in the project of National Socialism, a collective movement organised around the heroic and self-sacrificing values of *Preußentum*. Spengler's aloofness to the real force of historical development ensures that he must seek refuge in fatalist hypothesising: 'So it is that, blinded by prejudice, he looks past reality and fails to recognise his own children.'[74]

Von Leers's *Spenglers weltpolitisches System und der Nationalsozialismus* praises Spengler for his efforts in the struggle against the Weimar Republic, but, like Zweiniger, points out that Spengler and the Nazis were united in this struggle only 'in the negative' – that is, when it came to what they were against.[75] When it comes to positive proposals regarding the future, they part company. In order to make this point, von Leers distinguishes between the 'positive' Spengler of 1919 and the 'pessimist' Spengler of 1933. For von Leers, Spengler's *Prussianism and Socialism* had established him among the German people 'not only the reputation of a highly talented and original mind, but also the reputation of somebody who showed the way to new shores'.[76] The Spengler of 1919 possessed some kind of understanding of how to overcome the class struggle and create a strong Germany, but now he seems utterly indifferent to this perspective. Now he ignores the plight of the masses and stands up for the interests of those above instead. Von Leers compliments Spengler for the profound insights of his concept of Caesarism, but argues that simply because a Caesar emerged in the Roman world, it does not follow that it will happen again in modern conditions.

But how much truth is there to these accusations? What about von Leers's claim that the Spengler of 1933 has broken with the more optimistic nationalist ideas of Prussian socialism he first outlined in 1919? It is to these questions that we will now turn by discussing the significance of *The Hour of Decision* in relation to Spengler's ideas on race and Prussian socialism.

## *Rasse* and the Jews

Having arrived at this point, it is worth taking a closer look at the question of how Spengler understands the role of the Jews in Germany. The so-called Jewish question rages through Europe in the 1920s and 1930s, with German nationalist discourse often proceeding from the understanding that Jewish customs and traditions are simply incompatible with modern European life.[77] In order to arrive at a rounded understanding of Spengler's thought on race and the Jews, let us briefly take a step back from an exclusive focus on *The Hour of Decision* in order to discuss his ideas on the issue across his career as a whole. We can then establish how his final published text relates to this understanding.

In Chapter 3, we pointed out that, for the Spengler of *Prussianism and Socialism*, race is more of a metaphysical than a biological category. This rejection of biological conceptions of race is also evident in one of the most memorable statements against *völkisch* and Aryan-centric understandings of race in Volume 2 of *The Decline of the West*. Discussing the uselessness of analysing skulls – let alone measuring them, as the Nazis later would – in gaining an understanding of past societies and different peoples, Spengler writes:

> In fact, the racial expression of a human head is compatible with all conceivable skull forms. What is decisive is not the bones, but the flesh, the gaze, the facial expressions. Since the Romantic age there has been talk of the Indo-Germanic race. But are there Aryan and Semite *skulls*?[78]

Moreover, we have seen that Spengler is a consistent critic of the political aims and methods of the *völkisch* movement. Here, it is worth recalling an important footnote from *Rebuilding the German Reich*, in which he writes:

> And, incidentally, how petty, shallowly restricted and disgraceful the German sentence 'Jews out!' looks alongside the English one: 'Right or wrong, my country!' The former is a mere negation and completely underestimates the fact that one of the most dangerous *anti-German* traits – the tendency to internationalist and pacifist infatuation, the hatred of authority ... precisely have deep roots in the

German essence. Members of one's *own* race are always more dangerous than those of *another*, who precisely in their status as a minority will always prefer to adapt if they are seriously given the choice.[79]

This quote clearly demonstrates Spengler's rejection of slogans calling for the removal of the Jews from Germany. Yet he appears to do so on the assumption that the Jews are not part of what he calls one's '*own* race' (*die eigene Rasse*). This allows him to make the case that it is not the *Jews* that the Germans should be concerned about, but rather the weakness, pacifism, liberalism and other 'anti-German' traits among the *Germans* themselves. What does Spengler mean by this? Is his contention not based on anti-Semitic tropes and stereotypes?

In *The Decline of the West*, Spengler claims that the Jewish outlook and way of experiencing the world is the product of Arab or Magian culture (ca. 0–1000 AD). It is thus fundamentally different from the modern Faustian outlook. Magian culture coheres around the prime symbol of the cave. It is a culture defined by close communal ties – the *consensus omnium* of its adherents – and their isolation from those outside. The Jews have been able to survive as a people well beyond the existence of the Magian world precisely because of this cohesion. Regarding the lack of a homeland for Jews living in the *Abendland*, for instance, Spengler argues:

> But the West-European-American section of the Jewish *consensus*, which largely absorbed the other sections and tied them to its fate, has now fallen into a young *Zivilisation*, without connection to any piece of land, after it had cut itself off, ghetto-like, for centuries and thus had been able to save itself. It is thereby scattered and is heading towards dissolution. But the fate of this grouping is one *not within Faustian culture, but Magian culture*.[80]

For Spengler, then, Jewish otherness is not biological in nature, but historical-metaphysical: the Jews reflect an outmoded manner of existence that revolves around community, protection and cave-like isolation, not the Faustian drive for expansion and infinity. The skull-measuring racism of the National Socialists is nowhere to be found, but the assumption of Jewish *otherness* is fundamental. This assumption occasionally spills over into some of the problematic statements he makes on the Jews throughout his career, such as his criticism of the 'English-Judaic' thought of Marx and Bentham or his derogatory remarks on Spinoza, whose thought is dismissed using classically anti-Semitic clichés.[81]

Another example of Spengler's postulation of Jewish otherness comes in a letter to Hans Klores in 1915, in which he writes: 'we must not be fussy about who we call on [to strengthen the cause of the German nation], even if that means talented Jews'.[82] Such prejudiced language is not restricted to his correspondence. In *Rebuilding the German Reich*, for instance, he argues how nations can draw on leaders of foreign origins who become leading examples of 'their own' during acute crises. He mentions Russia's Catherine the Great, who was German; France's Napoleon, who was Italian; and Britain's Disraeli, who was a Jew.

On closer inspection, therefore, while Spengler's views are far removed from the biological and eugenic anti-Semitism of the National Socialists, his metaphysical generalisations about the 'Jewish way of life' as a nonsimultaneous (*ungleichzeitig*) hangover from Magian culture are clear manifestations of anti-Semitism. 'Metaphysical' racism is still a form of racism, as metaphysical categories and distinctions only acquire meaning with reference to the social context in which they are conceived and employed. His understanding revolves around an essentialising view of the Jews that, as part of the typecasting of cultures in his morphology of world history more generally, relies on tropes and stereotypes that are typical of his time and milieu.

How does this understanding find reflection in *The Hour of Decision*, however? In this text, Spengler equates a strong race to a people that is ready to assert itself on the world stage: 'it is not only an inexhaustible birth rate that makes up a strong race, but also the harsh selection imposed by the obstacles of life, such as disaster, illness and war' (121). Crucial in this respect are the Prussian values of coherent leadership. This can act as a role model for all in society to emulate. Accordingly, Spengler again distinguishes between his conception of *race* and more biological understandings: 'I repeat: the race that one has, not the race to which one belongs. The one is ethos, the other is zoology' (122, fn. 32). It is precisely this ethical or political understanding of race that can explain why, paradoxically, Spengler dismisses the Nazis as belonging to an alien race (*fremde Rasse*) alongside others (including, of course, the Jews): 'Nothing is as non-German, as non-Germanic, as this party mob [the Nazis] – they are Jewish, Slavic ... anything but Nordic'.[83]

In making the case for a Prussian understanding of leadership and an overhaul of the values of the German nation, *The Hour of Decision* abounds with radically racialised rhetoric that is largely absent from Spengler's *Prussianism and Socialism* and *Rebuilding the German Reich*, and blurs his distinction between biology and ethos. We thus find an array of concepts more commonly associated with the National Socialists: 'the deformed', 'those who are wayward and inferior in body and soul', 'human vermin' and 'subhumans' (*Untermenschen*) feature throughout *The Hour of Decision*.[84] Moreover, his historical distinction between the peoples of the *Abendland* and those of other cultures is expressed in terms of skin colour for the first time in his career, with the *white* world lining up against its *coloured* counterpart.

This evolution in Spengler's rhetoric could be explained with reference to the dominance of these ideas at the time. However, a better explanation – one that has not been considered in the secondary literature – is that he is seeking to win over those in the right-wing authoritarian nationalist movement (*nationale Bewegung*) who entertain racist or anti-Semitic views. The abundance of blood and race are therefore best understood *both* as rhetorical devices similar to those we have located in several of his writings *and* as points of reference for Spengler to outline his own views on these issues.

As we have seen above, however, *The Hour of Decision* is not well placed to present his alternative for Germany. Hitler's rise to the position of Chancellor renders the book out of date by the time it is published, and it only refers to National Socialism by name in the hastily compiled Introduction. Hence, Spengler does not always clearly establish where he differs from Hitler and his ideas. This is particularly the case when it comes to aspects of politics in which Spengler's critique of Faustian *Zivilisation* appears to overlap with aspects of National Socialism. One example is the supposed interplay between the forces of *finance* and *the masses*, which are 'international' in nature and thus undermine the bonds of nation and state. Especially given that Spengler considers the workers' movement and finance capital to be alien forces, such a view overlaps with the Nazi understanding of the economy.[85] Spengler does not stress the Jewish aspect of these phenomena – and is criticised by von Leers for this[86] – but the idea that both are inimical to the German nation is nonetheless present.

Similarly, while Felken is correct to stress that Spengler's understanding of global politics has no place for a biological hierarchy of peoples along the lines of the Nazi categories of races that create culture, races that destroy it, and races that support it,[87] Felken overlooks how a form of hierarchy is implicitly present in Spengler's attitude towards 'the coloured people of Java, Rhodesia and Peru' (96). These peoples, as we have seen, pose an imminent threat to the culture of the hypostatised white peoples.

Hence, *The Hour of Decision* places much more emphasis on the – already problematic – understanding of race and Jewishness in Spengler's other works. It does so precisely in an attempt to highlight how his conception of races and cultures is fundamentally different from that of National Socialists, but largely fails in doing so.

But how does *The Hour of Decision* discuss the *socialism* of National Socialism, and what does this reveal about the evolution of his political thought? These are the final questions to which we must now turn.

## Socialism and Shifting Priorities

It is apparent that the text's foregrounding of the baleful consequences of the revolution from below ensures that it is one of Spengler's most elitist publications. Whereas in *Prussianism and Socialism* he sought to win over the nationalist sections of the working classes, in *The Hour of Decision* such a project is dismissed as a concession to the revolution from below. Moreover, in contrast to *Rebuilding the German Reich*, *The Hour of Decision* avoids making detailed suggestions for the future of the German state, beyond the observations about how Caesarism must learn to hold the masses in contempt, not to organise amongst them.

We have already seen how Johann von Leers points to Spengler's purported change of heart regarding Prussian socialism and how he thereby attempts to undermine Spengler's claims of being an all-seeing prophet. In *The Hour of Decision*, Spengler appears to anticipate that he will be criticised precisely on the question of socialism. Seeking to have the final say on *Prussianism and Socialism*, he writes in *The Hour of Decision*: 'A certain upbringing is necessary for this, which I have called Prussianism and which, for all I care, you might call "socialist"' (123). Further: 'What I described years ago as "Prussianism" is important – it has after all, just stood the test of time – and not any kind of "socialism"' (123). Whereas *Prussianism and Socialism* was replete with ideas of war socialism (*Kriegssozialismus*) and state planning, now Spengler claims that capitalism and socialism are mere 'slogans': '"capitalism" is not at all a form of economy or a "bourgeois" way of making money. It is a way of seeing things' (79). Hence, he does not need to explain what he understands by them in any detail, 'because you do not define slogans' (65). In this attempt to present his ideas on socialism as consistent across his career from 1919 to 1933, Spengler could perhaps have also referred to the distinction he made in *Prussianism and Socialism* between *ethical* socialism as the universal moral imperative of Faustian culture and *economic* socialism as a manifestation of urban thinking-in-money in *Zivilisation*. He could have added that his socialism never had anything to do with economics, as it is merely a variant on English trader philosophy, of which Marxism is the purest embodiment: 'Marxism is the capitalism of the working class', as he puts it in 1919.[88]

Yet neither Spengler's talk of socialist 'upbringing' regarding *Prussianism and Socialism* nor a reference to the two *forms* of socialism can obscure the fact that he has changed his mind on the question of socialism by 1933. We have already seen how and why he moved away from socialist ideas in *Rebuilding the German Reich*, but in his last work it becomes clear that socialism 'in all its forms' (105) no longer holds any significance in his thought. This is most evident in a small but significant amendment to the claim, first outlined in *Prussianism and Socialism*, that Marxism is the capitalism of the working class. *The Hour of Decision* modifies this quote to maintain that socialism *tout court* is the capitalism of the lower classes, not just its Marxist debasement: 'Socialism is nothing more than the capitalism of the lower classes' (79). Whereas in 1919 Spengler was attempting to salvage socialism from Marx and to channel it into German-nationalist perspectives, he is now trying to rescue Germany and the white world from socialism of all stripes. He even claims that the age of socialism (1840–1940) is coming to an end and thus no longer views it as a necessary expression of Faustian culture, as he does in *The Decline of the West*. Whereas in 1919 he invoked the purportedly Prussian/Germanic virtue of 'one for all and all for one' to convey a semi-utopian sense of what can be achieved by a strong Prussian state of the future, by 1933 he is emphasising the 'truly Germanic' virtue of self-reliance and strength (more of an 'English' virtue in 1919, it should be recalled), not the welfarism and dependency on others that he sees as poisoning the German economy.

The lack of discussion about his ideal Spenglerian state of the future and the absence of the rhetoric of Prussian socialism in *The Hour of Decision* have ensured that it has been mainly received as a disconsolate text. It is often cited as proof of the author's (increasing) pessimism, a 'tragic twilight chapter to the life and work of this unusual thinker'.[89] After all, Spengler appears to be arguing that the great decision facing the *Abendland* is no longer one between English capitalism and Prussian socialism, but rather between the politics of an enlightened elite preserving all that is healthy and vital, and the continued baleful influence of the masses and politics and economics. The outcome could be the collapse of this world under the weight of its own contradictions long *before* his predictions in *The Decline of the West* suggest it might.

*The Hour of Decision* may lack the utopian-nationalist ideas of *Prussianism and Socialism* and the constitutional plans for Caesarism in *Rebuilding the German Reich*, but Spengler nonetheless holds fast to the idea that the German nation – again, with what he views as the right leadership – can tap into its potential and the brilliance that lies dormant within it in order to avert a possible downfall of the Western world. He remains convinced that the best Germans are awaiting the arrival of a man who can deploy power ruthlessly precisely because of his continued conviction that Germany can become the harsh, unswerving power to lead the world in a fashion analogous to Rome in the ancient world.

Spengler is clearly frustrated that National Socialism has emerged as the victorious movement from the array of contradictory trends, tendencies and factions that is the *nationale Bewegung*. He feels that his ideas in *Prussianism and Socialism* have been misunderstood and misappropriated by the National Socialists, but we have shown how the ambiguities in his concept of Prussian socialism must invariably have caused confusion among friend and foe alike. Spengler's conviction that his ideas have been misunderstood can only hold true if we, following the man himself, view his political thought as the ready-made incarnation of his philosophy of history that is largely unresponsive to the events unfolding around him. Spengler was no opportunist in the sense of somebody who profited from the Nazi regime. However, his political principles and judgements are always subordinate to making the best of the *opportunities* he sees as emerging on the horizon. As we have shown in this chapter, *The Hour of Decision* is not conceived as (and nor is it published early enough to be) a text that can exploit the possibilities presented by the overthrow of the Weimar Republic. This is the tragedy of Spengler's interaction with National Socialism: his horror at the consequences of the dictatorship that he partially predicted with his theory of history and championed in his politics of decline. Spengler is no Nazi and his political thought cannot be viewed as that of a forerunner whose thought links the events of 1919 and 1933: he is one of many authoritarian and anti-democratic thinkers who aspire to dictatorial forms. The Nazis do not turn out to be the force of Caesarism he believes must emerge victorious. But Spengler the self-professed prophet never seems to have predicted how the bloody end of the party-political life he held in such contempt could have such devastating consequences for German society and culture. This fundamental failing of his life's work is one he never honestly accounts for and one that, for all his brilliant insights into the nature of the human condition, taints his legacy to this day.

## Notes

1. See, *inter alia*, Hughes, *Oswald Spengler: A Critical Estimate*, 120–36; Felken, *Oswald Spengler: Konservativer Denker zwischen Kaiserreich und Diktatur*, 184–233; Farrenkopf, *Prophet of Decline: Spengler on World History and Politics*, 234–68; Maaß, *Oswald Spengler. Eine politische Biographie*, 93–98.
2. Vollnhals, 'Praeceptor Germaniae. Oswald Spenglers politische Publizistik', 178.
3. Cf. Felken, *Oswald Spengler*, 244.
4. Maaß, *Oswald Spengler*, 9 and 10.
5. Felken, *Oswald Spengler*, 225.
6. Struve, *Elites against Democracy: Leadership Ideals in Bourgeois Political Thought in Germany, 1890–1933*, 270.
7. Ibid.
8. Cf. Koktanek, 'Spenglers Verhältnis zum Nationalsozialismus in geschichtlicher Entwicklung', 50.
9. The condescending words of Hindenburg in August 1932, cited in Pyta, *Die Weimarer Republik*, 139.
10. On Spengler and Fauconnet, see Engels, '"Das Gescheiteste, was überhaupt über mich geschrieben ist". André Fauconnet und Oswald Spengler'.
11. Spengler to André Fauconnet, 15 March 1927, in Spengler, *Briefe 1913–36*, 517.
12. Gregor Strasser to Spengler, 2 June 1925, in ibid., 392.
13. Cf. Koktanek, 'Spenglers Verhältnis', 51.
14. Cited in Felken, *Oswald Spengler*, 188.
15. This is not to imply that Goebbels was not genuinely interested in Spengler's ideas. As Peter Longerich has shown, Goebbel's understanding of 'socialism' was influenced by Spengler's *Prussianism and Socialism*; Longerich, *Goebbels: A Biography*, 48–49.
16. This account of Strasser's life leans on Tartsch, *Denn der Mensch ist ein Raubtier*, 60–64. A different perspective on Strasser's political convictions is offered by Peter D. Stachura, who

claims that Strasser's '"socialism" was vacuous, amounting to little more than an emotionally based, superficial, petty-bourgeois anti-capitalism'; Stachura, *Gregor Strasser and the Rise of Nazism*, 10.
17. Gregor Strasser to Spengler, 8 July 1925, in Spengler, *Briefe 1913–36*, 397.
18. Gregor Strasser to Spengler, 2 June 1925, in ibid., 392.
19. Koktanek, *Spengler in seiner Zeit*, 308; Felken, *Oswald Spengler*, 191.
20. Koktanek, 'Spenglers Verhältnis', 49.
21. Spengler to Albert Knittel, 14 February 1933, in Spengler, *Briefe 1913–36*, 682.
22. Cf. Koktanek, 'Spenglers Verhältnis', 51. Like 'drummer', 'trumpet' was a derogatory term for Hitler at the time.
23. Cf. Felken, *Oswald Spengler*, 191.
24. Cf. ibid., 192.
25. Cf. Koktanek, *Spengler in seiner Zeit*, 427.
26. Cf. ibid., 438.
27. Demandt somewhat spuriously asserts that Spengler 'bumped into' Hitler in Bayreuth and that 'the *Führer*'s monologue on the political incompetence of Protestantism stifled their discussion'; Demandt, *Untergänge des Abendlandes. Studien zu Oswald Spengler*, 46.
28. Boyd, *Travellers in the Third Reich*, 142.
29. Cf. Koktanek, 'Spenglers Verhältnis', 51.
30. Cf. ibid.
31. Cf. Felken, *Oswald Spengler*, 194. Osmančević claims that Hitler and Spengler agree to convene on a monthly basis; Osmančević, *Oswald Spengler und das Ende der Geschichte*, 98.
32. Cf. Koktanek, 'Spenglers Verhältnis', 51.
33. Cf., ibid., 52.
34. Spengler to Alfons Sack, 25 November 1933, in Spengler, *Briefe 1913–36*, 716.
35. Spengler, '*Ich beneide jeden, der lebt*'. *Die Aufzeichnungen 'Eis heauton' aus dem Nachlaß* (Düsseldorf: Lilienverlag, 2007), 32.
36. Spengler to Adolf Hitler, 18 August 1933, in ibid., 699.
37. Naeher, *Oswald Spengler*, 128.
38. On this, see Felken, *Oswald Spengler*, 219.
39. He also speculates as to the longer future of the world order, not least in the form of a potential conflict between Russian state socialism and American state capitalism; cf. ibid., 204.
40. Spengler, *The Hour of Decision, Part One: Germany and World-Historical Evolution*.
41. Maaß, *Oswald Spengler. Eine politische Biographie*, 91.
42. Tartsch, *Denn der Mensch ist ein Raubtier. Eine Einführung in die politischen Schriften und Theorien Oswald Spenglers*, 199.
43. Hughes, *Oswald Spengler: A Critical Estimate*, 127. Markus Henkel argues that: 'There is no evidence that Spengler's writings were banned during the Third Reich'; Henkel, *Nationalkonservative Politik*, 30. It should also be noted that two editions of Spengler's writings were posthumously published during the Nazi regime.
44. Hughes, *Oswald Spengler: A Critical Estimate*, 127.
45. Thöndl, 'Das Politikbild von Oswald Spengler (1880–1936) mit einer Ortsbestimmung seines politischen Urteils über Hitler und Mussolini', 427.
46. Emphasis added to highlight Spengler's shifting understanding of *all* forms of 'worker socialism' as English.
47. Spengler, *Der Untergang des Abendlandes*, 1004.
48. Thöndl, '"Wie oft stirbt das Abendland?" Oswald Spenglers These vom zweifachen Untergang', 262.
49. Cf. Felken, *Oswald Spengler*, 220.
50. The reception of Spengler's work by Mussolini in particular and Italy more generally is usefully surveyed in Thöndl, *Oswald Spengler in Italien: Kulturexport politischer Ideen der 'Konservativen Revolution'*.
51. Henkel, *Nationalkonservative Politik*, 376.

52. Fischer writes: 'Rumor had it that before the two men separated, Hitler asked Spengler for one final bit of advice. Spengler is said to have responded cryptically: "Watch your Praetorian guard!"' This warning would certainly be consistent with Spengler's conception of the need for Caesarism to stand above the influence of the masses on politics, but Fischer does not provide any proof for this assertion and so it should be treated with caution; Fischer, *History and Prophecy: Oswald Spengler and the Decline of the West*, 74.
53. 'Ever since Hitler had asserted himself against Strasser, his growing movement increasingly found support among Germany's large industrialists'; Koktanek, *Oswald Spengler in seiner Zeit*, 308.
54. Cited in Felken, *Oswald Spengler*, 229.
55. Cited in ibid., 219.
56. Cited in ibid., 227.
57. Cited in ibid., 228.
58. Maaß, *Oswald Spengler*, 91.
59. Engels, Otte and Thöndl, *Der lange Schatten Oswald Spenglers. Einhundert Jahre Untergang des Abendlandes*, 7–13 (13).
60. Farrenkopf, *Prophet of Decline*, 236; 3.
61. Koktanek, 'Spenglers Verhältnis', 53.
62. Felken, *Oswald Spengler*, 197.
63. von Leers, *Spenglers weltpolitisches System und der Nationalsozialismus*, 27.
64. Gründel, *Jahre der Überwindung. Umfassende Abrechnung mit dem 'Untergangs'-Magier – Aufgabe der deutschen Intellektuellen – weltgeschichtliche Sinndeutung des Nationalsozialismus: ein offenes Wort an alle Geistigen*.
65. Koktanek, 'Spenglers Verhältnis', 54.
66. Koktanek, *Spengler in seiner Zeit*, 222.
67. See, *inter alia*, Horneffer, *Oswald Spengler – wie ich ihn sehe*; Krumm, *Der deutsche Sozialismus nach Hitler. Spengler und der Aufstieg des Nationalsozialismus*; Muhs, *Spengler und der wirtschaftliche Untergang Europas*.
68. Zweiniger, *Spengler im Dritten Reich. Eine Antwort auf Oswald Spenglers Jahre der Entscheidung*'; von Leers, *Spenglers weltpolitisches System und der Nationalsozialismus*.
69. For a useful collection of essays on the Nazi regime's ideological appeal and incorporation of utopian ideas, see Brockhaus (ed.), *Attraktion der NS-Bewegung*.
70. Zweiniger, *Spengler im Dritten Reich*, 9.
71. Ibid., 9.
72. Ibid., 10.
73. Ibid. This is a distinction that, as we saw in Chapter 2, Spengler makes in *The Decline of the West*.
74. Zweiniger, *Spengler im dritten Reich*, 11.
75. von Leers, *Spenglers weltpolitisches System*, 5.
76. Ibid.
77. The first three chapters of Francis R. Nicosia's study provide more context on issues of Nazism and anti-Semitism in the Kaiserreich and the Weimar Republic; Nicosia, *Zionism and Anti-Semitism in Nazi Germany*.
78. Spengler, *Der Untergang des Abendlandes. Umrisse einer Morphologie der Weltgeschichte*, 2 vols (1997 [1923]), 710.
79. Spengler, *Neubau des deutschen Reiches*, 18, fn. 1, emphasis added.
80. Spengler, *Der Untergang des Abendlandes*, 960, emphasis added.
81. Spengler's linking of Jewish and English thought in Bentham and Marx was removed from later editions of *Der Untergang des Abendlandes*; Spengler, *Der Untergang des Abendlandes. Erster Band: Gestalt und Wirklichkeit* (1920 [1919]), 206, 190. The denunciation of Spinoza, by contrast, was not; Spengler, *Der Untergang des Abendlandes*, 533.
82. Spengler to Hans Klöres, 14 July 1915, in Spengler, *Briefe 1913–36*, 44.
83. Cf. Vollnhals, 'Praeceptor Germaniae. Oswald Spenglers politische Publizistik', 195.

84. Cf. ibid., 191.
85. As depicted in the Nazi electoral poster from the early 1930s, entitled 'Tod der Lüge' ('Death of the Lie'), in which a Nazi member can be seen wringing the neck of a snake emblazoned with the words 'Marxism' and 'high finance'.
86. Von Leers, *Spenglers weltpolitisches System und der Nationalsozialismus*, 32.
87. Felken, *Oswald Spengler*, 230.
88. Spengler, *Preußentum und Sozialismus*, 75.
89. Farrenkopf, *Prophet of Decline*, 235.

# Conclusion

In this volume, we have advanced three main arguments. First, we have challenged the view that Spengler was a philosophical pessimist whose historical schema was straightforwardly determinist and implied a fatalist *diagnosis* of the decline of the Western world. We have shown that this reading of Spengler's work is particularly prominent in the handful of English-language discussions of his ideas. This approach is almost invariably based on a one-sided focus on, and misreading of, his major work *The Decline of the West*. This book was far from a 'post-mortem' of the West (Klaus P. Fischer), nor was it the output of a 'prophet of doom and gloom' (John Fennelly). By contrast, we have shown how Spengler aimed to outline a rigorously informed historical consciousness with which to address the manifold political tasks he identified within an age of wars and uprisings. Informed by this new understanding, the individuals and groupings he saw as the driving force of history could navigate the tides of history, instead of being swept aside by them ('Ducunt fata volentem, nolentem trahunt'). Depending on the circumstances in which he employed the term, *Untergang* not only referred to his idea that all historical formations would eventually die, but was also used as a rhetorical device to express the urgency with which the remaining problems of the West (*das Abendland*) must be solved.

Second, by shifting the focus from *The Decline of the West* to an analysis of Spengler's political activities and writings, our volume – the first such English-language work – has contributed to a more rounded understanding of Spengler as a well-connected and influential public intellectual. We have shown how he – in contrast to Alexander Demandt's claim that 'those who know what is going to happen do not say what should be done'– did in fact develop an informed political project, a *prognosis* of establishing a German-led socio-political order *within* the process of decline. While it did not amount to a single overarching, holistic programme across his career, this venture was a serious and interventionist one, which was geared towards his country going down in history (in both senses of the phrase) as a modern-day Rome. For this reason, we have demonstrated how the claims that Spengler was an isolated independent scholar (Jürgen Naeher), a political sciolist who 'made something of a fool of himself' during his career (Fennelly) or a philosopher who was overwhelmed by the unforgiving world of politics (Paul Hoser) are simplistic and one-sided. We have referred to this lifelong political project as Prussianism (*Preußentum*), in which his attachment to the German nation and his understanding of politics as the preserve of an enlightened elite intertwined. Both evolved in response to the major events of his life. In other words, our contextualisation, summary and analysis of his major political publications and activities have been able to explain how and why the content of his nationalist, anti-democratic and authoritarian project assumed different forms across his career: from his Prussian *socialism* of 1919 through to his contribution to the emergence of a German Caesar in 1924 and his extended discussion of the relationship between Caesarism and fascism in 1933. All the while, we have taken into consideration Spengler's historical method and his motivations, context as well as content, in the development of his ideas.

Third, doing so has allowed us to make a significant contribution to the understanding of Spengler the politician. As opposed to the limited literature that does engage with his political project, we have not treated his political thought as a fixed and static entity across his career (Detlef Felken), in which a text such as *Rebuilding the German Reich* contains nothing that was not already present in *Prussianism and Socialism* (Thomas Tartsch). Nor have we approached it as merely the extension of his philosophy of world history (Ernst Stutz). Instead, by contextualising Spengler's political works and writings, we have been able to highlight both the continuities and discontinuities within his political thought between 1919 and 1933. In contrast to the thinkers who note a 'classically conservative dimension' (Domenico Conte) to Spengler's politics or a Tory understanding of state and society (Markus Henkel) in the mid-1920s, we have demonstrated how Spengler's radical opposition to liberal democracy was an unswerving feature of his thought from 1918 onwards. At the same time, we have highlighted the enduring significance of Caesarism – both as a historical prediction and as the basis of his politics of decline – from 1922 onwards. We have thereby questioned John Farrenkopf's idea that it is 'simplistic' to view Spengler as an anti-democratic thinker, as well as Henkel's description of Spengler's 'openly declared belief in an (unbeloved) pluralistic democracy'. By closely tracing Spengler's pragmatism and flexibility in applying some of the core tenets of his philosophy of world history to his political work, we have been able to show what was specific about his politics vis-à-vis other trends on the German far right in his time. In so doing, we have been able to locate the strengths and shortcomings of more nuanced discussions of Spengler's politics in the secondary literature: to wit, H. Stuart Hughes's distinction between short-term optimism and long-term pessimism in his ideas; Farrenkopf's notion that Spengler gradually moved from qualified optimism to outright pessimism; Sebastian Maaß's idea that Spengler was a thinker of 'heroic realism'; and Martin Falck's location of 'utopian traits' in Spengler's thought.

Ultimately, our discussion of Spengler's politics of decline challenges his self-stylisation as a historical seer. As he put it: 'I see more clearly than others because I think independently – free of parties, schools of thought and interests. I have foreseen how things developed organically, according to fate [*schicksalhaft*] and how they will continue to develop.'[1] By contrast, we have shown not only how very few of Spengler's predictions came to fruition in his life, but also how his political thought partly developed in response to the particular interests he was pursuing at any given point: whether in the form of his commitment to an alliance between the aristocracy and nationalist-minded workers in 1919 or in his role as a lobbyist for German industrial interests in the 1920s. We have also shown how misleading is Spengler's Preface to his *Political Writings*, in which he claimed that he has never modified, or felt the need to modify, anything of fundamental importance he has ever written: 'I may say, without beating about the bush, that I have not been wrong on any issue of significance.'[2] Our study has shown Spengler as a pragmatist who sought to uphold, and intellectually justify, his life's mission of a German rebirth in a variety of ways. This overriding aim carried perhaps even more weight than any metaphysical claims or historical consistency in his thought: both were duly amended in response to contingent and often confusing events, not just in anticipation of them. While Spengler claims that his method is based not on 'sentimental romanticism', but on purportedly objective 'sober facts and deliberations',[3] we have seen how it is impossible to understand his political ideas and actions without taking into account his own feelings, aims and desires – particularly his German nationalism.

As the changing theorisation of socialism across his career underlines, Spengler was more than willing to modify or dispense with earlier ideas in order to adapt best to the opportunities he saw before him. His ideological relationship with fascism is thus a fitting place to conclude this publication. This relationship brings to the fore a recurring frustration in Spengler's political career: his attempts to impose a rigorous worldview on his life and times – even when this was done with what Ernst Bloch has deemed outright opportunism – did not always yield the outcomes Spengler desired. This was particularly true of his experience as a thinker of the right-wing authoritarian nationalist movement (*die nationale Bewegung*). This movement was a bewilderingly heterogeneous spectrum of conflicting ideas and ideologies about how to overthrow the Weimar Republic, from which the National Socialists eventually emerged victorious. We have demonstrated that, for all the common ground he shared with Hitler and his allies, Spengler was no National Socialist. However, nor could he be counted amongst the 'most prominent critics' (David Engels, Max Otte and Michael Thöndl) of the Nazis after 1933. His entire political career aimed at the establishment either of dictatorial political forms or ones that could best facilitate the emergence of a dictator in Germany. That National Socialism represented the 'wrong kind' of dictatorship should not obscure this basic fact.

The centrality of authoritarianism to Spengler's politics of decline has important implications for the assessment of his legacy as a thinker. Theodor Adorno once wrote that 'the forgotten Spengler takes his revenge by threatening to be right'.[4] By showing Spengler's political thought in all its complexity and contradictions across his career, this study will hopefully make it more difficult for subsequent generations to cast him as the all-seeing historical prophet he always sought to portray himself as. Spengler was a fascinating, provocative and astute thinker, but our discussion of his political ideas has shown that he was more of a pragmatist than a prophet, more of a realist than a 'prophet of decline' (Farrenkopf) who was 'able to see like Cassandra and was just as scandalous and lonely' (Koktanek). Spengler's insights into humanity's efforts to grasp the world around it remain brilliant, but they were always the product of a thinker who was steeped within the mentality of his age, not of a thinker writing 'from timeless heights'.[5] His ideas are both a diagnosis of the problems and tensions within the modern world and an occasionally disturbing reflection of them.

## Notes

1. Spengler, 'Vorwort', in *Politische Schriften 1919–1926*, 14.
2. Ibid., 7.
3. Spengler to André Fauconnet, 15 March 1927, in Spengler, *Briefe 1913–36*, 517.
4. Adorno, 'Spengler nach dem Untergang', 115.
5. Spengler, *Der Untergang des Abendlandes. Umrisse einer Morphologie der Weltgeschichte*, 47.

# Bibliography

## Works by Spengler

1904, 'Heraklit', in Oswald Spengler, *Reden und Aufsätze*, 4th edn (Berlin: Contumax, 2016), 4–44.
1910, 'Der Sieger', in Spengler, *Reden und Aufsätze*, 45–49.
1914, 'Zum Problem der modernen christlichen Kunst', in Martin Falck (ed.), *Zyklen und Cäsaren. Mosaiksteine einer Philosophie des Schicksals* (Kiel: Regin, 2013), 155–60.
1917, 'Spengler, 'Krieg, Drama und Roman', in Falck (ed.), *Zyklen und Cäsaren*, 161–67.
1920, 'Einführung zu Ernst Droems *Gesängen*', in Spengler, *Reden und Aufsätze*, 50–57.
1920 [1919], *Untergang des Abendlandes. Umrisse einer Morphologie der Weltgeschichte. Erster Band: Gestalt und Wirklichkeit* (Munich: Beck, unveränderte Auflage, 1920).
1920 [1919], *Preußentum und Sozialismus* (Munich: Beck, 1920).
1921, 'Pessimismus?', in Spengler, *Reden und Aufsätze*, 58–71.
1922, 'Das Doppelantlitz Rußlands und die deutschen Ostprobleme', in Oswald Spengler, *Politische Schriften 1919–1926* (Leipzig: Manuscriptum, 2009), 112–28.
1922, 'Moderne Kriegsführung', in Falck (ed.), *Zyklen und Cäsaren*, 258–60.
1924, 'Aufgaben des Adels', in Spengler, *Reden und Aufsätze*, 79–84.
1924, 'Das Verhältnis von Wirtschaft und Steuerpolitik seit 1750', in Spengler, *Politische Schriften 1919–1926*, 283–94.
1924, *Die Revolution ist nicht zu Ende*, Schriften an die Nation, 35 (Oldenbourg: Stalling, 1924).
1924, 'Frankreich und Europa', in Spengler, *Reden und Aufsätze*, 72–78.
1924, *Neubau des deutschen Reiches* (Munich: Beck, 1924).
1924, 'Neue Formen der Weltpolitik', in Spengler, *Politische Schriften 1919–1926*, 155–78.
1924, 'Neue Regierungsformen', in Falck (ed.), *Zyklen und Cäsaren*, 271–74.
1924, 'Nietzsche und sein Jahrhundert', in Spengler, *Reden und Aufsätze*, 98–110.
1924, 'Plan eines neuen Atlas Antiquus', in Spengler, *Reden und Aufsätze*, 85–92.
1924, 'Politische Pflichten der deutschen Jugend', in Spengler, *Politische Schriften 1919–1926*, 128–54.
1924, 'Staatsdienst und Persönlichkeit', *Die Polizei: Fachzeitschrift für die öffentliche Sicherheit mit Beiträgen aus der Deutschen Hochschule der Polizei*, 21 (1924), 276–79.

1924, 'Zehn Jahre nach Kriegsausbruch', in Falck (ed.), *Zyklen und Cäsaren*, 320–21.
1926, 'Zur Entwicklungsgeschichte der deutschen Presse', in Spengler, *Reden und Aufsätze*, 111–13.
1926, 'Das heutige Verhältnis zwischen Weltwirtschaft und Weltpolitik', in Spengler, *Politische Schriften 1919–1926*, 295–319.
1927, 'Einführung zu einem Aufsatz Richard Kornherrs über den Geburtenrückgang', in Spengler, *Reden und Aufsätze*, 120–21.
1927, 'Vom deutschen Volkscharakter', in Spengler, *Reden und Aufsätze*, 116–19.
1933, Spengler, 'Das Alter der amerikanischen Kulturen', in Spengler, *Reden und Aufsätze*, 122–30.
1934, 'Der Streitwagen und seine Bedeutung für den Gang der Weltgeschichte', in Spengler, *Reden und Aufsätze*, 122–30.
1934, *The Hour of Decision. Part One: Germany and World-Historical Evolution*, translated by Charles Francis Atkinson (New York: A.A. Knopf, 1934).
1935, Oswald Spengler, Willi Schmid and Peter Dörfler (eds), *Unvollendete Symphonie. Gedanken und Dichtung von Willi Schmid* (Munich: Oldenbourg, 1935).
1935, 'Zur Weltgeschichte des zweiten vorchristlichen Jahrtausends', in Spengler, *Reden und Aufsätze*, 139–258.
1936, 'Ist Weltfriede möglich?', in Spengler, *Reden und Aufsätze*, 259–60.
1941, *Gedanken* (Munich: Beck, 1941).
1961 [1933], *Jahre der Entscheidung. Erster Teil: Deutschland und die weltgeschichtliche Entwicklung* (Munich: Beck, 1961).
1963, *Briefe 1913–36* (Munich: Beck, 1963).
1965, *Urfragen. Fragmente aus dem Nachlaß* (Munich: Beck, 1965).
1966, *Frühzeit der Weltgeschichte. Fragmente aus dem Nachlaß* (Munich: Beck, 1966).
1997 [1923], *Der Untergang des Abendlandes. Umrisse einer Morphologie der Weltgeschichte*, 13th edn (Munich: dtv, 1997).
2007, *'Ich beneide jeden, der lebt'. Die Aufzeichnungen 'Eis heauton' aus dem Nachlaß* (Düsseldorf: Lilienverlag, 2007).
2009, *Politische Schriften 1919–1926* (Leipzig: Manuscriptum, 2009).
2013 [1931], 'Der Mensch und die Technik. Beitrag zu einer Philosophie des Lebens', in Falck (ed.), *Zyklen und Cäsaren*, 368–406.

## Secondary Literature

Adorno, Theodor W., 'Spengler nach dem Untergang', *Der Monat*, 20 (1950), 115–28.
Agard, Oliver, and Barbara Beßlich (eds), *Kulturkritik zwischen Deutschland und Frankreich (1890–1933)* (Frankfurt am Main: Peter Lang, 2016).
Baltzer, Armin, *Untergang 'oder' Vollendung. Spenglers bleibende Bedeutung* (Göttingen: Elsner, 1956).
Barry, John, 'The "Waste Land": A Possible German Source', *Comparative Literature Studies*, 9(1) (1972), 129–12.
Bernstein, Eduard, *Ferdinand Lassalle und seine Bedeutung für die Arbeiterklasse. Zu seinem vierzigsten Todestage* (Berlin: Vorwärts, 1904).
Beßlich, Barbara, *Wege in den 'Kulturkrieg'. Zivilisationskritik in Deutschland 1890–1914* (Darmstadt: Wissenschaftliche Buchgesellschaft, 2000).

———, 'Untergangs-Mißverständnisse. Spenglers literarische Provokationen und Deutungen der Zeitgenossen', in Gangl, Merlio and Orphälders (eds), *Spengler. Ein Denker der Zeitenwende*, 29–52.

Birkenmaier, Anke, *Versionen Montezumas. Lateinamerika in der historischen Imagination des 19. Jahrhunderts. Mit dem vollständigen Manuskript von Oswald Spenglers 'Montezuma. Ein Trauerspiel' (1897)* (Berlin: de Gruyter, 2011).

Bloch, Ernst, 'Spengler als Optimist', in *Philosophische Aufsätze zur objektiven Phantasie*. Werkausgabe, Vol. 10 (Frankfurt am Main: Suhrkamp, 1969), 192–97.

———, 'Spenglers Raubtiere und relative Kulturgärten', in *Erbschaft dieser Zeit*. Werkausgabe, Vol. 4 (Frankfurt am Main: Suhrkamp, 1985), 318–29.

Bollenbeck, Georg, *Tradition, Avantgarde, Reaktion. Deutsche Kontroversen um die kulturelle Moderne 1880–1945* (Frankfurt am Main: Fischer, 1999).

Bolz, Norbert, *Auszug aus der entzauberten Welt. Philosophischer Extremismus zwischen den Weltkriegen*, 2nd edn (Munich: Fink, 1991).

Boterman, Frits, *Oswald Spengler en 'Der Untergang des Abendlandes'. Cultuurpessimist en politiek activist* (Assen: Van Gorcum, 1992).

———, *Oswald Spengler und sein 'Untergang des Abendlandes'* (Cologne: SH-Verlag, 2000).

Boyd, Julia, *Travellers in the Third Reich* (London: Elliot & Thompson, 2017).

Boyle, Nicholas, *Goethe: The Poet and the Age. Volume II: Revolution and Renunciation* (Oxford: Oxford University Press, 2003).

Breysig, Kurt, 'Der Prophet des Untergangs', *Velhagen & Klasings Monatshefte*, 35(7) (1921), 261–70.

Brockhaus, Gudrun (ed.), *Attraktion der NS-Bewegung* (Essen: Klartext, 2014).

Broué, Pierre, *The German Revolution 1917–1923* (London: Merlin Press, 2005 [1971]).

Canning, George, *Memoirs of the Life of the Rt. Hon George Canning*, Vol. 2 (London: Thomas Tegg, 1830).

Carey, John, *The Intellectuals and the Masses: Pride and Prejudice among the Literary Intelligentsia, 1880–1939* (London: Faber & Faber, 1992).

Carr, William, *Hitler: A Study in Personality and Politics* (London: Edward Arnold, 1995).

Conte, Domenico, *Oswald Spengler. Eine Einführung* (Leipzig: Leipziger Universitätsverlag, 2004).

Dakin, Edwin Franden (ed.), *Today and Destiny: Vital Excerpts from the 'Decline of the West' of Oswald Spengler* (New York: A.A. Knopf, 1940).

de Berg, Henk, *Freud's Theory and Its Use in Literary and Cultural Studies* (Rochester, NY: Camden House, 2003).

de Berg, Henk, and Duncan Large (eds), *Modern German Thought from Kant to Habermas: An Annotated German-Language Reader* (Rochester, NY: Camden House, 2012).

de Winde, Arne et al. (eds), *Tektonik der Systeme. Neulektüren von Oswald Spengler* (Heidelberg: Synchron, 2016).

de Winde, Arne, Sven Fabré, Sientie Maes and Bart Philipsen, 'Geschichtete Geschichten. Spengler zur Einführung', 10–16.

Demandt, Alexander, *Untergänge des Abendlandes. Studien zu Oswald Spengler* (Cologne: Böhlau, 2017).

Demandt, Alexander, and John Farrenkopf (eds), *Der Fall Spengler. Eine kritische Bilanz* (Cologne: Böhlau, 1994).

Drascher, Wahrhold, 'Begegnungen mit Oswald Spengler', in Koktanek (ed.), *Spengler-Studien. Festgabe für Manfred Schröter zum 85. Geburtstag*, 9–31.
Eisner, Freya, 'Kurt Eisners Ort in der sozialistischen Bewegung', *Vierteljahrshefte für Zeitgeschichte*, 43(3) (1995), 407–35.
Eisner, Kurt, *Wilhelm Liebknecht. Sein Leben und Wirken* (Bremen: Europäischer Literaturverlag, 2012 [1900]).
Engels, David, '"Das Gescheiteste, was überhaupt über mich geschrieben ist". André Fauconnet und Oswald Spengler', in Gasimov and Lemke Duque (eds), *Oswald Spengler als europäisches Phänomen. Der Transfer der Kultur- und Geschichtsmorphologie im Europa der Zwischenkriegszeit 1919–1939*, 105–56.
———. *Auf dem Weg ins Imperium. Die Krise der Europäischen Union und der Untergang der römischen Republik. Historische Parallelen* (Munich: Europa Verlag, 2014).
———. (ed.), *Oswald Spenglers Geschichtsmorphologie heute* (Berlin: Manuscriptum, 2020).
———. *Oswald Spengler: Werk, Deutung, Rezeption* (Stuttgart: Kohlhammer, 2021).
Engels, David, Max Otte and Michael Thöndl, 'Einhundert Jahre *Untergang des Abendlandes (1918–2018)*', in Engels, Otte and Thöndl (eds), *Der lange Schatten Oswald Spenglers*, 7–13.
Engels, David, Max Otte and Michael Thöndl (eds), *Der lange Schatten Oswald Spenglers. Einhundert Jahre Untergang des Abendlandes*, Schriftenreihe der Oswald Spengler Society for the Study of Humanity and World History (Berlin: Manuscriptum, 2018).
Engels, Friedrich, 'Zur Kritik des sozialdemokratischen Programmentwurfes', in Karl Marx and Friedrich Engels, *Werke*, Vol. 22, 227–40.
Falck, Martin (ed.), *Zyklen und Cäsaren. Mosaiksteine einer Philosophie des Schicksals* (Kiel: Regin, 2013).
Farrenkopf, John, 'The Transformation of Spengler's Political Philosophy', *Journal of the History of Ideas*, 52(3) (1991), 463–85.
———. 'Klio und Cäsar. Spenglers Philosophie der Weltgeschichte im Dienste der Staatskunst', in Demandt and Farrenkopf (eds), *Der Fall Spengler. Eine kritische Bilanz*), 45–73.
———. *Prophet of Decline: Spengler on World History and Politics* (Baton Rouge: Louisiana State University Press, 2001).
Felken, Detlef, *Oswald Spengler. Konservativer Denker zwischen Kaiserreich und Diktatur* (Munich: Beck, 1988).
Fennelly, John F., *Twilight of the Evening Lands: Oswald Spengler – A Half Century Later* (New York: Brookdale Press, 1972).
Fischer, Klaus P., *History and Prophecy: Oswald Spengler and the Decline of the West* (New York: Peter Lang, 1989).
Fischer, Torben, and Matthias N. Lorenz (eds), *Lexikon der 'Vergangenheitsbewältigung' in Deutschland. Debatten und Diskursgeschichte des Nationalsozialismus nach 1945*, 3rd edn (Bielefeld: Transcript, 2015).
Föllmer, Moritz, and Rüdiger Graf (eds), *Die 'Krise' der Weimarer Republik. Zur Kritik eines Deutungsmusters* (Frankfurt am Main: Campus, 2005).
Frölich, Paul, Graf Ernst Reventlow and Arthur Moeller van den Bruck, *Schlageter. Eine Auseinandersetzung* (Berlin: Vereinigung Internationaler Verlag-Anstalten, 1923).
Gangl, Manfred, Gilbert Merlio and Markus Orphälders (eds), *Spengler. Ein Denker der Zeitenwende* (Frankfurt: Peter Lang, 2009).

Gasimov, Zaur, and Carl Antonius Lemke Duque (eds), *Oswald Spengler als europäisches Phänomen. Der Transfer der Kultur- und Geschichtsmorphologie im Europa der Zwischenkriegszeit 1919–1939* (Göttingen: Vandenhoeck & Ruprecht, 2013).
Goethe, Johann Wolfgang von, *Der Versuch die Metamorphose der Pflanzen zu erklären* (Gotha: Ettingersche Buchhandlung, 1790).
Graf, Rüdiger, 'Die "Krise" im intellektuellen Zukunftsdiskurs der Weimarer Republik', in Moritz Föllmer and Rüdiger Graf (eds), *Die 'Krise' der Weimarer Republik. Zur Kritik eines Deutungsmusters* (Frankfurt am Main: Campus, 2005), 77–106.
Graham, Ilse, *Goethe: Portrait of the Artist* (Berlin: Walter de Gruyter, 1977).
Gründel, Günther, *Jahre der Überwindung. Umfassende Abrechnung mit dem 'Untergangs'-Magier – Aufgabe der deutschen Intellektuellen – weltgeschichtliche Sinndeutung des Nationalsozialismus: ein offenes Wort an alle Geistigen* (Breslau: W. G Korn, 1934).
Günther, Albrecht Erich, 'Wandlung der sozialen und politischen Weltanschauung des Mittelstandes', *Der Ring*, 4(22) (1931), 408–10.
Gusejnova, Dina, 'Der Prophet als Parfum. Das Spenglersche am europäischen und amerikanischen Modernismus', *Zeitschrift für Weltgeschichte*, 15(1) (2014), 141–61.
Henkel, Markus, *Nationalkonservative Politik und mediale Repräsentation. Oswald Spenglers politische Philosophie und Programmatik im Netzwerk der Oligarchen (1910–1925)* (Würzburg: Nomos, 2012).
Herf, Jeffery, *Reactionary Modernism: Technology, Culture and Politics in Weimar and the Third Reich* (Cambridge: Cambridge University Press, 1984).
Heuss, Theodor, *Kriegssozialismus* (Berlin: Deutsche Verlags-Anstalt, 1915).
———. 'Das Geschäftsprojekt des Diktators', ÖVW 16.37, 14 July 1924, 1135–37.
Hilberg, Raul, *Die Vernichtung der europäischen Juden*, Vol. 3 (Frankfurt: Fischer, 1990).
Horneffer, Ernst, *Oswald Spengler – wie ich ihn sehe* (Stuttgart: Frommann, 1934).
Hörste-Phillips, Ulrike, *Joseph Wirth 1879–1956. Eine politische Biographie* (Paderborn: Schöninghausen, 1998).
Hoser, Paul, 'Ein Philosoph im Irrgarten der Politik. Oswald Spenglers Pläne für eine geheime Lenkung der nationalen Presse', *Vierteljahrshefte für Zeitgeschichte*, 38(3) (1990), 435–58.
Hughes, H. Stuart, *Oswald Spengler: A Critical Estimate* (New York: Charles Scribner's Sons, 1952).
Huntington, Samuel, *The Clash of Civilizations and the Remaking of World Order* (New York: Simon & Schuster, 1996).
———. *Kampf der Kulturen. Die Neugestaltung der Weltpolitik im 21. Jahrhundert* (Munich: Goldmann, 1998).
Joll, James, 'Two Prophets of the Twentieth Century: Spengler and Toynbee', *Review of International Studies*, 11(2) (1985), 91–104.
Kamphausen, Georg, *Die Erfindung Amerikas in der Kulturkritik der Generation von 1890* (Weilerswist: Velbrück Wissenschaft, 2002).
Kautsky, Karl, 'Republic and Social Democracy in France', in Lewis (ed.), *Karl Kautsky on Democracy and Republicanism*, 157–269.
Klemperer, Klemens von, *Germany's New Conservatism: Its History and Dilemma in the Twentieth Century*, 2nd edn (Princeton: Princeton University Press, 1968).
Koktanek, Anton Mirko, 'Spenglers Verhältnis zum Nationalsozialismus in geschichtlicher Entwicklung', *Zeitschrift für Politik*, 13(1) (1966), 33–55.

———. *Oswald Spengler in seiner Zeit* (Munich: Beck, 1968).
———. (ed.), *Spengler-Studien. Festgabe für Manfred Schröter zum 85. Geburtstag* (Munich: Beck, 1965).
Kolb, Eberhard, *The Weimar Republic* (London: Routledge, 2001).
Krebs, Wolfgang, *Die imperiale Endzeit – Oswald Spengler und die Zukunft der abendländischen Zivilisation* (Berlin: Rhombos, 2008).
Kroll, Joe Paul, '"A Biography of the Soul": Oswald Spengler's Biographical Method and the Morphology of History', *German Life and Letters*, 62(1) (2009), 67–83.
Kroner, Richard, and Georg Mehlis (eds), *Logos. Internationale Zeitschrift für Philosophie der Kultur*, 9(2) (1921).
Krumm, Paul, *Der deutsche Sozialismus nach Hitler. Spengler und der Aufstieg des Nationalsozialismus* (Leipzig: Das Neue Deutschland, 1934).
Lassalle, Ferdinand, *Was nun? Zweiter Vortrag über Verfassungswesen* (Zurich: Meyer & Zeller, 1863).
———. 'Offenes Antwortschreiben an das Zentralkommitee zur Berufung eines Allgemeinen Deutschen Arbeiterkongresses', in Ferdinand Lassalle, *Gesammelte Reden und Schriften*, Vol. 3 (Berlin: Paul Cassirer, 1919 [1863]), 41–107.
Leers, Johann von, *Spenglers weltpolitisches System und der Nationalsozialismus* (Berlin: Junker und Dünnhaupt, 1934).
Lenin, Vladimir Ilych, 'Theses for an Appeal to the International Socialist Committee and All Socialist Parties'. Retrieved 4 February 2022 from https://www.marxists.org/archive/lenin/works/1916/dec/25.htm.
Lensch, Paul, *Drei Jahre Weltrevolution* (Berlin: Fischer, 1918).
Lewis, Ben, 'The Four-Hour Speech and the Significance of Halle', in Ben Lewis and Lars T. Lih (eds), *Zinoviev and Martov: Head-to-Head in Halle* (London: November Publications, 2011), 7–36.
———. 'Bebel's Forgotten Legacy', *Weekly Worker*, 959, 25 April 2013, 8.
———. 'The SPD Left's Dirty Secret', *Weekly Worker*, 1016, 26 June 2014, 10–11.
———. (ed.), *Karl Kautsky on Democracy and Republicanism* (Leiden: Brill, 2019).
Lewis, Ben, and Lars T. Lih (eds), *Zinoviev and Martov: Head-to-Head in Halle* (London: November Publications, 2011)
Longerich, Peter, *Goebbels: A Biography* (London: Vintage, 2015).
Lübbe, Hermann, *Politische Philosophie in Deutschland* (Munich: dtv, 1974).
———. 'Oswald Spenglers "Preußentum und Sozialismus" und Ernst Jüngers "Arbeiter"', in Alexander Demandt and John Farrenkopf (eds), *Der Fall Spengler. Eine kritische Bilanz* (Cologne: Böhlau, 1994), 129–52.
Lukács, Georg, *Die Zerstörung der Vernunft* (Berlin: Aufbau-Verlag, 1954).
Ludz, Peter Christian (ed.), *Spengler heute. Sechs Essays mit einem Vorwort von Hermann Lübbe* (Munich: Beck, 1980).
Maaß, Sebastian, *Oswald Spengler. Eine politische Biographie* (Berlin: Duncker & Humblot, 2013).
Maehl, William Harvey, *Shadow Emperor of the German Workers* (Philadelphia: American Philosophical Society, 1980).
Marx, Karl, *Value, Price and Profit* (New York: International Publishers, 1969).
———. *Capital Volume I* (London: Penguin, 1990).
———. 'Critique of the Gotha Programme', in Marx and Engels, *Selected Works*, Vol. 3, 13–30.
Marx, Karl, and Friedrich Engels, 'The Communist Manifesto', in Marx and Engels, *Selected Works*, Vol. 1, 98–137.

———. *Selected Works*, Vol. 1 (Moscow: Progress Publishers, 1969).
———. *Selected Works*, Vol. 3 (Moscow: Progress Publishers, 1970).
———. *Werke*, Vol. 22 (Berlin: Dietz, 1972).
Merlio, Gilbert, 'Urgefühl Angst', in Spengler, *'Ich beneide jeden, der lebt'. Die Aufzeichnungen 'Eis heauton' aus dem Nachlaß*, 89–123.
———. 'Spenglers Geschichtsmorphologie im Kontext des Historismus und seiner Krise', in Gangl, Merlio and Orphälders (eds), *Spengler. Ein Denker der Zeitenwende*, 129–44.
Merlio, Gilbert, and Daniel Meyer (eds), *Spengler ohne Ende. Ein Rezeptionsphänomen im internationalen Kontext* (Frankfurt am Main: Peter Lang, 2014).
Meyer, Arnold Oskar, *Bismarcks Glaube im Spiegel der Lösungen und Lehrtexte* (Munich: Beck, 1933).
Möller, Horst, 'Geschichte im Dienste der Zeitkritik', in Peter Christian Ludz (ed.), *Spengler heute* (Munich: Beck, 1980), 49–73.
Muhs, Karl, *Spengler und der wirtschaftliche Untergang Europas* (Berlin: Junker & Dünnhaupt, 1934).
Naeher, Jürgen, *Oswald Spengler* (Reinbek bei Hamburg: Rowohlt, 1984).
Neurath, Marie, and Robert S. Cohen (eds), *Otto Neurath: Empiricism and Sociology* (Boston, MA: Reidel, 1973).
Neurath, Otto, 'Anti-Spengler', in Marie Neurath and Robert S. Cohen (eds), *Otto Neurath: Empiricism and Sociology* (Boston, MA: Reidel, 1973), 158–213.
Nicosia, Francis R., *Zionism and Anti-Semitism in Nazi Germany* (Cambridge: Cambridge University Press, 2008).
Niekisch, Ernst, *Gewagtes Leben. Begnegungen und Begebnisse* (Cologne: Kiepenhauer & Witsch, 1958).
Noske, Gustav, *Von Kiel bis Kapp. Zur Geschichte der deutschen Revolution* (Berlin: Verlag für Politik und Wirtschaft, 1920).
Nübel, Christoph, *Die Mobilisierung der Kriegsgesellschaft* (Münster: Waxmann, 2008).
Osmančević, Samir, *Oswald Spengler und das Ende der Geschichte* (Vienna: Turia & Kant, 2007).
Paul, Jean, 'Die unsichtbare Loge', in Jean Paul, *Werke*, Vol. 1, 2nd edn (Berlin: G. Reimer, 1822 [1793]).
Pyta, Wolfram, *Die Weimarer Republik* (Wiesbaden: Verlag für Sozialwissenschaften, 2004).
Radek, Karl, 'Leo Schageter, der Wanderer ins Nichts', in Hermann Weber (ed.), *Der deutsche Kommunismus. Dokumente 1915–1945* (Cologne: Kiepenheuer & Witsch, 1964), 142–47.
Ringer, Fritz K., *The Decline of the German Mandarins: The German Academic Community, 1890–1933* (Lebanon, NH: University Press of New England, 1990).
Rollinger, Robert, and Sebastian Fink (eds), *Oswald Spenglers Kulturmorphologie – eine multiperspektive Annäherung* (Wiesbaden: Springer VS, 2018).
Rühle, Jürgen, 'Haßliebe zu den niederen Dämonen: Ernst Niekisch und der Nationalbolschewismus', in *Literatur und Revolution – die Schriftsteller und der Kommunismus* (Cologne: Kiepenhauer & Witsch, 1960), 192–206.
Schäfer, Karen, *Die Militärstrategie Seeckts* (Berlin: Frank & Timme, 2016).
Schmidt, Jürgen, *August Bebel. Kaiser der Arbeiter* (Zurich: Rotpunktverlag, 2018).
Schröter, Manfred, *Der Streit um Spengler. Kritik seiner Kritiker* (Munich: Beck, 1922).

Seeck, Otto, *Geschichte des Untergangs der antiken Welt* (Berlin: Siemenroth, 8 vols, 1910–1921).
Shakespeare, William, *Julius Caesar*. Edited by Martin Spevack and revised with a new introduction by Jeremy Lopez (Cambridge: Cambridge University Press, 2017).
Sontheimer, Kurt, 'Der Tatkreis', *Vierteljahrshefte für Zeitgeschichte*, 7(8) (1959), 229–60.
——. *Antidemokratisches Denken in der Weimarer Republik. Die politischen Ideen des Nationalismus zwischen 1918 und 1933* (Munich: Nymphenburger, 1962).
Sozialdemokratische Partei Deutschlands (ed.), *Protokoll über die Verhandlungen des Parteitages der Sozialdemokratischen Partei Deutschlands. Abgehalten zu Essen vom 15. bis 21. September 1907* (Berlin: Vorwärts, 1907).
Stachura, Peter D., *Gregor Strasser and the Rise of Nazism*, 2nd edn (Abingdon: Routledge, 2015).
Strasser, Peter, *Spenglers Visionen. Hundert Jahre Untergang des Abendlandes* (Vienna: Braumüller, 2018).
Struve, Walter, *Elites against Democracy: Leadership Ideals in Bourgeois Political Thought in Germany, 1890–1933* (Princeton: Princeton University Press, 1973).
Stutz, Ernst, *Die philosophische und politische Kritik Oswald Spenglers* (Zurich: Wiedikon, 1958).
Tartsch, Thomas, *Denn der Mensch ist ein Raubtier. Eine Einführung in die politischen Schriften und Theorien Oswald Spenglers* (Norderstedt: Books on Demand, 2001).
Thöndl, Michael, 'Das Politikbild von Oswald Spengler (1880–1936) mit einer Ortsbestimmung seines politischen Urteils über Hitler und Mussolini', *Zeitschrift für Politik*, Neue Folge, 40(4) (1993), 418–43.
——. '"Wie oft stirbt das Abendland?" Oswald Spenglers These vom zweifachen Untergang', in Manfred Gangl, Gilbert Merlio and Markus Orphälders (eds), *Spengler. Ein Denker der Zeitenwende*, 251–72.
——. *Oswald Spengler in Italien: Kulturexport politischer Ideen der 'Konservativen Revolution'* (Leipzig: Leipziger Universitätsverlag, 2010).
Tyrell, Albrecht, *Vom 'Trommler' zum 'Führer': Der Wandel von Hitlers Selbstverständnis zwischen 1919 und 1924 und die Entwicklung der NSDAP* (Munich: Fink, 1975).
Vogt, J., 'Rezenzion zu Oswald Spengler, "Briefe 1913–36"', *Historische Zeitschrift*, 199(2) (1964), 459–63.
Vogt, Stefan, 'Strange Encounters: Social Democracy and Radical Nationalism in Weimar Germany', *Journal of Contemporary History*, 45(2) (2010), 253–81.
Vollnhals, Clemens, 'Praeceptor Germaniae. Oswald Spenglers politische Publizistik', in Demandt and Farrenkopf (eds), *Der Fall Spengler. Eine kritische Bilanz*, 171–97.
Wagner, Jannis, '"Weltmacht oder Niedergang". Wilhelmische Mentalität, extreme Emotionen und Bilder des Kommenden am Beispiel Oswald Spenglers', *Zeitschrift für Geschichtswissenschaft*, 63 (2015), 930–48.
Weiß, Volker, 'Rezension zu S. Maaß, *Oswald Spengler. Eine politische Biographie*'. Retrieved 4 February 2022 from http://www.hsozkult.de/publicationreview/id/rezbuecher-21730.
——. *Die autoritäre Revolte. Die Neue Rechte und der Untergang des Abendlandes* (Hamburg. Klett-Cotta, 2017).
Ziemann, Benjamin, *War Experiences in Rural Germany 1914–1923* (Oxford: Berg, 2007).
Zweiniger, Arthur, *Spengler im Dritten Reich. Eine Antwort auf Oswald Spenglers 'Jahre der Entscheidung'* (Berlin: Oldenburg, 1933).

# Index

Abassid caliphate, 51
Absolutism, 4, 50, 136
Adorno, Theodor W., 1, 30, 40n8, 176
aesthetics, 1, 44, 48, 51, 53, 55
Albers, August, 12, 28n16
Alcibiades, 55
Alexander the Great, 53–4
Allies, 89, 144
American cultures, 22
American hegemony, 36
analogy (*Analogie*), 37, 52–55, 72, 81, 126
*ancien regime,* 50
Ancient Greece, 18, 23, 43–4, 53, 56, 63, 140n8. *See also* Apollonian culture
ancient history, 1, 13
Angst, 8, 26n12
animal world, 10, 46, 65n4
anti-communism, 88, 92, 116
anti-German ideology, 92, 163–4
anti-nature (*Widernatur*), 20
anti-Semitism, 5, 88, 131, 147, 150, 164–6, 171n77. *See also* racism
Apollonian culture, 43, 48–52, 56, 63, 72–3, 75
　prime symbol of, 43, 45
Aquinas, Thomas, 48

Arabian culture, 43, 49, 62, 164.
　*See also* Magian culture
archetypal plant, (*Urpflanze*) 46
Archimedes, 53
aristocracy, 17, 48, 87, 91–2, 100, 104, 120, 130, 136, 155, 175.
　*See also* nobility
aristocratic leadership, 78–9, 108
Asia, 14, 22–3, 133, 153
atheism, 51, 70
Atkinson, Charles F., 15
Augustine, 49
Augustus, 56
Aurelius, Marcus, 25n1, 52
authoritarian politics, 4, 12, 15, 39, 75–6, 82–3, 87, 92, 101, 107, 111n36, 159, 165, 169, 174–6. *See also* Caesarism
authoritarian socialism, 99. *See also* Prussian socialism
autumn, 48–50, 70, 126. *See also* cultures

Babylonian culture, 22, 43, 65n3
Bach, Johann Sebastian, 50
Bacon, Francis, 49
Baeumler, Alfred, 156
Baltzer, Armin, 32, 38
Battle League (Kampfbund), 123, 125, 132

Bavaria, 87, 115–16, 120, 147–8
　and secession, 124
　socialist republic of, 88
　State Commissioner of, 121
Bavarian People's Party, 22, 115
Bayreuth Festival (July 1933), 149–50, 158, 170n27
Bebel, August, 9–10, 102–4, 130
Beer Hall Putsch (October 1923), 4, 15, 21, 122, 146–7. *See also* March on Berlin
Beethoven, Ludwig van, 50
Bentham, Jeremy, 94, 164, 171n81
Berlin, 9, 15, 88, 113, 115, 120–3
Bernstein, Eduard, 105
biology, 47, 52–3, 57, 62, 95
　and evidence-based methods of, 47
birth rates, 19, 56
Bismarck, Otto von, 7, 24, 76, 81, 104, 127, 150, 159
　and worker protection laws, 103
Blankenburg, 7
Boterman, Frits, 33
bourgeoisie, 48–9, 63, 84n14, 91, 103, 110n23, 144
bourgeois intelligentsia, 49
bourgeois materialism, 90, 167. *See also* thinking-in-money
Boyle, Nicholas, 46, 65n6
Braumüller, Wilhelm, 12, 41n60
bread and circuses (*panem et circenses*), 69, 79
Brecht, Bertolt, 56
breeding (*Zucht*), 128
Britain, 11, 85n20, 88, 106
　and global supremacy, 101
Brutus, 81
Buddhism, 53, 90

Caesarism, 3–5, 15–17, 61, 73–4, 78
　and constitutional framework for, 50–1, 168–9
　and final state form of, 139
　and formation of, 61, 73, 109, 117, 135, 137
　as core value of Spengler's politics, 15, 74, 77–81, 83, 114, 134–5, 138–9, 145, 148, 155, 157–9, 167–9, 174
　as historical diagnosis, viii, 38, 68, 133, 145, 173, 176
　as historical prognosis, 39, 64, 67–8, 74–6, 78, 173
　in Faustian civilisation, 61, 80, 134, 138, 144
　in Germany, 83, 114, 138–40, 145, 157–8, 162, 174
　in Italy, 157–8
Caesar, Julius, 51, 54, 71, 79
Calvin, John, 49
Cassandra, 24, 176
Cassius, 81
cause and effect, 52, 54. *See also* rationalist historiography
Centre Party (*Deutsche Zentrumspartei*), 89, 115
ceramics, 22
Chamberlain, Houston Stewart, 150
chariot, 22
Charlemagne, 58
C. H. Beck Publishing House, 12, 15, 66n20, 88
China, 51, 60–1, 156
　and Warring Sates Period (ca. 475–221 BC), 51
Christianity, 49, 53, 59, 70
　and early form of (*Urchristentum*), 59
　and the Protestant Reformation, 49
　in the 'East', 59

in the 'West', 59
cities, 50, 69–71
Civilisation (*Zivilisation*), 18, 35, 37, 47–51, 54, 61, 67–76, 78–80, 82–3, 84n8, 90–1, 93, 96, 100, 106–9, 112n54, 113, 116, 119, 128, 135, 138, 156, 164, 166–7
civilising imperialism, 132
civil peace (*Burgfrieden*), 91–3, 101, 105, 119
civil service, 127–8
civil war, 88
class egoism, 95
class struggle, 155, 162
Classical world, 45, 52, 56. *See also* Apollonian culture
Clausewitz, Carl Philipp Gottlieb, von 126
Cluny St. Odilo, fifth Benedictine Abbot of, 59
colonialism, 16, 75, 79, 156
command economy, 100
commoners, 50, 69
common sense, 72
communism, 51, 88, 103, 110n23, 144, 148, 150, 157
Communist Party of Germany (KPD), 118–19, 121, 151
Conservative Revolution (*konservative Revolution*), 14, 36–7, 81, 93, 114–15
Conte, Domenico, 36, 114, 174
contingency (*Zufall*), 80, 138
contrapuntal music, 43
Cosmann, Paul Nikolaus, 117, 124
countryside, 48, 50
coups, 4, 75, 122, 134, 147
crisis, 21, 61, 71, 88, 121, 124, 139, 146
  and rhetoric of, 61, 73–4
  as opportunity, 19, 120–2, 125

Cromwell, Oliver, 50, 153
Crown Prince Rupprecht of Bavaria, 115, 140n9
Crusades (1096-1291), 48–9
cult of science, 51
cultures, 10, 18, 20–3, 42–5, 53–6, 65n2, 98, 156, 164–6
  and birth of, 48, 57–8, 61, 76, 83
  and co-existence of, 57
  and cross-fertilisation, 59
  and death of, 30, 46, 61, 76, 98
  and development of, 46–7, 60, 71, 76
  and expressions of life (*Lebensäußerungen*), 43, 47
  and fate of (*Schicksal*), 76
  and final phase of, 8, 54, 61, 69–72, 74–5, 79–80
  and four seasons of, 47–52, 60
  and fulfilment (*Vollendung*), of 52, 60
  and historical transmission, 63, 66n22
  and life-cycles of, 65n14, 67
  and 'pre-established' patterns, 57
  and prehistory (*Vorzeit*) of, 47, 51, 57
  and relations between, 54–5, 57, 82
  and the '*Kultur*' phase of, 48, 77
  and the 'reformation' period of, 49, 60
  and three phases of, 47
  as plants, 59, 66n20
cultural pessimism (*Kulturpessimismus*), viii, 68, 75
Cuno, Heinrich, 102
Cuno, Wilhelm, 119–20
Cyaxares, 54

Darwin, Charles, 9, 20
debating clubs, 128, 137
decadence, 8, 56, 69, 119, 133, 135, 156
demagogues, 157
Demandt, Alexander, 34–5, 56, 74, 83, 149, 170n27, 173
democracy, 2, 4, 16, 69–70, 72, 78, 84n14, 85n20, 87, 89, 106–8, 112n60, 128, 133, 135, 137–8, 148, 158, 174
   and inbuilt tendency towards dictatorship, 51, 78, 81, 94
   and overthrow of, 15, 51, 73, 78–9, 82
   as deception, 51, 72, 79
   the end of, 73, 78, 80, 114, 119, 133–5, 138–9
Democritus, 50
Descartes, René, 49, 53
*Deutsche Allgemeine Zeitung*, 102
dictatorial political forms, 5, 16, 99, 134, 158, 169, 176
dictatorship, 5, 51, 83, 102, 121, 134, 136, 157–9, 169, 176
   of capital, 72, 79, 100, 121
   of civil servants, 100
   of the proletariat, 100
*Die Glocke* (*The Bell*), 101–2
*Die Rote Fahne* (*Red Flag*), 118
Dionysus, 49, 54
discipline, 77, 90, 152, 155
Discobolus of Myron, 43, 56
decline (*Untergang*), 14, 61–2, 74, 173
*Die Tat*, 101, 111n33, 148
Dilthey, Wilhelm, 54
Doric columns, 48, 52–3, 71
Dostoevsky, Fyodor, 14
Drascher, Wahrhold, 32
Droem, Ernst (Adolf Weigel), 13
Duchy of Weimar, 31

Düsseldorf, 10, 17, 19
dystopianism, 73

Ebert, Friedrich, 121
economic growth, 92
economic socialism, 89–91, 94, 102, 110n16, 130, 167. *See also* ethical socialism
education (*Bildung*), 127–9, 133, 142n65
egalitarianism, 87, 89
Egypt, 22, 43, 45, 52–3, 60, 62, 65, 129
eighteenth century, 4, 64, 93, 138, 154
*Eis Heauton*, 8–9
Eisner, Kurt, 88, 110n6,
elections, 72, 75, 77–9, 134, 136–7, 155
   of 1932, 146
   of March 1933, 148–9
   of May 1924, 125,
eleventh century, 64
Eliot, Thomas Stearns, 1, 15
elite, 2, 15, 39, 51, 81, 87, 115, 120, 127–30, 138–9, 154–5, 160, 168, 174
Engels, David, 37–8, 176
England, 11, 92, 101–4, 130, 133
   and Prussia, 101–4,
   and sham of parliamentarism, 136
   and Viking roots, 93–5, 101
English political economy, 95
English thought, 171n81. *See also* individualism
Enlightenment, 50, 70, 128
Entente powers, 116
epistemology, 44, 71
Escherich, Georg, 88, 116
estates, 17, 48–51, 69, 91, 96, 127, 136

ethical socialism, 89–90, 93–4, 107, 108, 110n16, 130, 167. *See also* economic socialism
ethics, 44–5, 54–5, 71, 90, 94, 100, 165
Eton, 128, 137
Eurocentrism, 43, 50
    and Spengler's critique of, 62, 64
Europe, 14, 16, 21, 23, 42, 49–50, 57–8, 60, 62–4, 72, 75, 92–3, 104, 116, 132–3, 139, 146, 154, 160, 163–4
European Union, 37
executive branch of government, 99–100, 126, 136, 138
expansionism, 16, 48, 94
extraparliamentary right, 88, 115, 147

facts (*Tatsachen*), 54, 57, 65n19, 72, 80, 147, 153, 175
Falck, Martin, 34, 175
Farrenkopf, John, 12, 26n3, 31, 34, 39, 86, 106–7, 112n60, 160, 174–6
fascism, 21, 140, 144–5, 151, 154–5, 157, 162, 174–5
    as transitional form, 157
    in Germany, 119, 140, 152, 156
    in Italy, 35, 139, 152, 156
    in its elitist form, 157, 158
    in its plebeian form, 155, 157–8
fate (*Schicksal*), 24, 45, 54, 62, 69, 71, 75, 80, 90, 109, 164, 175
fatherland, 104, 123, 162
Fauconnet, André, 146
Faustian culture, 3, 34, 51–2, 54, 57, 59–64, 68–9, 74, 90, 106, 114, 167–8
    and destiny of, 98, 107
    and ethics of, 132
    and moral dynamism, of 89
    and unique historical consciousness of, 63
Faustian civilisation, 61, 64, 94
    as age of war and revolution, 82
    and remaining tasks of, 64, 68, 82, 107, 173
    and the struggle between nations, 91, 93–5, 156
    and the struggle within nations, 95, 156
    dynamics behind, 3, 67
Feder, Gottfried, 131
Fennelly, John F., 23, 31, 173–4
feudalism, 92, 100
Feuerbach, Ludwig, 51
Final Solution, 19. *See also* Jewish question
finance capital, 17, 36, 130–1, 155, 166
First World War, 11, 17, 29, 32, 69, 71, 75, 87, 93, 98, 101, 104-7, 141n32. *See also* war
Fischer, Klaus P., 31, 78, 158, 171n52, 173
Förster-Nietzsche, Elisabeth, 123–5
    and role at the Nietzsche Foundation Archive, 22
formlessness, 46, 51, 73, 76, 78–9, 91, 126. *See also Urseelentum*
forms (*Gestalten*), 44, 46–8, 52, 54–5, 58. *See also Gestaltenlehre*
form-sense (*Formgefühl*), 45
France, 11, 16–17, 119, 150, 153, 165
    and history of, 4, 42, 70, 75, 126, 138–9
    as world power, 11, 16–17, 92, 130, 132

Frederick the Great, 50, 92, 99, 150
Frederick William I, 94, 103, 159
free trade, 94, 155
Freikorps, 116, 147
French Revolution, 40, 70, 75, 126,
   and Directory Period of, 126, 138
   and gilded youth (*jeunesse dorée*), 126, 139
Freud, Sigmund, 65n1, 84n8
Freyer, Hans, 107
Fukuyama, Francis, 37

GÄA-Gesellschaft, 115, 118, 141n23
Galilei, Galileo, 49
Gauss, Carl Friedrich, 53
Gerlich, Fritz, 124, 142n52
German army, 12, 92, 120–2, 129
German Democratic Party (DDP), 89
German Historical School, 129
German historicism, 54
Germanic Catholicism, 48–9, 52–3
German-led world order, viii, 34, 173. *See also* hegemony
'German Michel', 94, 128
German National People's Party (DNVP), 115, 148
Germanness (*Deutschtum*), 105–7, 132
   and metaphysics of, 106
German Revolution, 24, 36, 87–8, 92, 114, 126, 148
   of 1848, 89
   of 1914, 91, 119 (*see also* civil peace)
   of 1918, ix, 24, 36, 87–8, 92, 114, 126, 148

German socialist state, 87, 99. *See also* Prussian socialist state
Germany, viii, 1, 5, 7, 11–14, 16–19, 21, 24, 32, 35, 78, 87, 89, 90, 99–101, 103–5, 109, 114–16, 118, 121, 129–33, 137–8, 152–4, 156–7, 159, 162–4, 168, 176
   and democratisation of, 89, 106, 128, 135
   and discourse of national renewal, 14, 29, 99, 103, 107, 114, 138
   and intellectual discourse, viii, 69
   and rebirth of, 51, 68, 80–3, 89, 92–3, 98, 116–17, 125–7, 137, 139, 144, 159, 166
   and soul of, 131
   and three paths of development of, 100
   as modern-day Rome, 83, 168
   as the 'last nation of the West', 4
   as the leading Faustian nation, 64, 80–3, 133, 153–4, 160
German youth, 16, 71, 106, 123, 125–8
General Council of the International Workingman's Association, 97
General German Workers' Association (ADAV), 104
*Gestaltenlehre* (theory of forms), 44. *See also* Goethe
global economic crash (1929), 19, 21, 146, 155. *See also* Wall Street crash
global power politics, 4, 133, 154. *See also* imperialism
God, 48, 81. *See also* the divine

Goebbels, Joseph, 5, 147
   and Spengler, 30, 147, 149, 161, 169n15
Goethe, Johann Wilhelm Friedrich von, 8, 13, 18, 23, 31, 56, 65n6, 75, 83, 102, 139, 150
   and the principles of natural inquiry, 52
   comparative method of, 46–7, 52, 60
Gothic cathedrals, 48, 53, 71
Grantzow, Adele, 7, 12
great men of history, 51. See also strongmen
Gründel, Günther, 161
Günther, Albert Eric, 81
Gusejnova, Dina, 40n8

Haeckel, Ernst, 9
Halle, 9–10
Hamburg, 10–11, 16, 21, 37, 149, 152
Hamburger Überseeclub, 115
Hanfstaengl, Ernst, 150
Hartzfeld, Sophie von, 105
Harz region, 7
Hauptmann, Gerhart Johann Robert, 56
Hegel, Georg Wilhelm Friedrich, 30, 50, 57, 63, 65n19, 81
Heidegger, Martin, 149
Hellenism, 51, 71
Henkel, Markus, 26n12, 28n69, 36, 41n46, 111n39, 114, 135, 137–8, 140n6, 141n42, 141n48, 142n65, 170n43, 174
Henry I, 54
Heraclitus, 10, 76, 105
Herzog, Bodo, 32
Heuss, Theodor, 111n31, 139
High Cultures, 20–1. See also Cultures.

Hilferding, Rudolf, 120
Hindenburg, Paul von, 56, 65n18, 92, 149, 169n9
historical change, 3, 10, 39, 67, 162
   and inevitability of, 76
historical pseudomorphosis, 66n22
historiography, 42, 55, 61, 105, 144
history
   and four stages of before High Cultures (a, b, c and d), 20
   subjects of, 76, 80
Hitler, Adolf, 5, 15, 21, 156, 161–2
   and censorship of Spengler's works, 153, 159
   and meeting with Spengler in July 1933, 150–1, 158, 171n52
   and Spengler, 37, 100–1, 122–5, 140, 142n80, 145–51, 154, 159, 161, 166, 176
   and trial of (1924), 123, 125
Hohenzollern monarchy, 78, 108
Hoffmann, Adolf, 120
Holocaust, 30
home front, 91–2
homeland (*Heimat*), 38, 164
homology (*Homologie*), 52–4
honour, 77–8, 88, 129, 134, 155
Hugenberg, Alfred, 15, 115, 118, 120
   and the 'Hugenberg press', 115
Hughes, H. Stuart, 31, 109, 153–4, 174
Humboldt, Wilhelm von, 128

Icarus, 56
ideology, 64, 82, 91, 96, 98, 99, 101, 105–6, 109, 154, 157–8

imperialism, 30, 57, 64, 71, 75–6, 89–90, 101, 108, 132, 156. See also global power politics
*Imperium Germanicum,* 89. *See also* German-led world order
Indian Culture, 18, 23, 43, 61–2, 90, 156
individualism, 93–4, 106
Indo-Germanic race, 163
industrialists, 15, 32, 39, 81, 83, 115, 149, 171n53
industrial warfare, 4, 75
instinct, 55, 94–6, 98, 108
intellectual epochs, 53,
intermaxillary bone (*os intermaxillare*), 46–7, 60
internationalism, 89, 108, 163
Islamic world, 61. *See also* Magian culture

Jewish Question, 5, 19, 63, 95, 111n24, 146, 163–6
Jünger, Ernst, 34, 86, 88, 110n1
*Julius Caesar,* 81
Jung, Edgar Julius, 107
Juni-Klub, 81, 115
Junkers, 105
Junker-bourgeois coalition, 138

Kahr, Gustav von, 22, 115, 120–4, 140n9, 159
Kafka, Franz, 56
Kaiser Maximilian, 156
Kaiserreich, 33, 136. *See also* Second Reich and Wilhelmine Empire
Kaiser Wilhelm, 136
  and abdication of, 78, 92
Kant, Immanuel, 50, 65n1, 112n54
Kapp, Wolfgang, 105, 120
Klöres, Hans, 164
knightly ideals, 48, 73, 93–4

Knittel, Albert, 149
Knittel, Else, 149
Knopf, Charles, 12, 25
Koktanek, Anton Mirko, 20, 32–3, 38, 125, 134–5, 137, 141n24, 141n42, 142n52, 148, 159–60, 176
Kolb, Eberhard, 125
Kornhardt, Hildegard (Spengler's sister), 7, 23, 26n3, 65n2, 150
Kornherr, Richard, 19
Krebs, Wolfgang, 36
Krupp, Gustav, 15, 115

labour, 10, 96, 130
  and alienation, 97
  and ethical value of, 95, 100
  division of, 97
  as special commodity, 96–7
landowners, 81
Lassalle, Ferdinand, 104–5
law, 103, 121, 128–9, 133
League of Nations, 160
*l'art pour l'art,* 51
Leers, Johann von, 160–3, 166–7
Leibniz, Gottfried Wilhelm, 57
Leipzig, 102, 149
Lenin, Vladimir Ilych, 82, 100, 132, 134–5, 158
Lensch, Paul, 101–2, 105, 108, 111n39
left-wing politics, 12, 148, 154
*lèse-majesté,* 103, 136
Lettow-Vorbeck, Paul von, 115
libel, 117, 120, 148
liberal constitutional models, 128
liberalism, 91, 104, 154
  in Germany, 92–3, 164
living standards, 19, 129
Locke, John, 50
*Logos,* 13
Lossow, Otto von, 122
Ludz, Peter Christian, 33

Lübbe, Hermann, 33–4, 106, 112n54
Lüttwitz, Walter von, 105
Lukács, Georg, 30, 106
Luther, Martin, 49

Maaß, Sebastian, 37, 41n52, 114, 135, 137–9, 144, 153, 175
Machiavelli, Niccolò di Bernardo dei, 34, 118
machinery, 17, 20, 79, 96
Magian culture, 43, 49, 51, 59, 164–5
Manchesterism, 155. See also free trade
Mann, Thomas, 1, 29–30
March on Berlin, 122–23. See also Beer Hall Putsch
martial law, 121
Marx, Karl, 51, 63, 81, 97, 99, 164, 167, 171n81
　and Spengler's critique of, 90–6, 104
Marxist socialism, 90–3, 95–6, 101–3, 130, 132–3, 167. See also economic socialism
Marx, Wilhelm, 125
materialism, 18, 51, 70, 78, 90–1, 96. See also thinking-in-money
mathematics, 9–10, 13
Meister Eckhart, 93
metaphysical bonds, 69, 76
metaphysics, 1, 3, 5, 19–20, 43–4, 49, 51, 58–9, 62–3, 69–70, 89, 94–5, 106–7, 132, 163–5, 175
　of light, distance and sight, 10, 44, 57–8
Metternich, Klemens von, 24
Mexican culture, 8, 43, 65n3, 156
Meyer, Eduard, 13
Middle Ages, 42, 49, 63
military defeat, 1, 17, 24, 29, 89

military service, 9. See also conscription
Mirabeau, comte de, 153
modernity, 42, 63, 70, 83, 154
modern press, 72–3, 84n14, 119
modern warfare, 14–15
Möller, Horst, 33, 105
monarchy, 78, 89, 108
　reinstatement of, 99, 103, 115
　Spengler's attitude towards, 78, 89, 101, 137–9, 143n85
money, 14, 17, 36, 90, 95, 97, 102, 117–18, 131, 155, 167
　and the rule of in civilisation 50–1, 69, 72, 78–9, 90–1, 94, 99, 154
Morocco, 11, 154
morphology, 36, 71–2, 74, 80, 98
　and function, 46–7, 52–5, 73
　and position, 11, 46–8, 52–3, 60
　of history, 38, 44, 53–60, 62–4, 87–8, 106–9, 165
　of plants, 46–53
Moscow, 7, 14
Mozart, Wolfgang Amadeus, 50
*Münchner Neueste Nachrichten*, 124
Münzing, Hermann, 122
Muhammad, 49–50, 53. See also Islamic world
music, 13, 43–5, 50, 53, 75
Mussolini, Benito, 35, 82, 135, 139–40, 156–8
　and review of Spengler's *Hour of Decision*, 158
　as 'true ruler' of Italy, 21, 51, 134–5, 139, 157–8
mutations in human history, 20
myth, 44–5, 48, 56

Naeher, Jürgen, 8, 33, 73, 110n9, 174

Napoleon I, 53, 55, 75, 126, 138, 151, 165
Napoleon III, 7
National Bolshevism, 101, 117
National Directorate (*Direktorium*), 15–16, 113
nationalism, 2, 4, 9, 14, 16, 18, 33–5, 37, 39, 64, 82–3, 86, 88–9, 92, 95, 101–2, 105–7, 113–7, 119–20, 125, 133, 144, 150, 162–3, 167–8, 174–5
National Socialism, 5, 16, 21–22, 30, 37, 83, 95, 101, 117, 123, 131–2, 140, 142n80, 144–9, 151–4, 156, 158–62, 165–6, 168–9, 175–6
National Socialist German Workers' Party (NSDAP), 124, 144, 146–9, 161
   and Hannover Conference of (1926), 147
   and 'left' wing of 22, 147
nation of culture (*Kulturnation*), 83
Natorp, Paul, 106
natural sciences, 9, 47
nature, 20–21, 52, 55
Naumann, Friedrich Joseph, 87, 108
Nazi regime, 22, 141n42, 145–6, 149, 151, 159, 161, 169
   and early peace rhetoric of, 160
Nazi seizure of power, ix, 121, 146, 152–3, 159
Neurath, Otto, 65n18, 82
Newton, Isaac, 47
Niekisch, Ernst, 101, 111n36
Nietzsche, Friedrich, 13, 30, 76–7
   and decadence, 69
   and legacy of, 123, 126
   and Spengler, 8, 13, 18, 22–3

Night of the Long Knives (June 1934), 22, 158. *See also* purges
nihilism, 13, 70
nobility, 49–50, 69, 72, 77–8, 80, 155
non-estate (*Nichtstand*), 69, 91
non-parliamentary dictatorship, 121
Nordic, 53, 59, 165
North German Confederation, 136
November Revolution (1918), ix, 24, 101, 103–4, 114, 123, 141n32, 147. *See also* German Revolution of 1918

October Revolution (1917), 30
October uprising (1923), 121
Old Testament prophets, 24
Olympian gods and goddesses, 48
organic community (*Gemeinschaft*), 93
Organisation Escherich (Orgesch), 88, 116
Osmančević, Samir, 8–9, 35, 55, 68, 170n31
Oswald Spengler Society for the Study of World History, 37
otherness, 5, 164
Otte, Max, 37–8, 176

pacifism, 23, 163–4
paganism, 59
painting, 4, 45, 75
*panta rhei*, 10, 75. See also Heraclitus
paramilitary groupings, 88, 110n9, 115–16, 141n35, 147. *See also* extraparliamentary right
parliament, 10, 19, 72, 75, 77–8, 81, 84, 89, 91–2, 100, 102, 115–16, 121, 127, 134–8, 147, 157. *See also* democracy

Papen, Franz von, 115, 148
Paris, 7
patriotic associations (*vaterländische Verbände*), 116
Patriotische Gesellschaft, 21
*Paulskirche*, 89
peace, 23, 75, 89, 92, 98. *See also* pacifism
peasantry, 48, 69, 91, 105
Petersburg, 14
philosophy, 10, 24, 31–3, 35, 49, 65n1, 69, 75, 78, 82, 95, 103, 106, 112n54, 118, 128
 of life, 20, 62
 of power, 104
physiognomic tact, 55
Plato, 31, 50
plebeianism, 16, 21, 123, 157–9
Plenge, Johann, 106
plutocrats, 73. *See also* dictatorship
poetry, 4, 7, 13, 45, 55, 69, 75, 128
political parties, 17, 76–7, 91, 119, 157
political process, 76, 153
political socialism, 110n16. *See also* economic socialism
politically 'in condition' (*in Verfassung*), 77
politics of decline, viii, 2–4, 6, 14, 25, 38–9, 42, 68, 74, 77, 82–3, 169, 174–6
politics on the grand scale (*Großpolitik*), 133
politics on the small scale (*Kleinpolitik*), 133–4
Polygnotus, 53
polytechnic education, 128
populism, 146
postcapitalism, 100
*post-histoire*, 35
Potsdam Day (21 March 1933), 145, 149

Praetorian Guard, 158, 171n52
prejudice, 5, 24, 42, 50, 162, 164
pre-Socratic thinkers, 49
*Preußentum*, 4, 39, 87, 132, 149, 162, 167, 174. *See also* Spengler's political alternative
*Preußische Jahrbücher*, 13
press barons, 78, 81, 113
press freedom, 88
priesthood, 48, 69
 as living symbol of space, 49
primal estates (*Urstände*), 48
primal form (*Urform*), 46–7
prime symbol (*Ursymbol*), 43–5, 53, 58, 156, 164
primitive human condition (*Urmenschentum*), 58, 76
print media, 116–17
propaganda, 15, 100, 102, 120, 150, 161
property, 77, 129–31, 134. *See also* ownership
Protestant church, 150
Prussia, 89, 96, 108, 123, 127, 152
 and England, 90, 93–6, 130
Prussian civil servants, 98–100, 103, 127–9, 133
Prussian collectivity, 90, 94, 102, 159, 165
Prussian discipline, 90, 96, 160, 165
Prussian socialism, 4, 13, 87–9, 92–9, 101, 103, 105–7, 109, 130, 132, 146, 149, 161, 163, 167–8, 174
Prussian socialist state, 99, 104–5, 109, 168
Punic Wars, 11
puritanism, 49, 53
purges, 22, 157–9
putsch, 105, 120, 122–4, 134. *See also* coup

Pythagoras, 49–50, 53

race (*Rasse*), 2, 5, 62–4, 95, 98, 132, 146, 156, 161, 163–6
   and Aryan-centric understandings of, 62, 163
   and biology, 62–3, 156, 165
   and metaphysics, 95, 161, 164–5
   as ethos, 165
   as rhetorical device, 166
   as zoology, 165
   in the spiritual sense, 94
race struggle (*Rassenkampf*), 156
racial hierarchies, 62
racialism, 21, 62, 95
racism, 5, 16, 21, 123, 156, 164–5, 166
Rathenau, Walther, 87, 100, 141n35
rationalism, 14, 18, 55, 69, 84n8, 91, 96, 100, 154
rationalist historiography, 55
*Realpolitik*, ix, 3, 39, 76, 118, 132–3
reason, 50, 70, 84n8. *See also* rationalism
recorded history, 46–7
Reichskanzler, 151
Reichstag fire (27 February 1933), 150
religion, 1, 13, 49, 59, 62, 70, 127
reparations, 16, 116, 119–20, 132
republic, 88–9, 94, 99, 116, 120–1
republicanism, 15, 91, 99–100, 102, 116, 126
Reusch, Paul, 15, 32, 115, 118–20, 140n19, 149
revanchism, 16, 132
Reventlow, Ernst Graf zu, 117–18, 140n18
rhetoric, 72–4

Rhodes, Cecil, 79, 81–2, 134–5
right-wing extremism, 120
right-wing nationalist movement (*nationale Bewegung*), 2, 4, 9, 113, 150, 166, 168, 175
right-wing press, 15, 117, 124
Rococo period, 50
Roman imperialism, 57
Roman Republic, 37, 51, 56 71, 79
Roman Senate, 129
Rome, 75, 83, 89, 168, 173
   'Golden Age' of, 56
   rise of, 11
rootlessness, 69, 72, 155
Rousseau, Jean-Jacques, 50
Ruhr region, 115, 119–20, 141
rural way of life, 69. *See also* peasantry
Russia, 10–11, 14, 82, 104, 130, 132, 134, 154, 165, 170n39
Russian Bolshevism, 18, 130, 133, 154–5
Russian Revolution (1917), 88, 101. *See also* October Revolution

Sack, Alfons, 151
Savigny, Friedrich Karl von, 129
Saxony, 121
scepticism, 70, 96, 98, 158, 162
Schiller, Friedrich, 56
Schlubach, Roderich, 149
Schröter, Manfred, 29, 32
science, 9, 45–51, 55–6, 58, 62–3
sculpture, 43, 53, 56
second chamber (Staatsrat), 137
Second Millennium BC, 22
Second Reich, 108. *See also* Kaiserreich; Wilhelmine Empire
second religiousness (*zweite Religiösität*), 70
Second World War, 2, 23, 29–30. *See also* war

Seeckt, Hans von, 120–3
Seißer, Hans von, 122
self-denial, 77. *See also* honour
'self-determination of the people', 79
Seneca, 82
Sepoy uprising, 156
seventeenth century, 4, 49, 93
Shakespeare, William, 56, 129
Sièyes, Emmanuel-Joseph, 69
'Signor', 149–50. *See also* Spengler, Oswald
simultaneousness (*Gleichzeitigkeit*), 50, 52–3, 55, 57
small-state politics (*Kleinstaaterei*), 121, 124, 152
sexual enlightenment, 56
Smuts, Jan, 116
Social Democratic Party of Germany (SPD), 88–9, 91–2, 120–1, 130–1, 141n35
   and anti-imperialist wing of, 101
   and Essen Congress of (1907), 104
   and factional politics of, 99–101
   and parliamentary fraction of, 91
   and Spengler, 102–5
   and war credits vote in 1914, 91
socialism, 2–5, 9, 12–13, 16, 84n14, 86–109, 110n16, 130–4, 137, 139, 147–8, 155, 157, 159, 163, 166–8, 169n15, 174–5
socialist republic, 88
social question (*die soziale Frage*), 108
social rank, 96
Socrates, 50
Sombart, Werner, 106
sophism, 50

soul (*Seele*), 14, 42, 45–6, 49, 51, 53, 57–60, 62, 69–70, 81, 83, 94, 96, 98, 131, 137, 152, 165
South Africa, 116, 134
southern cultures, 22. *See also* Babylon and Egypt
Soviet Russia, 132, 134
soviets, 88
Spahn, Martin, 115, 117
special calling (*Beruf*), 96
Spengler, Adele, 7
Spengler, Bernhard, 7
Spengler Debate (1920), 13, 29
Spengler, Hildegard (Spengler's niece), 23
Spengler, Julius, 8
Spengler, Oswald Arnold Gottfried
   and anxiety, 8–9, 26n12
   and clandestine press headquarters (*Pressezentrale*), 116–19, 124
   and 'coloured peoples', 152, 154, 156, 165–6
   and constitutional proposals, 16, 133, 136, 138
   and 'Copernican revolution', 42
   and essentialism, 62, 94, 156, 165
   and fatalism, viii, 1, 3, 13, 38, 61, 72–3, 109, 162, 173
   and feelings of loneliness, 9, 24–5, 33, 176
   and 'heroic realism', 37, 134, 139, 175
   and 'Hindenburg style', 56, 65n18
   and 'invisible lodge', 119, 141n24
   and journalism, 10, 34, 88, 109, 117
   and legacy of viii, 5–6, 25, 35, 37, 67, 169, 176

and life 'purpose', of 9
and 'manly pessimism', 31
and meta history, ix, 3, 135, 145
and methodological bias of, 55–6, 108
and misogyny, 8
and objective truth, 55, 72
and optimism, viii, 21, 31, 39, 68, 70, 109, 118, 163, 175
and paradox in historical method of, 63–4
and pessimism, 1, 3, 8, 13–14, 17, 21, 31, 34, 36, 61, 68, 73, 75, 109, 162, 168, 173, 175
and political alternative (see also Preußentum), 1, 4, 15, 39, 68, 74, 77, 80, 87, 91
and political leadership, 16, 32, 68, 77–8, 80–1, 83, 86, 108, 127, 135
and political writings, 2, 6, 31–2, 34, 39, 61–2, 67–8, 77, 109
and pragmatic conservatism, 6, 16, 107, 132, 135, 139, 146
and predicting the future, 3, 24, 39, 60, 64, 127, 154, 160
and return to research, 18, 126
and shortcomings in theory of history, 61–4
and stages within career of, 9, 24, 36, 78
and the 'Coloured World Revolution', 152
and theory of world history, viii, 13, 18, 83
and the 'White World Revolution', 152, 154–5
and 'Tory Conservatism', 16, 36, 77, 114, 134–5, 174

and typecasting of cultures, 62, 165
and understanding of space and time, 43–5
and 'white peoples', 154, 156, 166
as historical actor, 1, 9, 73, 82, 109
as isolated doomsayer, 6, 8, 14, 23–4, 33–8, 68, 109, 146–8, 159–60, 167, 169, 173, 176
as lobbyist for German industry, 115, 132, 175
as networker, 2, 15, 39, 115
as opportunist, 4, 108, 12–2, 145, 168
as philosopher of history, 2, 7, 31–33, 35, 39, 55, 68, 76, 118, 128, 145, 159, 168
as political philosopher, 2, 77, 119, 135
as politician, viii, 34, 36, 88, 98, 174
as proto-Nazi, 62, 144–5
as publicist, 2, 4, 113
as public speaker, 4, 15–16
autobiographical fragments of, 8–9, 25n1, 26n3
family environment of, 7–9
utopianism of, 107–8, 148, 162, 168, 175
voluntarism of, 39, 64, 103
sport, 51, 133
spring, 48–9, 52, 57, 59. See also cultures
stab-in-the-back myth (Dolchstoßlegende), 92
Stahlhelm, 116
stasis, 43, 56
state bureaucracy, 15, 127, 133, 139
state of the future, 99

statesmanship, 16, 71, 80, 126–7, 160
Stinnes, Hugo, 15, 115, 120, 147
stocks and shares, 17
stoicism, 82
Strasser, Gregor, 5, 22, 146–8, 159, 161, 169n16
Strasser, Otto, 107
Strasser, Peter, 38
stream of existence (*Strom des Daseins*), 58
Stresemann, Gustav, 116, 119–25
strongmen, 3, 51. *See also* Caesarism; great men of history
Struve, Walter, 78, 87, 91, 103, 138, 140n8, 143n86, 145, 159
Sturmabteilung (SA), 22
Stutz, Ernst, 32–3, 36, 68, 174
suffrage, 108, 136
summer, 48–9, 60. *See also* cultures
supreme command, 99
surface phenomena, 56
symbols, 42–5, 48–9, 53, 57–8. *See also* prime symbol
syndicalism, 102
Syracuse, 31

Talleyrand-Périgord, Charles-Maurice de, 118, 151
Taiping Rebellion, 156
Tartsch, Thomas, 36, 77, 114, 137, 153, 174
taxation policy, 115, 130
technics (*Technik*), 20
technocratic politics, 136
technology, 20, 71, 79, 100, 156
teleology, 42, 63, 144
tenth century, 57–8
Teutonic Knights, 94. *See also* Prussia
*The Decline of the West* (*Der Untergang des Abendlandes*), vi, viii, 1–4, 9–13, 15–16, 20, 22, 24, 29, 31, 32, 34, 37–9, 42–3, 46, 56–7, 59–61, 63–4, 67–8, 70–1, 73–80, 82–3, 86–7, 91, 94–5, 102, 107–9, 116, 132, 134, 139, 155, 163–4, 168, 173
  and potential relevance of today, 2
  and various editions of, 12, 15, 24, 59, 66n20, 110n13
  as bestseller, 1
  as the focal point of Spengler studies, viii
the divine, 48, 50
the masses (*die Masse*), 51, 69, 72, 77, 79, 109, 154–60, 162, 166–8, 171n52
theory of colours (*Farbenlehre*), 47
the people (*das Volk*), 69, 162
*The Times*, 129
thinking-in-money (*das Denken in Geld*), 51, 72, 78, 90–1, 97, 167
think tanks, 118
Thöndl, Michael, 37–8, 154, 156, 176
Thuringia, 121
tide of history, 1, 68, 81
Tirpitz, Alfred von, 115
Tolstoy, Leo, 14
Torgler, Ernst, 151
Toynbee, Arnold, 1, 15, 27n35
trader philosophy, 95, 106, 167. *See also* England
trade unions, 87, 91, 97, 101–5, 131
tradition, 4, 69, 77–80, 91, 94, 101, 134, 138, 155, 160, 163
tragedy of humanity, 21
Treaty of Versailles, 115, 161
triad of Antiquity-Middle Ages-Modernity, 42, 63
Troeltsch, Ernst, 106
Troy, 52

true ruler (*Herrscher*), 21, 52, 135, 157. *See also* Mussolini, Benito
Tsar of Russia, 7
twentieth century, 35, 38, 107, 112n54, 153
twenty-first century, 34

unlimited space, 43
uprisings, 15, 64, 75, 79, 88, 122–3, 150, 152, 156, 173
utilitarianism, 51

Valley, Anton Graf von Arco auf, 88
van den Bruck, Arthur Wilhelm Ernst Victor, 14, 93, 115, 118
van Rijn, Rembrandt, 53
Völkischer Block, 147. *See also* NSDAP
*völkisch* ideology, 16, 21, 83, 102, 123, 126, 147, 163. *See also* racism
Vogt, Stefan, 107
Vollnhals, Clemens, 34, 107, 145
Voltaire, 50
von Keyserling, Hermann Alexander Graf, 13
von Ranke, Leopold, 54–5, 60, 83
Vico, Giambattista, 30
Vienna, 12
Vikings, 93–5, 101. *See also* England
Vistula, 14

wage labour, 97
wages, 96–7, 103
    and state setting of, 100, 130
Wagner, Siegfried, 150
Wagner, Winnifried, 149
Wäninger, Carl, 116
war, 4, 11–2, 14–15, 35, 57, 64, 75–9, 83, 88–92, 100, 102–6, 126, 139, 152, 160, 165, 173

Warburg, Max, 115
War Department of Raw Materials (Kriegsrohstoffabteilung), 100
war-ready state, 77
war socialism (*Kriegssozialismus*), 100, 167
Wall Street crash, 146. *See also* global economic crash
wealth, 17, 33, 79, 95–7, 131
    and unequal distribution of, 97
Weapons and Munitions Procurement Office (WuMBA), 100
Weber, Max, 87, 108
Weimar Republic, viii, 1–2, 4, 6, 14, 18, 36, 67, 73–4, 83, 86, 88–9, 99, 102, 105, 109, 113–16, 118–22, 125–6, 130–1, 137, 144, 148, 162, 169, 175
    and constitution of, 4, 15, 88, 121, 138
    and leading lights of, 6
    and relative stabilization of, 125
Weiß, Volker, 37, 41n52
Western democracies, 3, 106
Western world, viii, 11, 19, 31, 52, 64, 68, 156. *See also* Faustian culture
    and degeneration of, 23, 52
    and final days of, 1–3, 14, 39, 73, 75, 78, 168, 173
Wilhelmine Empire. *See also Kaiserreich* and Second Reich
will to power, 93, 104, 158. *See also* Faustian culture
Winnig, August, 102, 105
winter, 48, 51–2, 61, 65n12, 67–74. *See also* cultures
Wirth, Joseph, 141n35
women's rights, 56, 102
working class, 87, 91, 92, 95, 97, 99, 103–5, 108, 115, 120, 147, 154, 167

and rule of, 99
and 'sensible' part of, 92, 102
and strike action, 95, 97
as the 'radical nothing', 91, 155
world-feeling, 45, 49–50, 90, 93
world of facts (*Tatsachenwelt*), 72
world-outlook (*Weltanschauung*), 5, 44

world revolution, 148, 152, 154–5
workers' and soldiers' council, 88–9. *See also* soviets
Würzburg, 125, 139

Zehrer, Hans, 107
Zweiniger, Arthur, 161–2

www.ingramcontent.com/pod-product-compliance
Lightning Source LLC
Chambersburg PA
CBHW051544020426
42333CB00016B/2092